YEADON'S REGISTER

of

L N E R

LOCOMOTIVES

Volume Forty-Nine Part B

Classes N8, N9, N10, N11, N12, N13, N14 & N15

YEADON'S REGISTER OF L.N.E.R. LOCOMOTIVES - VOLUME 49B

EDITORS NOTE AND ACKNOWLEDGEMENTS

Welcome to *Yeadon's Register of LNER Locomotives* Volume 49B featuring the North British and North Eastern 0-6-2T classes - N8, N9, N10, N11, N12, N13, N14, and N15.

We are now down to the penultimate volume in this long running series and at 160 pages it is packed with hundreds of illustrations to help the reader follow the fortunes of the above named classes. In the previous volume we indicated that nine classes would be covered in 49B but due to a slight techincal hiccup, only eight appear; N18 class will instead be featured in Volume 50 along with all the bits and pieces that have been put to one side over the twenty year production period of the Register. That final volume promises to be a rather interesting tome.

Since the passing of Willie Yeadon, we have relied heavily on the support of Eric Fry to iron out some of the bumpy irregularities which can, and do, surface from time to time. Not only has Eric steered us through the awkward bits, he has made sure the 'easy' bits have been correct and ready for publication. Our thanks to Eric are immeasurable.

In its new home at the Hull History Centre, the Yeadon Collection is well and truly looked after for future generations of historians, students of railway history, and modellers who strive for perfection. Judy Burg and her staff will help new readers settle in to trawl through the vast collection which was accumulated by Willie Yeadon over sixty years of research into LNER locomotive matters. The place is certainly worth a visit because the Register has only really scratched the surface of the archive.

Once again the photographic contributors have given us a huge lift in helping to illustrate every change in each class. Thank you gentlemen wherever you may be.

Amadeus Press continue to provide the expertise which culminates with a finished product we are proud of and which hopefully you are proud to own.

By the time this volume reaches Ontario the severe Canadian winter will be all but over, so hopefully it will help to brighten the days even more for Jean and Simon. One more to go.

As usual, we thank you the reader last but then you are the final link in the chain which started so long ago in Holderness Road.

Besides the balance of the 0-6-0T engines, the few 4-4-0T classes, and the last N, Volume 50 will contain the histories of the petrol, diesel and electric motive power accumulated or inherited by the LNER during its twenty-five year lifetime.

The catalogue reference for the locomotives featured in this volume are as follows:
DYE 1/59; DYE 1/60; DYE 1/61; DYE 2/7; DYE 2/14; DYE 2/15; DYE 2/16; DYE 2/18; DYE 2/19.

The Yeadon Collection is available for inspection and anyone who wishes to inspect it should contact -
Hull History Centre
Worship Street
Freetown Way
Hull
HU2 8BG
A catalogue of the Yeadon Collection is available.

First published in the United Kingdom by
BOOK LAW PUBLICATIONS 2011 in association with Challenger
382 Carlton Hill, Nottingham, NG4 1JA
Printed and bound by The Amadeus Press, Cleckheaton, West Yorkshire.

INTRODUCTION

CLASS N8

For a class of only sixty-two engines there were a surprisingly large number of variations in their mechanical aspect, not to mention use of both saturated and superheated boilers. None of these differences were covered by class parts under LNER ownership.

The first ten engines were built in 1886 to the design of T.W. Worsdell. This was his second design for the North Eastern Railway and introduced a new wheel arrangement to the company. Joy valve gear was used and the cylinders were 18in. x 24in. They were classified 'B' by the NER.

Having spent time working at Crewe under Webb, Worsdell had become enthusiastic about compound expansion of steam and soon tried this out on the Great Eastern before coming to the NER. In 1888 he had two more 0-6-2 tanks built, one a 2-cylinder compound using 18in. and 26in. cylinders, whilst the other engine was to his original simple design, built for cost comparison. On the longer runs on which these tank engines were then used, the compound showed a superiority in efficiency, and fifty more were built down to 1890.

Once these 0-6-2 tanks slid down the scale of use and were engaged in shunting and short distance goods work, the advantage first shown disappeared, this being exacerbated by the difficulty in starting the compounds. After the retirement of T.W. Worsdell, who was succeeded by his brother Wilson Worsdell, the decision was taken to discard compound working on the 0-6-2Ts, as well as other classes. Between 1902 and 1912 all the compound 0-6-2Ts were rebuilt to simple expansion.

The first three rebuilds were to the original design, with 18in. x 24in. cylinders, Joy valve gear and slide valves. After that a more complex rebuilding was undertaken with larger cylinders, 19in. x 26in. (which required a new crank axle), Stephenson valve gear and 8¾in. diameter piston valves. To avoid fitting a new crank axle some of the rebuilds retained 24in. stroke, but still with Stephenson gear and piston valves. Seven of the original simple engines also figured in these rebuildings. The final thirteen rebuilds from compound to simple reverted to the original plan with 18in. x 24in. cylinders and Joy valve gear with slide valves. Then, in 1915, superheated boilers began to be fitted, but only to those engines which had piston valves.

At the time of Grouping Class N8 consisted of five distinct varieties, which were:
1) 18in. x 24in. cylinders, Joy gear, slide valves, saturated – total 19. Nos.14, 185, 215, 216, 238, 271, 287, 351, 371, 428, 509, 528, 573, 683, 857, 858, 860, 1105, 1168.
2) 19in. x 24in. cylinders, Stephenson gear, piston valves, saturated – total 6. Nos.136, 212, 346, 445, 523, 1152.
3) 19in. x 24in. cylinders, Stephenson gear, piston valves, superheated – total 24. Nos.76, 210, 267, 284, 345, 348, 349, 503, 504, 515, 531, 535, 780, 809, 856, 859, 861, 862, 863, 959, 961, 1072, 1091, 1165.
4) 19in. x 26in. cylinders, Stephenson gear, piston valves, saturated – total 5. Nos.74, 350, 864, 1104, 1145.
5) 19in. x 26in. cylinders, Stephenson gear, piston valves, superheated – total 8. Nos.213, 218, 219, 293, 373, 855, 1124, 1127.

No alterations to cylinders dimensions or type of motion were made after Grouping and when engines with slide valves and Joy gear required renewal of cylinders, Darlington provided the original type. No.9392 (ex 573) survived until 1955 still with Joy valve gear.

Nos.74, 346, 350, 523 and 1152, from groups 2 and 4 above received superheaters soon after Grouping. By 1932 it

---

N8 Class Numerical Index

Orgin. No.	1946 No.	Brake at Group.	Page No.	Orgin. No.	1946 No.	Brake at Group.	Page No.	Orgin. No.	1946 No.	Brake at Group.	Page No.
14	—	S	11	349	—	S	23	857	—	S	17
74	9375	S	14	350	—	S	23	858	—	S	17
76	9394	W	32	351	—	S	23	859	9377	S	17
136	9387	W	26	371	—	S	20	860	—	W	17
185	—	S	11	373	—	S	23	861	9378	W	17
210	9371	W	11	428	—	S	11	862	9379	S	17
212	9372	W	11	445	—	S	26	863	9380	W	20
213	—	W	20	503	9374	S	14	864	9381	W	20
215	—	S	29	504	—	S	11	959	—	S	35
216	—	W	29	509	—	S	29	961	9398	W	35
218	—	W	29	515	9391	S	32	1072	9393	S	32
219	9382	S	20	523	—	S	26	1091	9399	S	38
238	—	S	29	528	—	S	14	1104	9400	W	38
267	9395	W	35	531	—	S	11	1105	9389	S	29
271	9396	S	35	535	9373	S	14	1124	—	S	23
284	—	S	20	573	9392	S	32	1127	9386	S	26
287	—	S	35	683	—	S	20	1145	—	S	26
293	9401	S	38	780	9397	S	35	1152	9385	S	26
345	9390	S	29	809	—	S	32	1165	—	S	14
346	9383	S	23	855	—	W	14	1168	—	S	32
348	9384	W	23	856	9376	W	14				

Darlington was responsible for building fifty of the sixty-two strong class of North Eastern Railway 0-6-2T which became LNER Class N8. They were built from June 1886 to May 1890 but the last forty engines, built from December 1888 were originally compounds. By 1912 however, all had been rebuilt to simple expansion. Note the original small tanks, all of which had been enlarged from 1240 to 1500 gallons by 1904.

The twenty engines which were to become LNER Class N9 were built at Darlington between May 1893 and February 1894. Numbered 1617, 1618, 1640 to 1655, 383 and 1705, they originally had side tanks holding 1241 gallons plus a well tank of 130 gallons capacity. The 4ft 5$\frac{1}{2}$in. deep bunker held two tons of coal. However, during the early 1900s higher sided tanks holding 1500 gallons and 5ft 0in. deep bunkers for 2$\frac{1}{2}$ tons of coal, began to be fitted and seventeen were like this at Grouping.

The twenty engines which became LNER Class N10 were all built at Darlington between October 1902 and April 1903. In order of building they were numbered: 1321, 1667, 1683, 1697, 1774, 89, 429, 1109, 1112, 1132, 1138, 1148, 1317, 1706, 1710, 1699, 1707, 1711, 1785 and 1716. These were the tank version of Class J25.

In February 1901 the Hull & Barnsley Railway bought from Kitson & Co. of Leeds, five tank engines they had built to this design for the Lancashire Derbyshire & East Coast Railway (*see* also Volume 49A, Class N6), who were unable to pay for them. On being taken into H&B stock, as Nos.97 to 101, only small changes were made, screw couplings were replaced by three-link loose type as this class was not used for passenger trains. Also fitted were some brackets put under the cab roof and for which purpose has not been discovered. They were given the classification N11 by the LNER.

was realised that the expense of such equipment on Class N8 was not justified and when reboilering was necessary saturated boilers were often used. Nevertheless, twenty-three still carried superheated boilers at withdrawal and in fact the last N8 to survive, No.69390 (ex 345) still had one when withdrawn in October 1956.

The boilers on Class N8 were usable also on the J21, J25, N9 and N10 classes, a total of 423 engines. They were freely interchangeable between these classes. During the mid thirties a lot of redesign work was done by Darlington on the boilers it managed, a change to single plate instead of three-ring barrels being made. For Diagram 67 the first five new ones were superheated and designated 67B and only one went eventually to Class N8, No.69377 from July 1949 to March 1952. It could be recognised by the position of the safety valves being four inches further forward.

More redesign work produced the 67A type, in both saturated and superheated form. As well as having the safety valves in the new position, the dome was set 1ft 9in. further back. Twenty-three N8s carried 67A boilers from 1941 onwards.

Early in the 1900s higher sided tanks and bunkers were fitted to the entire class.

Steam brake only was fitted when the engines were new. From 1899 to 1902 fifteen were converted to Westinghouse, plus another one in 1906 and a final three during 1922-23. Under the LNER Unification of Brakes Programme these nineteen all received vacuum ejectors in 1929-30.

The remaining forty-three N8s were steam brake throughout their lives. Of the dual fitted engines, nine remained so. Between 1943 and 1947 another nine had their Westinghouse brake removed and were converted to steam brake, whilst retaining vacuum ejectors. One other became steam brake only.

In March 1939 a most unusual renumbering took place. No.855 had been withdrawn on 31st December 1938 and arrived at Darlington on 17th January 1939 to be cut up. Before this had been done No.856 arrived on 31st January for repair and by mistake was sent to North Road scrap yard and broken up. To put matters straight No.855 was reconditioned and renumbered 856. The blunder could not however be totally disguised because 855 had 26in. stroke cylinders whereas 856 had 24in. cylinders, and so officialdom marked the history sheet for the latter "26in. stroke cylinders from 855 engine" – only marginally true as it was the entire locomotive and not just the cylinders that came from 855!

No.503 had been turned out as No.9 in 1888 but was renumbered in January 1914 when its original number was required for one of the NER's new electric locomotives.

Under the LNER general renumbering scheme which began in 1946 (although it had been drawn up in July 1943), the thirty surviving N8s became 9371 to 9387 and 9389 to 9401. The missing number 9388 would have gone to No.45 but it was scrapped before this could be done. All thirty engines survived at Nationalisation but due to subsequent withdrawals only nineteen received 60000 series numbers. The random allocation of the original NER numbers requires a table (included on page 1) to aid identification of the 1946 numbers.

Initially allocated to working goods and mineral trains over medium distances, the N8 replaced a number of older 0-6-0 tender engines doing the same duties. By Grouping however they themselves had been relegated to short goods runs and shunting and by which time they could be found at sheds located the length and breadth of the old NER territory. About a third of the class were stationed in Hull with the rest in general spread thinly, either singly or in pairs, at a dozen or more depots; the few exceptions were East Hartlepool, Sunderland and Waskerley

which had four, five and seven respectively. By the outbreak of WW2 nearly half of the class had been condemned and those surviving were still spread over the entire NE area from Tweedmouth to Selby and from Starbeck to Hull. When BR was created there were, remarkably, still thirty members of N8 class still operational and they were now concentrated at just five sheds with Dairycoates having the bulk at twenty engines. The rest were in the Tyne and Wear area. Tyne Dock had two used for banking duties and it was one of these, No.69390, which became the last N8 in service but in October 1956 it too was condemned and N8 class was extinct.

CLASS N9

The last of T.W.Worsdell's Class B (LNER N8) two-cylinder compound 0-6-2 tanks were built in 1890. When more engines of this type were required, WilsonWorsdell was in command. He was not in favour of compounds and instead opted for a conventional simple design with 19in. x 26in. cylinders, Stephenson motion and slide valves. Twenty Class N (LNER N9) were built during 1893-94.

They were otherwise similar to Class B having the same boiler, and the bunker and side tanks were of the same size as on the final series of Class B.

Early in the 1900's higher side tanks and bunker began to be fitted, but the process was never completed and three engines, Nos.1645, 1648 and 1652, were never altered.

Originally numbered 1617, 1618 and 1640 to 1655, 383 and 1705, they were given numbers 9410 to 9429 under the 1946 scheme, although No.1645 failed to take up its new number 9417 due to early withdrawal. Seventeen of the class entered BR service, but only five of them received 60000 series numbers.

Withdrawal took place between 1946 and 1955.

LNER Diagram 67 boilers were carried, standard with those on classes J21, J25, N8 and N10. Exchanges took place with all of these classes. The redesigned Diagram 67A type, recognisable by the position of the dome set 1ft 9in. further back, was fitted to ten of the class during 1942-49, and all retained this type to withdrawal. The other ten ran throughout their lives with the Diagram 67 type.

Intended for goods and mineral traffic, steam brake only was provided when new. The ability to move fish vans and similar vehicles led to Nos.1654 and 1655 being changed to Westinghouse brake in 1900. Six more followed in 1911-12 and a final pair in 1922-23.

The 1928 Unification of Brakes Programme resulted in these ten engines having vacuum apparatus added during 1928-31. Four of the ten engines with train brakes remained dual fitted until withdrawal, but between 1944 and 1947 the other six had their Westinghouse pumps removed and were then fitted with combined automatic steam and vacuum brakes.

By Grouping this class too was well distributed over the old North Eastern. Eight sheds shared their services from Hull to Blaydon with East Hartlepool having six under its roof, alongside the other 0-6-2Ts. Shunting and short trip working pre-occupied most of the class but some, such as a pair at Annfield Plain, were employed on mineral trains; others worked on banking duties. Between 1923 and the outbreak of WW2, the class managed to further spread itself out, albeit for short periods, to another sixteen different sheds. A couple worked both passenger and goods services on branch lines such as Allendale, Amble, and Richmond. Pre-war, a few even managed to get some passenger work in running over sections of the ECML whilst working services between York and Pickering.

Because of the 1943 requirement to concentrate certain classes at a particular shed or group of sheds, County Durham became their final area of operation working the pick-ups, and shunting. No.69429 became the last of class for a few weeks in the summer of 1955 but it too was condemned in July and another ex NER class became extinct.

CLASS N10

In 1902 the NER decided to build twenty more 0-6-2T engines, which proved to be the final batch. The design was changed slightly in that 4ft 7¯in. wheels instead of 5ft 1¯in. were used. The new engines were in fact a tank version of the contemporary class P1 (LNER J25) 0-6-0 tender engines, classified U.

The boiler was standard with Class J25, as well as the earlier J21, N8 and N9 engines. Tanks and bunker were larger in size than on classes N8 and N9 as built (most of these were later altered to correspond in this respect with the N10s). Withdrawal occurred during the years 1948 to 1962.

None were ever superheated, and there were many interchanges of boiler with the above mentioned classes.

The redesigned Diagram 67A boiler began to be fitted to Class N10 in 1939 and all ran with this type to withdrawal, except for No.9103 (ex 1706) which was withdrawn in 1948 still with Diagram 67 boiler. Nos.69093 and 69102 briefly reverted to the 67 type in early BR days, before once again carrying a 67A boiler.

Originally numbered between 89 and 1785 in the NER list, all twenty were renumbered 9090 to 9109 in 1946. All entered BR service although No.9103 did not last long enough to get its BR number.

Although designed for goods work the class was equipped with the Westinghouse brake, useful at times for moving carriage stock. The LNER added vacuum ejectors between 1928 and 1932. Then, in 1944, removal of the Westinghouse brake together with vacuum ejector began and by 1947, eighteen of the class had steam brake only, limiting them to freight duties. During 1947 second thoughts prevailed and Nos.9092 and 9095, although losing their Westinghouse brake, were changed to steam and vacuum.

During 1950/54 three of the steam brake only engines (Nos.69096, 69100 and 69108) had their ejectors refitted making a total of five so equipped.

Like the other two NER 0-6-2t classes, the N10s could be found all over the former North Eastern system at Grouping but only at eight sheds, Dairycoates having the bulk of them at seven engines, later boosted to eight when No.1148 joined them from Selby in 1925. Neville Hill had four up to 1925 when it lost No.1710 to Tweedmouth. By the outbreak of war in 1939 none of the class was allocated to sheds south of Durham but ironically they were still distributed to just eight depots. The movement to new sheds continued throughout WW2 but all of them were kept north of the Tees except No.1148 which was allocated to Northallerton from March 1943 to March 1944, and again from 1945 to 1951. In late 1947 there was an influx to Hull again when five went to Dairycoates, followed by six others in 1948-49. Most of the class undertook goods and shunting work but during August 1942 Heaton employed Nos.89 and 1683 on passenger turns along with some of the Sunderland complement. However, by 1944 their somewhat brief time hauling passenger trains was brought to a close when the relevant braking equipment was stripped from them.

Three of the class survived in 1962 but in April of that year Class N10 became extinct too when Nos.69097, 69101 and 69109 were all condemned.

CLASS N11

In February 1901 five radial tanks were acquired by the Hull & Barnsley Railway. They were the first radial tanks purchased by the company and were numbered 97 to 101. They were designed and built by Kitson & Co. and had been ordered by the Lancashire, Derbyshire & East Coast Railway as the final series of their A class (LNER N6). The first of the five was actually delivered to Tuxford as their No.29 but was immediately returned to the makers because the railway company could not afford to pay, the order for all five being cancelled.

Fortunately for all concerned, the H&B had an urgent need for more powerful tank engines to work the Denaby branch and they agreed to purchase the five engines from Kitson's. They differed markedly from existing H&B designs in having domed instead of straightback boilers, square topped cabs and squat built-up chimneys.

The LDECR and H&B engines all became LNER property in 1923 but were classified separately as N6 and N11 because by then there were significant differences between them. The former had all been rebuilt with Belpaire firebox boilers whereas Class N11 was still running with the original round top type.

When the H&B was taken over by the NER in April 1922 the boilers of these engines were already twenty-one years old and in need of replacement. Darlington designed a new domed boiler based on the saturated type used on Class D17 though they were unable to make it interchangeable with that or any other class. A batch of five such boilers was constructed during 1923 and put to work between September 1923 and November 1924. They became Diagram 66 on the LNER and no further boilers were built for class N11, which was condemned during the period 1943 to 1946 when the boilers became life expired.

As supplied by Kitson, the engines were equipped with vacuum brakes for both engine and train working but before Grouping this had been removed in favour of steam brakes for the engine only, a situation which then remained unchanged until withdrawal.

Their initial employment on the Denaby branch saw them banking heavy coal trains to the main line junction at Wrangbrook. They also worked passenger trains on the branch until those services ceased in September 1903. After that they worked miner's trains on the eleven mile branch until an unknown date when the vacuum ejectors were probably removed although the arrival of the 0-8-0 tender engines of Class Q10 saw them relegated to yard work. By Grouping four were allocated to Springhead shed and one to Cudworth, the Hull engines working the yard at Springhead and trip working to Alexandra docks. In 1927 the Springhead engines moved to Dairycoates and the same four fluctuated between those two sheds for some years until No.2482 went to join No.2481 at Cudworth in 1937. No.2479 went to work at Hartlepool in 1930 but returned to Hull six years later.

The first act of the NER was to add 3000 to the running numbers of the H&B locomotives in order to avoid confusion with their own stock. However, when the LNER took over, these new numbers conflicted with the new company's numbering scheme introduced in February 1924 in which the GNR stock also had 3000 added to their existing numbers. Consequently the entire surviving H&B stock was quickly renumbered again into the series 2405 to 2542 (which followed on from the highest NER number). The five N11 class engines became Nos.2478 to 2482. Only the last four survived long enough to be included in the 1943 renumbering scheme when Nos.9085 to 9088 were allocated but never carried. In May 1946 the last member of the N11 class was condemned.

Nine engines, Hull & Barnsley Railway Nos.102 to 110, were built by Kitson & Co. during November and December 1901. They were supplied with domeless boilers, vacuum brake for both engine and train, and were fitted with three coal rails. This is the condition in which the NER took them over on 1st April 1922. All nine still had the 1901 built boiler. They were classified N12 on the LNER.

The ten engines which became LNER Class N13 were built for the H&BR by Hawthorn, Leslie & Co. at Newcastle during the five months from November 1913 to March 1914. The first five were regarded as being replacements and so became Nos.13, 15, 18, 23 and 27. They were similar to N12 class but had their boilers pitched 1½in. higher and their tanks held 2000 instead of 1558 gallons.

The six engines which became LNER Class N14 were built by the North British Locomotive Co., Hyde Park Works, Glasgow and were delivered in September 1909. Numbered 858 to 863, they had short cabs and were intended primarily to be used as bankers on the Cowlairs incline from Glasgow (Queen Street) station, hence the provision of slip couplings. Except for No.863, the others spent almost their entire lives on these duties. Note the lock-up safety valves on the dome.

CLASS N12

The second class of 0-6-2 tank engines built for the H&B consisted of nine engines built by Kitson & Co. to the design of Matthew Stirling. Numbered 102 to 110, they were put to traffic at the end of 1901. Earlier in that year the five stop-gap 0-6-2Ts had also been bought from Kitson's (see N11). Other than having the same wheel arrangement the two classes bore little resemblance to each other. Stirling's engines followed his long held ideas on design, with their domeless, straightback boilers and rounded cabs with wrap over roof. However, the leading dimensions were similar, i.e. cylinder size and boiler pressure, but as the Stirling engines had 4ft 6in. coupled wheels, and the Kitson design 4ft 9in., the latter were slightly less powerful.

The new 0-6-2Ts were required at the coal producing end of the H&B system to work the feeder branches, including the new Wath branch which came into use early in 1902.

Nos.102 to 110 became NER 3102 to 3110 in 1922 and LNER 2483 to 2491 in 1924.

An 0-6-0T class (LNER J75) for shunting work was introduced at the same time as the new 0-6-2T (though constructed by Yorkshire Engine Co.) and carried the same boiler size.

The domeless pattern of boiler on Class N12 had been introduced in 1892 by Stirling on his three 5ft 0in. 0-6-0T engines (LNER J80). This size boiler was also standard on Class J75 and on the later N13 class, an eventual total of 38 engines. It became Diagram 71A on the LNER.

Except for those on Class N13, most of these boilers were worn out and in urgent need of replacement when the NER took over in 1922. As a temporary measure, in June 1923 No.3104 (ex 104) was given a NER boiler (LNER Diagram 69) built in 1917 off '901' class 2-4-0 No.156. Except for the barrel being three inches longer, this boiler was of similar size to the H&B one, but of course had a dome.

Meanwhile five sets of boiler material which were on hand at Springhead works were sent to Darlington for completion. These were of the original domeless pattern (Diagram 71A). Four of these boilers when completed were put on Nos.3110, 3109, 2489 and 2486 (110, 109, 108, 105), three at Darlington between November 1923 and April 1924, whilst one was sent back to Springhead for fitting to No.2489 in February 1924, and consequently differed in getting a different smokebox to those done at Darlington. The fifth boiler went to a Class J75 engine.

For further renewals Darlington redesigned the 71A boiler so as to incorporate a dome. This new design was called 71B and between September 1924 and January 1925 Nos.2483, 2484, 2487 and 2488 (ex 102, 104, 106 and 107) were fitted with this pattern, which completed the renewal programme for Class N12.

The situation then in 1925 was as follows:
Diag. 69 (domed) No.2485.
Diag. 71A (domeless) Nos.2486, 2489, 2490, 2491.
Diag. 71B (domed) Nos.2483, 2484, 2487, 2488.

There were several subsequent changes. In 1934 No.2484 reverted to a domeless 71A type and No.2486 changed from 71A to 71B. Also in that year No.2487 received a third hand Diagram 69 boiler (built 1916) off Class J80 No.2449 which had originally been on '901' class 2-4-0 No.352, so Nos.2485 and 2487 then became alike.

From their introduction in 1901, these nine engines were allocated to Cudworth shed from where they worked the various branches connected to the collieries. Besides coal haulage, they

were engaged in banking and working passenger services. Even at the Grouping they continued in that employment although one engine had moved to Hull temporarily. From 1927 their days in the coalfield were numbered and many of the class went to work elsewhere although their presence at Cudworth was usually represented by a couple of the class. The Derwent Valley Light Railway hired an N12 for a few months from October 1927. The following year the DVLR required another N12 and from then until to 1938 a member of the class became a near permanent feature on that railway. Others went as far afield as Hartlepool, Ferryhill, Ardsley, Woodford and Tuxford to find suitable work but their options were lessened by the trade depression. In 1942 No.2486 returned to Springhead after five years at Tuxford and continued in the same employment – shunting wagons at the works.

Withdrawal of all but one of the N12 class took place during 1936-38. No.2486 lasted a further ten years and was withdrawn numbered 9089 in August 1948. The last of the straightback boilers went out of service when No.2489 was withdrawn in February 1937.

CLASS N13

On the H&B coal traffic for export continued to increase and this involved the opening in 1914 of the large King George dock at Hull. Consequently more locomotives were required by the company. Ten 0-6-2Ts were delivered from Hawthorn Leslie, Newcastle between November 1913 and February 1914. They were numbered 13, 15, 18, 23 and 27 (these five being regarded as replacements for old 0-6-0 tender engines, which were put on a duplicate list) and Nos.152 to 156 (added to Capital Stock).

Stirling kept to his ideas on design and the new engines differed only slightly from his earlier 0-6-2Ts. The main difference was an increase in tank size raising the water capacity from 1558 to 2000 gallons with a consequent increase in overall weight from 58 tons to 61 tons 9 cwt.

After becoming numbers 3013, 3015, 3018, 3023, 3027, and 3152 to 3156 in 1922, the LNER renumbered them: 2405, 2407, 2410, 2415, 2419, and 2533 to 2537 two years later. In 1946 they became 9110 to 9119 and under BR ownership all except 9110 received the prefix 6 to these numbers.

At the time the H&B was absorbed by the NER on 1st April 1922 the domeless boilers on these engines were only eight years old and therefore not in need of replacement. Nevertheless an early decision must have been made to provide them with domed boilers because the first LNER engine diagrams issued in 1924 showed a domed boiler of the 71B type.

It was not until September 1926 when No.2405 actually received a Diagram 71B boiler and it was another four years before the next N13 got one, the remaining N13s being reboilered between December 1930 and August 1934. None reverted to the 71A type.

The final 71B boilers were constructed in three batches, four in 1930, three in 1932 and three in 1934. They differed from those made previously in having a single plate barrel, vertical stays and flat valve regulator, and injectors below the footplate instead of the combination type. The Ross pop safety valves were mounted directly on the firebox, without a casing round the base as with the earlier 71B boilers.

From the outset this class was equipped with steam brake only and therefore never got involved in working passenger trains. Employed on transfer trips and shunting, the majority of the class were at Springhead shed with just two out at Cudworth when the LNER came in being. Things remained pretty much the same until 1942 when two of the Springhead engines went to Newport before moving back south to Selby. The bombing of Hull saw eight of the class move inland to either Neville Hill or Selby and just two N13 remained at Springhead – Nos.2410 and 2415, the former engine actually never left Springhead throughout its life. In 1946 Neville Hill housed five of the class whilst Selby had three but these latter engines went back to Hull during the year. Neville Hill kept hold of a few of its batch until withdrawal, the rest ending their days at Springhead.

All ten engines survived long enough to be taken over by BR in 1948, but No.9110 was withdrawn in June of that year. No more withdrawals took place until May 1952 and No.69114 was the last Hull & Barnsley locomotive in service when condemned in October 1956.

CLASSES N14 & N15

1909 was a busy time for the North British Railway Locomotive Department under the jurisdiction of W.Reid, four new classes being introduced during the second half of that year. These were the D29 Scott 4-4-0 and the small wheeled D33 version of it, and two tank engine designs, the G9 0-4-4Ts and N14 0-6-2 radial tanks. These shared the same pattern boiler and were turned out from the North British Locomotive Co. during September to November.

The twelve G9s were not subsequently added to, Reid turning instead two years later to a 4-4-2T design (Class C15), again using the same boiler.

The 0-6-2T was a new wheel arrangement for the NBR and proved to be most useful for a variety of work ranging from banking passenger trains up the notorious Cowlairs incline to yard shunting and shorter distance goods workings. They were a great advance over Holmes' forty 0-6-0Ts (Class J83) built in 1900-1 in that they were altogether larger and their increased coal and water capacity allowed them to remain at work longer before needing to stop for servicing. Consequently the 0-6-2T was adopted for further construction in preference to 0-6-0Ts of the J83 type until the end of the NBR, and into early LNER days.

Experience with the six N14s led to a slight modification to the design of the next batch of eighteen, turned out in 1910. The cab was lengthened at the expense of a small reduction in coal and water capacity. The LNER classified them N15. Construction of Class N15 continued, the final ten to NBR order not being delivered until the first three months after Grouping. Then, at a meeting of the new Locomotive Committee of the LNER on 22nd February 1923 it was recommended that twenty more be built "needed to replace old tender engines". The LNER Board agreed to this and they were turned out from Cowlairs between October 1923 and April 1924, the last locomotives to be built at that works. Incidentally, all the previous N15s had been constructed by outside contractors.

Class N14 were numbered as a series, 858 to 863, but in Class N15 each consecutive batch revisited lower numbers in the NBR range as replacements for old engines, except for the series 907 to 926 built in 1912.

Under the LNER 1946 renumbering scheme these engines took numbers 9120 to 9224 in order of construction, except for 9071 and 9219 which were completely misplaced as 9178 and 9185 respectively: 9071 (9178) was built in 1923 but appeared in the series constructed during 1916/17, whilst 9219 (9185) was put immediately before the 1920 series even though it was built in 1913. Nine N15s actually took numbers occupied previously by other members of the class (as detailed below),

whilst Nos.9225 and 9227 only moved a few digits to 9223 and 9224, like 9225 and 9227 in the table.

9142 became 9181 21/7/46	9398 became 9142 1/9/46
9154 became 9127 8/11/46	9917 became 9154 10/11/46
9165 became 9182 12/4/46	9224 became 9165 28/4/46
9166 became 9183 3/11/46	9229 became 9166 10/11/46
9209 became 9128 20/10/46	9052 became 9209 20/10/46*
9210 became 9129 20/1/46	9055 became 9210 27/1/46
9219 became 9185 18/2/46	9099 became 9219 3/3/46
9223 became 9164 3/11/46	9225 became 9223 3/11/46*
9224 became 9165 28/4/46	9227 became 9224 5/5/46.

* Note same day renumbering.

In addition N14 9863 became 9125 27th October 1946, this number having been carried by an N15, which was renumbered 9220 on 20th October 1946. A numerical index for Classes N14 and N15 can be found below.

When built the six engines of Class N14, together with the contemporary twelve G9s, had their safety valves mounted on the dome, whereas all the N15s had theirs on the firebox. All these boilers had the same dimensions and were interchangeable. New boilers were put into circulation between 1921 and 1950, all with safety valves on the firebox.

As a result of boiler exchanges and the construction of new boilers, all the N14s acquired safety valves on the firebox, as follows:
9858 – July 1931; 9859 – January 1923;
9860 – June 1923; 9861 – April 1925;
9862 – January 1926; 9863 – February 1925.
None ever reverted to dome mounted safety valves.

Meanwhile the following fifteen class N15 engines ran for a time with 1909-built boilers with safety valves on the dome, off classes N14 and G9:
9054 – November 1934 to April 1945.
9075 – February 1934 to January 1941.
9096 – November 1941 to June 1946.
9106 – March 1941 to February 1946.
69222* (9174) – May 1951 to March 1957.
9219 – October 1935 to September 1941.
9251 – April 1923 to December 1933.
9276* - November 1937 to December 1943.
9282 – August 1923 to March 1928.
9387* - May 1939 to July 1945.
9913 – July 1925 to March 1930.
9914* (9151) – August 1945 to May 1950.
9918 – March 1930 to December 1934.
9921 – August 1930 to July 1935.
* These engines had boilers from Class G9; the others came from N14 class.

It would appear that only six boilers with safety valves on the dome were used to achieve this:
B.226 off G9 9352 (w. 6/37), 9276 Nov. 1937 to Dec. 1943.
B.219 off G9 9351 Feb. 1938, 9387 Apr. 1939 to Jul. 1945, 9914 Aug. 1945 to May 1950, 69222 May 1951 to Mar. 1957.
B.309 off N14 9858 Jan. 1923, 9251 Apr. 1923 to Dec. 1933, 9075 Feb. 1934 to Jan. 1941.
B.310 off N14 9860 Jun. 1923, 9282 Aug. 1923 to Mar. 1928, 9918 Mar. 1930 to Dec. 1934.
B.271 ???? off N14 9863 Feb. 1925, 9397 Mar. 1925 to May 1934, 9054 Nov. 1934 to Feb. 1941, 9106 Mar. 1941 to Feb. 1946.
B.291 off N14 9861 Apr. 1925, 9913 Jul. 1925 to Mar. 1930, 9921 Aug. 1930 to Aug. 1935, 9219 Oct. 1935 to Sept. 1941, 9096 Nov. 1941 to Jun. 1946.

The first six engines of what was to become LNER Class N15 were built for the North British Railway by the North British Locomotive Co., Hyde Park Works, Glasgow in June 1910. They were numbered 7, 154, 209, 210, 251, and 282 and were fitted initially with Westinghouse brakes for train braking. These were the only air-braked N15 and the LNER made them Part 2 of the class. By Grouping Nos.251 and 282 had been fitted with vacuum ejectors also and between July 1924 and November 1925 the other four were also dual fitted.

It was quite usual for boilers in Scotland, where the water was kinder because of its softness, to last much longer than in England, hence the survival of several 1909 boilers into the forties and fifties. The last Diagram 81 boiler with dome mounted safety valves was taken off No.69222 in March 1957. No Diagram 81 boiler with valves on the dome ever had this arrangement altered to firebox mounting.

The six N14s and the initial six N15s had the Westinghouse brake only when built. Vacuum ejectors for alternative train braking had been fitted to five N14s and two of the N15s prior to Grouping and the remaining Westinghouse engines were dealt with during 1924-25. The six N15s were classified Part2 by the LNER.

All later built N15s were turned out with steam brake only, except for the ten built in 1920 which had also vacuum ejectors. This was short lived and the vacuum equipment was removed during 1922-23 for fitting to class J36 engines then being rebuilt. The steam brake N15s were classified Part 1 by the LNER. In March 1929 when additional engines were required to comply with new banking regulations on the Cowlairs incline following a run back collision at Queen Street, Nos.9029 and 9165 were converted from steam to Westinghouse plus vacuum ejector brake and were reclassified Part 2.

By April 1936 when further engines with continuous brakes were needed, the Westinghouse system was obsolete on the NB Section and Nos.9097 and 9166 were then equipped with vacuum combination to their existing steam brake. They were not reclassified and remained N15/1.

Similar fittings were applied to twelve other N15s during 1948-54, in some cases for marshalling braked goods trains at Niddrie and Leith Walk yards and in others as replacements for withdrawn engines on the Cowlairs incline duties. Also after

nationalisation the Westinghouse brake was replaced by steam (still with vacuum combination) on five engines of Class N15/2, leaving three unchanged to withdrawal. The six N14 also kept their Westinghouse and vacuum ejector braking system to withdrawal.

As with the two N15 altered in 1936, none of the later conversions had their class parts changed. In fact it would appear that latterly the authorities at Cowlairs had lost sight of the original purpose of the N15 class parts, i.e. N15/1 for goods engines and N15/2 for those with continuous brakes. Nevertheless the class parts survived in use in the Diagram Book Index right through to the withdrawal of the class, Nos.69126 to 69131, 69182 and 69188 being Part 2 and all the rest Part 1.

Except for two of the class sent to Doncaster and Annesley in 1924 as part of the so-called shunting trials, the N14 and N15 were firmly allocated in the central belt of Scotland with a few exceptions which went to Aberdeen, Carlisle and Tweedmouth. Shunting and trip working was their sole aim in life and they went about it admirably being involved in moving not only mixed goods trains but also heavy mineral trains over some awkward routes. BR put some at former LMS sheds in Scotland, mainly in the Glasgow area. A few got to Dundee and as far north as Keith but otherwise they stuck firmly to former NBR sheds.

Three N14s, Nos.9121, 9122 and 9123 were the first to be withdrawn in 1947. No.69124 went in 1950 and the last two, 69120 and 69125, in March 1954. All the N15 class entered BR service and no withdrawals took place until 1957 and was not completed until dieselisation was well under way in 1962.

CLASS N14 & N15 NUMERICAL INDEX

Orig. No.	1946 No.	Brake at Grp.	Page.	Orig. No.	1946 No.	Brake at Grp.	Page.
9007	9126	W	107	9387	9133	S	110
9019	9206	S	148	9388	9134	S	110
9020	9186	S	140	9389	9135	S	110
9022	9187	S	140	9390	9136	S	111
9023	9207	S	150	9391	9137	S	111
9029	9188	S	140	9392	9138	S	111
9031	9208	S	150	9393	9139	S	111
9047	9172	S	135	9396	9140	S	111
9049	9189	S	140	9397	9141	S	116
9052	9209	S	150	9398	9142	S	116
9054	9173	S	135	9399	9143	S	116
9055	9210	S	150	9453	9180	S	138
9060	9211	S	150	9519	9196	S	145
9061	9174	S	135	9520	9197	S	145
9065	9175	S	135	9521	9198	S	145
9067	9212	S	153	9522	9199	S	145
9069	9176	S	135	9523	9200	S	145
9070	9177	S	138	9524	9201	S	148
9071	9178	S	153	9525	9202	S	148
9074	9213	S	153	9526	9203	S	148
9075	9214	S	153	9527	9204	S	148
9076	9215	S	153	9528	9205	S	148
9077	9216	S	153	9858	9120	W+VE	101
9078	9217	S	155	9859	9121	W+VE	101
9079	9218	S	155	9860	9122	W+VE	101
9096	9190	S	143	9861	9123	W+VE	101
9097	9191	S	143	9862	9124	W+VE	101
9099	9219	S	145	9863	9125	W	103
9106	9192	S	143	9907	9144	S	116
9107	9193	S	143	9908	9145	S	116
9108	9194	S	143	9909	9146	S	120
9125	9220	S	155	9910	9147	S	120
9142	9181	S	138	9911	9148	S	120
9147	9221	S	155	9912	9149	S	120
9154	9127	W	107	9913	9150	S	120
9165	9182	S	138	9914	9151	S	120
9166	9183	S	138	9915	9152	S	123
9174	9222	S	157	9916	9153	S	123
9209	9128	W	107	9917	9154	S	123
9210	9129	W	107	9918	9155	S	123
9219	9185	S	130	9919	9156	S	123
9223	9164	S	130	9920	9157	S	126
9224	9165	S	130	9921	9158	S	126
9225	9223	S	157	9922	9159	S	126
9227	9224	S	157	9923	9160	S	126
9229	9166	S	130	9924	9161	S	126
9230	9167	S	133	9925	9162	S	130
9240	9195	S	145	9926	9163	S	130
9246	9168	S	133				
9251	9130	W+VE	107				
9252	9169	S	133				
9257	9170	S	133				
9259	9184	S	140				
9264	9171	S	133				
9276	9179	S	138				
9282	9131	W+VE	110				
9386	9132	S	110				

1946 & Original Numbers

1946 No.	Orig. No.	1946 No.	Orig. No.
9120	9858	9175	9065
9121	9859	9176	9069
9122	9860	9177	9070
9123	9861	9178	9071
9124	9862	9179	9276
9125	9863	9180	9453
9126	9007	9181	9142
9127	9154	9182	9165
9128	9209	9183	9166
9129	9210	9184	9259
9130	9251	9185	9219
9131	9282	9186	9020
9132	9386	9187	9022
9133	9387	9188	9029
9134	9388	9189	9049
9135	9389	9190	9096
9136	9390	9191	9097
9137	9391	9192	9106
9138	9392	9193	9107
9139	9393	9194	9108
9140	9396	9195	9240
9141	9397	9196	9519
9142	9398	9197	9520
9143	9399	9198	9521
9144	9907	9199	9522
9145	9908	9200	9523
9146	9909	9201	9524
9147	9910	9202	9525
9148	9911	9203	9526
9149	9912	9204	9527
9150	9913	9205	9528
9151	9914	9206	9019
9152	9915	9207	9023
9153	9916	9208	9031
9154	9917	9209	9052
9155	9918	9210	9055
9156	9919	9211	9060
9157	9920	9212	9067
9158	9921	9213	9074
9159	9922	9214	9075
9160	9923	9215	9076
9161	9924	9216	9077
9162	9925	9217	9078
9163	9926	9218	9079
9164	9223	9219	9099
9165	9224	9220	9125
9166	9229	9221	9147
9167	9230	9222	9174
9168	9246	9223	9225
9169	9252	9224	9227
9170	9257		
9171	9264		
9172	9047		
9173	9054		
9174	9061		

(above) The other twelve members of the class, numbered 503 (originally No.9), 74, and 855 to 864, were built at Gateshead between January and December 1888. All except No.74 were compound but had been rebuilt to simple expansion by February 1910.

Rebuilding from compound and application of superheaters created four distinct groups within the class. At Grouping nineteen of the class, Nos.14, 185, 215, 216, 238, 271, 287, 351, 371, 428, 509, 528, 573, 683, 857, 858, 860, 1105, and 1168 had 18in. x 24in. cylinders, Joy valve gear, slide valves, and were not superheated.

Six engines, Nos.136, 212, 346, 445, 523 and 1152 had 19in. x 24in. cylinders, piston valves below the cylinder, Stephenson gear and were also unsuperheated.

14

Darlington 1.

To traffic 6/1886.

REPAIRS:
?/?. ?/?—?/10/01.**G.**
?/?. ?/?—?/3/18.**G.**
Ghd. 19/5—13/10/24.**G.**
Ghd. 30/12/27—10/3/28.**G.**

BOILERS:
D456.
G109 ?/10/01.
G640 ?/3/18.
D1676 *(new)* 13/10/24.

SHEDS:
Sunderland.
Blaydon 7/10/31.

CONDEMNED: 21/4/32.
Cut up at Darlington.

531

Darlington 2.

To traffic 6/1886.

REPAIRS:
Dar. ?/?—?/11/04.**G.**
Piston valves fitted 9/08.
Dar. ?/?—?/6/21.**G.**
Dar. 29/6—31/8/23.**G.**
Dar. 29/9/26—20/1/27.**G.**
Dar. 19/3—14/5/29.**G.**
Dar. 8/5—23/6/31.**G.**
Dar. 8/5—11/6/34.**G.**
Dar. 11/6/37. *Not repaired.*

BOILERS:
D457.
G385 ?/11/04.
D1200 *(new. sup)* ?/6/21.
D551 *(ex855)* 11/6/34.

SHED:
Dairycoates.

CONDEMNED: 26/6/37.
Cut up at Darlington.

185

Darlington 3.

To traffic 7/1886.

REPAIRS:
??. ?/?—?/11/01.**G.**
??. ?/?—?/5/20.**G.**
Ghd. 20/10—17/12/23.**G.**
Ghd. 18/3—1/4/25.**L.**
Ghd. 27/11/28—21/1/29.**G.**
Ghd. 17/12/30—7/1/31.**L.**

BOILERS:
D468.
G111 ?/11/01.
D1089 *(new)* ?/5/20.

SHED:
Waskerley.

RENUMBERED:
185ᴅ 17/12/23.

CONDEMNED: 10/12/32.

210

Darlington 4.

To traffic 7/1886.

REPAIRS:
Dar. ?/?—?/9/02.**G.**
Piston valves fitted 9/08.
Dar. ?/?—?/9/20.**G.**
Dar. 1/12/22—21/3/23.**G.**
Dar. 11/9—30/11/25.**G.**
Dar. 16/3—8/5/28.**G.**
Dar. 27/3—22/5/30.**G.**
Vacuum ejector fitted.
Dar. 18/4—20/5/32.**G.**
Dar. 5—30/4/34.**G.**
Dar. 8/6—1/9/36.**G.**
Dar. 5/10—18/11/38.**G.**
Dar. 23/10—26/11/41.**G.**
Dar. 6—26/10/42.**L.**
Dar. 4/10—24/11/44.**G.**
Dar. 17/10—28/11/47.**G.**
Ghd. 8/3—19/4/48.**L.**
After rear end collision.
Ghd. 6/12/49—26/1/50.**C/L.**
After rear end collision.
Dar. 27/2/52. *Not repaired.*

BOILERS:
D469.
D1768 ?/9/02.
 D769 *(new, sup)* ?/9/20.
 D712 *(exJ25 1977)* 21/3/23.
 D679 *(ex76)* 30/4/34.
 D1387 *(exJ21 1572)* 1/9/36.
 D1511 *(ex1104, sat)* 18/11/38.
 D1676 *(ex862, sup)* 26/11/41.
 2190 *(ex9380)* 28/11/47.

SHEDS:
Dairycoates.
Neville Hill 12/2/34.
Dairycoates 28/3/43.
Heaton 14/12/47.

RENUMBERED:
9371 19/5/46.
69371 19/4/48.

CONDEMNED: 10/3/52.
Cut up at Darlington.

212

Darlington 5.

To traffic 8/1886.

REPAIRS:
??. ?/?—?/11/05.**G.**
Piston valves fitted 1/09.
??. ?/?—?/2/22.**G.**
Dar. 8/12/23—20/3/24.**G.**
Dar. 29/8—30/12/27.**G.**
Ghd. 5/1—12/2/29.**L.**
Vacuum ejector fitted.
Ghd. 27/5—10/7/30.**L.**
Ghd. 11/5—4/6/31.**L.**
Dar. 3/1—8/2/33.**G.**
Dar. 3—23/3/33.**N/C.**
Dar. 20/1—3/3/39.**G.**
Dar. 25/1—8/2/41.**N/C.**
Dar. 28/10—3/12/41.**G.**
Dar. 10/11—14/12/44.**G.**
Dar. 15/9—15/10/48.**G.**

BOILERS:
D470.
D1869 ?/11/05.
D1259 *(new)* ?/2/22.
D1934 *(ex445)* 8/2/33.
 2651 *(ex9400)* 15/10/48.

SHEDS:
Stockton.
East Hartlepool 18/2/26.
Dairycoates 8/7/37.
Heaton 14/12/47.

RENUMBERED:
9372 19/5/46.
69372 15/10/48.

CONDEMNED: 27/11/50.
Cut up at Darlington.

428

Darlington 6.

To traffic 8/1886.

REPAIRS:
??. ?/?—?/9/03.**G.**
??. ?/?—?/9/21.**G.**
Ghd. 13/8—5/11/25.**G.**

BOILERS:
D471.
G305 ?/9/03.
D1257 *(new)* ?/9/21.

SHED:
Waskerley.

CONDEMNED: 9/4/30.

504

Darlington 7.

To traffic 9/1886.

REPAIRS:
??. ?/?—?/7/02.**G.**
??. ?/?—?/8/19.**G.**
Piston valves fitted.
Ghd. 18/10—9/11/23.**L.**
Ghd. 28/2—13/6/27.**G.**
Ghd. 3/12/30—20/1/31.**G.**
Dar. 24/8—6/10/34.**G.**

BOILERS:
D472.
G170 ?/7/02.
D753 *(new, sup)* ?/8/19.
D746 *(ex862)* 13/6/27.

WORKS CODES:- Cow - Cowlairs. Dar - Darlington. Don - Doncaster. Ghd - Gateshead. Hls - Hull Springhead. RSH - Robert, Stephenson & Hawthorn. Str - Stratford. Yk - York.
REPAIR CODES:- **C/H** - Casual Heavy. **C/L** - Casual Light. **G** - General. **H**- Heavy. **H/I** - Heavy Intermediate. **L** - Light. **L/I** - Light Intermediate. **N/C** - Non-Classified.

11

Twenty-four engines were like the above six but had superheaters and extended smokebox. They were Nos.76, 210, 267, 284, 345, 348, 349, 503, 504, 515, 531, 535, 780, 809, 856, 859, 861, 862, 863, 959, 961, 1072, 1091 and 1165.

There were eight, Nos.213, 218, 219, 293, 373, 855, 1124 and 1127, with piston valves, Stephenson gear and superheaters but had 19in. x 26in. cylinders.

The other five, Nos.74, 350, 864, 1104 and 1145 also had 19in. x 26in. cylinders with piston valves below, and Stephenson gear but were not superheated.

(above) **No.69392 (ex573),** one of those with Joy's valve gear and slide valves, remained in that condition until withdrawal on 4th May 1955, when there were only four of the sixty-two left.

After Grouping five more had superheated boilers put on, Nos.74 (14th April 1924), 1152 (20th October 1924), 350 (2nd February 1927), 523 (25th February 1927) and 346 (21st March 1927), so that thirty-seven of the sixty-two were fitted with superheaters, all of the Schmidt type.

By 1930 it was decided the class did not need, or justify, the expense of superheater maintenance and replacement boilers for Nos.218 and 219 (both 31st August 1932) were new saturated type. Both however retained their extended smokebox. No.210 also ran without a superheater but only from 18th November 1938 to 26th November 1941. It was the only one to regain a superheater.

504 cont./
SHEDS:
Heaton.
Dairycoates 10/4/37.

CONDEMNED: 26/6/37.
Into Dar. for cut up 21/8/37.

528

Darlington 8.

To traffic 9/1886.

REPAIRS:
??. ?/?—?/5/03.**G.**
??. ?/?—?/7/21.**G.**
Ghd. 28/7—12/10/25.**G.**

BOILERS:
D473.
G304 ?/5/03.
D1256 *(new)* ?/7/21.

SHED:
Waskerley.

CONDEMNED: 11/12/29.

535

Darlington 9.

To traffic 10/1886.

REPAIRS:
??. ?/?—?/12/03.**G.**
??. ?/?—?/4/21.**G.**
Piston valves fitted.
Ghd. 7/6—16/8/23.**G.**
Dar. 7/10—31/12/25.**G.**
Dar. 8/8—26/9/28.**G.**
Dar. 4/8—26/9/30.**G.**
Dar. 23/6—16/8/33.**G.**
Dar. 22/1—23/3/36.**G.**
Dar. 24—27/3/36.**N/C.**
Dar. 15/2—29/3/39.**G.**
Dar. 9/6—22/7/41.**G.**
Dar. 15/4—15/5/43.**G.**
Dar. 17/2—24/3/45.**G.**
Dar. 22/8—3/10/47.**G.**

BOILERS:
D474.
D1776 ?/12/03.
D1192 *(new)* ?/4/21.
D411 *(ex1124)* 26/9/30.
2489 *(new)* 16/8/33.
2492 *(ex9394)* 3/10/47.

SHEDS:
Dairycoates.
Selby 3/10/39.

Heaton 20/7/40.
Dairycoates 28/3/43.

RENUMBERED:
9373 7/7/46.

CONDEMNED: 13/3/50.
Cut up at Darlington.

1165

Darlington 10.

To traffic 11/1886.

REPAIRS:
??. ?/?—?/8/03.**G.**
??. ?/?—?/8/21.**G.**
Piston valves fitted.
Dar. 28/5—26/8/24.**G.**
Dar. 16/5—20/7/28.**G.**
Ghd. 20/2—8/4/31.**G.**
Dar. 10/10—10/11/33.**G.**
Dar. 12/6—24/8/36.**G.**

BOILERS:
D475.
D1774 ?/8/03.
D1203 *(new, sup)* ?/8/21.

SHEDS:
Starbeck.
Tweedmouth 1/4/29.
Blaydon 28/3/39.

CONDEMNED: 12/7/39.
Laid aside and cut up at
Darlington November/December
1939.

Diagram 67A boiler.

503

Gateshead 1-88.

To traffic 1/1888.

REPAIRS:
??. ?/?—?/3/08.**G.**
*Rebuilt to simple with piston
valves.*
??. ?/?—?/7/21.**G.**
Ghd. 27/3—4/6/24.**G.**
Ghd. 15—25/9/24.**L.**
Ghd. 19/4—22/6/28.**G.**
Ghd. 17/5—20/6/32.**G.**
Dar. 13/3—19/4/39.**G.**
Dar. 3/7—15/8/41.**G.**
Dar. 8—29/1/44.**G.**
Dar. 4—31/5/46.**G.**
Ghd. 4/1—16/5/47.**L.**
After collision.

BOILERS:
G993.
G641 ?/3/08.
D1205 *(new, sup)* ?/7/21.
D1230 *(ex856)* 19/4/39.
3432 *(new, sat)* 29/1/44#.
3394 *(exJ25 2041)* 1/11/46#.

SHEDS:
Carlisle.
Borough Gardens 4--6/25.
Dairycoates 3/6/39.

RENUMBERED:
503 1/1/14 (ex No.9).
9374 31/5/46.

CONDEMNED: 28/3/49.
Cut up at Darlington.

74

Gateshead 2-88.

To traffic 3/1888.

REPAIRS:
??. ?/?—?/9/05.**G.**
Piston valves fitted.
Dar. 6/2—14/4/24.**G.**
Dar. 13/9—7/12/27.**G.**
Dar. 17/9—1/11/29.**G.**
Ghd. 17/10—14/11/32.**L.**
Dar. 25/11—22/12/33.**G.**
Dar. 15/7—12/8/38.**G.**
Dar. 7/1—13/2/41.**G.**
Dar. 20/12/43—5/2/44.**G.**
Dar. 24/10—23/11/46.**G.**

BOILERS:
G994.
G463 ?/9/05.
D1489 *(new, sup)* 14/4/24.
D755 *(ex213)* 22/12/33.
D753 *(ex293)* 12/8/38.
3436 *(new, sat.)* 5/2/44#.
3738 *(new)* 23/11/46#.

SHEDS:
Dairycoates.
Waskerley 22/5/30.
Dairycoates 30/6/39.

RENUMBERED:
9375 23/6/46.

CONDEMNED: 28/3/49.
Cut up at Darlington.

~ *Diagram 67B boiler.*

855

Gateshead 24-88.

To traffic 10/1888.

REPAIRS:
??. ?/?—?/1/00.**G.**
*Rebuilt to simple with piston
valves.*
??. ?/?—?/5/19.**G.**
Ghd. 17/8—7/9/23.**L.**
Ghd. 25/3—2/7/24.**G.**
Ghd. 23/5—16/8/27.**G.**
Ghd. 27/9—24/10/28.**L.**
Ghd. 17/12/29—4/2/30.**G.**
Vacuum ejector fitted.
Ghd. 3/5—6/6/32.**G.**
Dar. 20/4—18/5/34.**G.**

BOILERS:
G839.
D768 *(new, sup)* ?/5/19.
D711 *(exJ25 1968)* 2/7/24.
D551 *(ex293)* 4/2/30.
D712 *(ex210)* 18/5/34.

SHED:
Carlisle.

CONDEMNED: 31/12/38.
*Into Dar. for cut up 17/1/39 but
engine portion retrieved from
scrap yard and used for No.856
which had been cut up in
mistake.*

856

Gateshead 25-88.

To traffic 10/1888.

REPAIRS:
??. ?/?—?/7/00.**G.**
*Rebuilt to simple with piston
valves 2/08.*
??. ?/?—?/4/13.**G.**
??. ?/?—?/7/21.**G.**
Ghd. 16/9—11/11/24.**G.**
Ghd. 8/7—4/8/25.**L.**
Ghd. 11/6—18/8/27.**G.**
Ghd. 24/2—4/4/30.**G.**
Vacuum ejector fitted.
Ghd. 7/10—11/11/32.**G.**
Dar. 6/8—12/11/36.**G.**
Dar. 31/1—17/3/39.**G.**
*Reconstructed from No.855 - see
above.*
Dar. 2/2—20/3/42.**G.**
Dar. 19/3—7/6/45.**G.**
*Changed from Westinghouse to
steam brake (still with VE.).*
Dar. 29/3—17/4/47.**L.**

(above) Between October 1943 and June 1945 eight engines, Nos.74, 346, 503, 780, 856, 861, 1091 and 1152 lost both superheater and the extended smokebox. Replacement boilers were to Diagram 67A which had a single plate barrel on which the dome was 1ft 9in. further to the rear. No.780 became 9397 on 14th December 1946. Four more were similarly changed during BR days: Nos.69377 (8th March 1952), 69379 (23rd November 1949), 69394 (10th March 1950), and 69398 (18th January 1950).

(right) The last survivor of the class, No.69390 (ex 345), was still superheated to its withdrawal on 18th October 1956. From 12th June 1953 it carried a Diagram 67A boiler with the dome 1ft 9in. further back.

When boilers were given LNER Diagram numbers in June 1928, No.67 covered both saturated and superheated varieties. Those which were superheated had 18-element Schmidt type with circulating valve on the left hand side of the smokebox.

From 1933, new superheated boilers had Robinson type element and could be identified because element protection was by Gresley anti-vacuum valve situated behind the chimney. No.535 had this type of Diagram 67 boiler from 16th August 1933 to withdrawal on 13th March 1950.

Darlington's first essay at the redesign of Diagram 67 boiler was a change to a single plate barrel with dome position unaltered but with the safety valves moved four inches forward. Only five of these boilers were built, in the two month period from December 1936 to January 1937, and only one was used by an N8, No.69377 from 2nd July 1949 to 15th February 1952.

(below) All subsequent boilers were to Diagram 67A and all had rear dome and forward safety valve positions. Of the 120 saturated versions built from November 1938 to November 1947, N8 class got ten when new, and another ten when second-hand. As No.1091 (9399 from 24th February 1946), this engine had a new one from 14th October 1943.

856 cont./
Dar. 22/12/47—6/2/48.**G**.

BOILERS:
 G893 ?/7/00.
 D1769 ?/4/13.
 D1230 *(new, sup)* ?/7/21.
 D1489 *(ex348)* 17/3/39.
   3277 *(exJ21 1589,sat)*7/6/45#.

SHEDS:
Consett.
Neville Hill 17/7/39.
Dairycoates 28/3/43.
Neville Hill 15/8/48.
Dairycoates 17/10/48.

RENUMBERED:
 9376 27/10/46.
 ᴇ**9376** 6/2/48.

CONDEMNED: 27/2/50.
Cut up at Darlington.

_____

857

Gateshead 26-88.

To traffic 10/1888.

REPAIRS:
 ??. ?/?—?/4/04.**G**.
Rebuilt to simple.
 ??. ?/?—?/9/19.**G**.
Ghd. 17/8—10/9/23.**L**.
Ghd. 16/9—14/11/24.**G**.
Ghd. 23/5—24/8/27.**G**.
Ghd. 9/1—24/2/30.**G**.
Ghd. 24/2—20/3/31.**L**.
After collision.
Ghd. 23/9—28/10/32.**L**.
Dar. 13/8/35. *Not repaired.*

BOILERS:
G307 ?/4/04.
D889 *(new)* ?/9/19.

SHED:
Tweedmouth.

CONDEMNED: 15/8/35.
Cut up at Darlington.

_____

858

Gateshead 27-88.

To traffic 10/1888.

REPAIRS:
 ??. ?/?—?/10/01.**G**.
Rebuilt to simple 2/09.
 ??. ?/?—?/9/19.**G**.

Ghd. 29/5—7/8/24.**G**.
Ghd. 8/10—16/12/27.**G**.
Ghd. 29/4—8/6/31.**G**.
Dar. 16/3/36. *Not repaired.*

BOILERS:
 G108 ?/10/01.
 D884 *(new)* ?/9/19.
D1136 *(exJ21 104)* 8/6/31.

SHED:
Sunderland.

CONDEMNED: 20/3/36.
Cut up at Darlington.

_____

859

Gateshead 28-88.

To traffic 10/1888.

REPAIRS:
??. ?/?—?/12/03.**G**.
Rebuilt to simple with p.v. 6/08.
??. ?/?—?/2/21.**G**.
Dar. 22/12/22—15/2/23.**G**.
Dar. 22/4—2/6/24.**L**.
Dar. 25/9—29/11/24.**G**.
Dar. 3/5—10/8/27.**G**.
Dar. 25/11/29—11/1/30.**G**.
Dar. 20/9—28/10/32.**G**.
Dar. 4/3—11/4/35.**G**.
Dar. 8/3—22/4/38.**G**.
Dar. 25/10—23/11/40.**G**.
Dar. 3/11—4/12/43.**G**.
Dar. 7—9/12/43.**N/C**.
Dar. 13/11—21/12/46.**G**.
Dar. 4/6—2/7/49.**G**.
Dar. 4—6/7/49.**N/C**.
Dar. 15/2—8/3/52.**G**.

BOILERS:
 G306 ?/12/03.
D1190 *(new, sup)* ?/2/21.
 2650 *(new)* 11/4/35.
 2480 *(exJ25 2055)* 23/11/40.
 3328 *(exJ21 314)* 21/12/46#.
 2863 *(exJ25 5659)* 2/7/49~.
 25084 *(ex??, sat)* 8/3/52#.

SHEDS:
Selby.
Heaton 8/3/40.
Dairycoates 28/3/43.
Heaton 22/2/53.

RENUMBERED:
 9377 27/10/46.
 69377 2/7/49.

CONDEMNED: 28/6/55.
Cut up at Darlington.

_____

860

Gateshead 29-88.

To traffic 11/1888.

REPAIRS:
 ??. ?/?—?/1/07.**G**.
Rebuilt to simple 2/10.
 ??. ?/?—?/8/21.**G**.
Dar. 5/2—29/4/25.**G**.
Dar. 9/4—31/8/26.**L**.
Dar. 13/9—5/11/29.**G**.
Vacuum ejector fitted.
Dar. 14/2—8/3/33.**L**.
Dar. 28/7—6/10/33.**H**.
Dar. 5/11—13/12/34.**G**.
Dar. 22/1—3/3/36.**L**.
After collision.

BOILERS:
 G523 ?/1/07.
 G745 ?/8/21.
D1696 *(new)* 29/4/25.
D1142 *(ex136)* 13/12/34.

SHEDS:
Malton.
Neville Hill 21/7/32.
Dairycoates 12/2/34.

CONDEMNED: 26/6/37.
Into Dar. for cut up 16/8/37.

_____

861

Gateshead 30-88.

To traffic 11/1888.

REPAIRS:
??. ?/?—?/3/06.**G**.
Rebuilt to simple with p.v.
??. ?/?—?/5/15.**G**.
Dar. 26/10/22—30/1/23.**G**.
Dar. 2/10—31/12/25.**G**.
Dar. 3/7—31/8/28.**G**.
Dar. 28/4—19/5/30.**L**.
Vacuum ejector fitted.
Dar. 3/5—8/6/32.**G**.
Dar. 26/3—2/5/35.**L**.
After collision.
Dar. 29/1—9/3/37.**G**.
Dar. 17/7—26/8/40.**G**.
Dar. 18—25/9/42.**L**.
Dar. 31/8—14/10/43.**G**.
Dar. 4/11—5/12/47.**G**.
Ghd. 19/11—15/12/51.**G**.

BOILERS:
 G489 ?/3/06.
D437 *(new, sup)* ?/5/15.
D744 *(ex213)* 31/8/28.
D1198 *(ex284)* 9/3/37.

 3402 *(new, sat)* 14/10/43#.
 3397 *(exN10 9095)* 5/12/47#.
 25068 *(ex??)* 15/12/51#.

SHEDS:
Dairycoates.
Starbeck 3/3/26.
Dairycoates 24/6/26.
Selby 16/9/29.
York 31/1/38.
Consett 9/9/40.
Borough Gardens 29/12/44.
Tyne Dock 19/5/45.
Heaton 17/11/51.
Springhead 27/9/53.
Bridlington 6/12/53.

RENUMBERED:
 9378 20/10/46.
 69378 15/12/51.

CONDEMNED: 26/9/55.
Cut up at Darlington.

_____

862

Gateshead 31-88.

To traffic 11/1888.

REPAIRS:
 ??. ?/?—?/4/04.**G**.
Rebuilt to simple with p.v. 5/07.
 ??. ?/?—?/2/19.**G**.
Ghd. 30/7—24/8/23.**L**.
Ghd. 5/3—15/7/26.**G**.
Ghd. 10/1—5/2/29.**L**.
Ghd. 17/1—28/2/30.**G**.
Dar. 16/5—16/6/34.**G**.
Dar. 16/12/36—17/2/37.**L**.
Dar. 7/3—22/4/39.**G**.
Dar. 30/9—1/11/41.**G**.
Dar. 5/5—3/6/44.**G**.
Dar. 14/1—1/3/47.**G**.
Dar. 13—30/1/48.**L**.
After collision.
Dar. 25/10—23/11/49.**G**.
Dar. 16/10/52. *Not repaired.*

BOILERS:
 G313 ?/4/04.
 D746 *(new, sup)* ?/2/19.
 D747 *(ex348)* 15/7/26.
 D1200 *(ex531)* 16/6/34.
 D1676 *(exJ25 2076)* 22/4/39.
 D1197 *(ex293)* 1/11/41.
 3207 *(exJ25 5678)* 1/3/47#.
 3304 *(exN10 9091, sat)* 23/11/49#.

SHEDS:
Heaton.
Dairycoates 10/4/37.

Of the fifteen superheated Diagram 67A boilers, only one N8, No.345 got a new one from 9th June 1941 to 10th May 1947. From December 1946 five other N8 got second-hand superheated 67A's, No.9395 being so fitted from 22nd February 1947 to 18th August 1952 withdrawal.

New saturated boiler No.D1676 started work from 13th October 1924 on No.14 (*see* page 24, second from bottom) until the engine was withdrawn on 21st April 1932. It was then used by J25 No.2076 from August 1934 to October 1938 after which a surplus set of Schmidt elements was put in, with extended smokebox and steam circulating valve on its side. It then served No.862 from 22nd April 1939 to 30th September 1941 and No.210 from 26th November 1941 to 17th October 1947, and finally No.69401 from 12th March 1949 to 25th August 1951 when both engine and boiler were condemned.

By Grouping, the standard chimney had a plain top but seven were noted with a 'windjabber.' No.862 had that type from its superheating in February 1919 to at least March 1939. Note that its new 1939 boiler had Ross 'pop' valves apparently on a Ramsbottom mounting, and with that type of base cover.

Much more common was the chimney with a plain top, and Ramsbottom valves in a polished brass casing. Although 'pop' valves were standard from 1930, the Ramsbottom type could still be seen in use to August 1951 on No.69401.

The new superheater boiler put on No.504 in August 1919 had 'pop' valves but unlike No.862, its base cover was the more conventional type. No.504 remained in this painting until it went to Gateshead works on 28th February 1927.

Until late in 1931 the superheated engines had a continuous boiler handrail which curved above the top of the smokebox door.

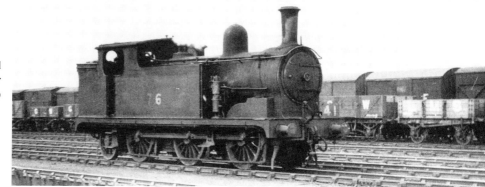

On the non-superheated engines, the handrails ended on the side of the smokebox, and there was a separate curved rail above the smokebox door.

From 23rd December 1931 on No.1091 a start was made altering the continuous rail to the three separate parts and nearly all are believed to have been so done. Ex works 4th August 1938, No.345 certainly had separate rails – see page 36, centre – yet as No.69390 – see page 25, top – it had reverted to continuous rail. No.69401 – see opposite, second from top – also finished its career with a continuous type.

862 cont./
RENUMBERED:
9379 16/6/46.
69379 23/11/49.

CONDEMNED: 20/10/52.
Cut up at Darlington.

_____

863

Gateshead 32-88.

To traffic 11/1888.

REPAIRS:
??. ?/?—?/3/07.**G.**
Rebuilt to simple with p.v.
??. ?/?—?/9/18.**G.**
Ghd. ?/?—13/6/22.**G.**
Ghd. 6/2--22/4/25.**G.**
Ghd. 8/7—13/9/29.**G.**
Vacuum ejector fitted.
Dar. 15/11/34—8/2/35.**G.**
Dar. 8/6—23/8/37.**G.**
Dar. 26/10—21/12/38.**H.**
Dar. 25/7—16/8/40.**L.**
Dar. 10/6—19/7/41.**G.**
Dar. 29/8—11/10/44.**G.**
Changed from Westinghouse to steam brake still with VE.
Dar. 1/10—21/11/47.**G.**

BOILERS:
G534 ?/3/07.
D693 *(new, sup)* ?/9/18.
D627 *(exJ21 1073)* 8/2/35.
D1342 *(exJ21 1515)* 19/7/41.
2190 *(exJ21 1609)* 11/10/44.
2192 *(exJ25 5662)* 21/11/47.

SHEDS:
East Hartlepool.
Alston 19/9/30.
Gateshead 1/5/33.
West Hartlepool 2/3/35.
Dairycoates 17/4/39.
Neville Hill 15/6/39.
Dairycoates 28/3/43.
Heaton 14/12/47.

RENUMBERED:
9380 10/11/46.

CONDEMNED: 21/11/50.
Cut up at Darlington.

_____

864

Gateshead 33-88.

To traffic 12/1888.

REPAIRS:
Rebuilt to simple with p.v.
??. ?/?—?/10/07.**G.**
Dar. 25/9/22—12/1/23.**G.**
Dar. 6/3—29/7/25.**G.**
Dar. 10/12/27—18/2/28.**G.**
Dar. 11/2—20/3/30.**G.**
Vacuum ejector fitted.
Dar. 29/9—3/11/32.**G.**
Dar. 18/11—23/12/35.**G.**
Dar. 15/12/37—2/2/38.**G.**
Dar. 2/7—2/8/40.**G.**
Dar. 22/9—20/10/43.**G.**
Dar. 3/4—17/5/47.**G.**
Changed from Westinghouse to steam brake, still with VE.
Dar. 14/9—20/10/49.**G.**
Dar. 11/9—17/10/52.**G.**
Dar. 28/10—6/11/52.**C/L.**

BOILERS:
G75.
G629 ?/10/07.
D1935 *(new)* 18/2/28.
D1518 *(ex445)* 23/12/35.
D1936 *(exN9 1649)* 20/10/43.
3416 *(ex9385)* 17/5/47.
3759 *(ex5695)* 20/10/49.
3759 reno.25100 17/10/52.

SHED:
Dairycoates.

RENUMBERED:
9381 20/10/46.
69381 20/10/49.

CONDEMNED: 29/6/55.
Cut up at Darlington.

_____

219

Darlington 61.

To traffic 12/1888.

REPAIRS:
??. ?/?—?/10/98.**G.**
Rebuilt to simple with p.v. 2/04.
??. ?/?—?/4/15.**G.**
Dar. 11/4—25/6/24.**G.**
Dar. 2/3—9/7/27.**G.**
Dar. 2/9—18/10/29.**G.**
Dar. 6/7—31/8/32.**G.**
Dar. 20/4—23/5/35.**G.**
Dar. 16/2—13/4/38.**G.**
Dar. 15/8—24/9/40.**G.**
Dar. 28/5—9/7/43.**G.**
Dar. 6/3—12/4/47.**G.**
Dar. 18/10—23/11/49.**G.**
Dar. 8—13/1/51.**N/C.**
Dar. 17/7/52. *Not repaired.*

BOILERS:
D655.
G832 ?/10/98.
D422 *(new, sup)* ?/4/15.
2363 *(new, sat)* 31/8/32.
D1268 *(exN10 89)* 23/5/35.
2364 *(ex218)* 24/9/40.
D1523 *(exJ25 2142)* 9/7/43.
2366 *(ex9396)* 12/4/47.
2366 reno.25037 13/1/51.

SHED:
Dairycoates.

RENUMBERED:
9382 12/5/46.
69382 23/11/49.

CONDEMNED: 17/7/52.
Cut up at Darlington.

_____

371

Darlington 62.

To traffic 12/1888.

REPAIRS:
??. ?/?—?/9/00.**G.**
Rebuilt to simple.
??. ?/?—?/5/12.**G.**
Dar. 29/10/24—29/1/25.**G.**
Dar. 25/1—30/3/28.**G.**

BOILERS:
D656.
6897 ?/9/00.
D91 *(new)* ?/5/12.

SHEDS:
Selby.
Dairycoates 16/9/29.

CONDEMNED: 21/5/31.
Cut up at Darlington.

_____

213

Darlington 63.

To traffic 12/1888.

REPAIRS:
??. ?/?—?/10/01.**G.**
Rebuilt to simple with p.v.
??. ?/?—?/2/18.**G.**
Dar. 3/8—20/10/23.**G.**
Dar. 30/12/25—29/4/26.**G.**
Dar. 27/11/28—25/1/29.**G.**
Vacuum ejector fitted.
Dar. 11/8—17/9/31.**G.**
Dar. 19/10—24/11/33.**G.**
Dar. 16/12/35. *Not repaired.*

BOILERS:
D657.
G115 10/01.
D744 *(new, sup)* ?/2/18.
D755 *(ex515)* 20/10/23.
D786 *(ex515)* 24/11/33.

SHED:
Neville Hill.

RENUMBERED:
213ᴅ 20/10/23.

CONDEMNED: 31/1/36.
Cut up at Darlington.

_____

284

Darlington 64.

To traffic 12/1888.

REPAIRS:
??. ?/?—?/9/06.**G.**
Rebuilt to simple with p.v.
??. ?/?—?/4/21.**G.**
Dar. 22/5—11/9/24.**G.**
Dar. 5/10—30/12/27.**G.**
Dar. 23/12/29—14/2/30.**G.**
Dar. 24/5—28/6/32.**G.**
Dar. 14/4—18/5/34.**G.**
Dar. 3/9/36. *Not repaired.*

BOILERS:
D658.
G515 ?/9/06.
D1198 *(new, sup)* ?/4/21.

SHED:
Dairycoates.

CONDEMNED: 3/10/36.
Cut up at Darlington.

_____

683

Darlington 65.

To traffic 12/1888.

REPAIRS:
??. ?/?—?/6/98.**G.**
??. ?/?—?/1/10.**G.**
Rebuilt to simple.
Ghd. 6/8—9/10/23.**G.**
Dar. 27/1—24/6/26.**G.**
Dar. 17/10—27/11/28.**G.**
Dar. 5/6—15/7/30.**N/C.**
Dar. 17/12/30—23/1/31.**N/C.**
Dar. 1/6—16/7/31.**G.**
Dar. 15/10—10/11/31.**N/C.**
Dar. 9/3—5/4/34.**G.**
Dar. 30/7—9/9/36.**G.**

(above) **At Grouping, the majority had a wheel and handle for fastening the smokebox door. By 1935 the wheel had almost entirely given place to a second handle although No.445 still had a wheel to January 1938.**

The smokebox door was almost flat, and had a broad rim which sealed by contact with a ring riveted to the front of the smokebox.

Beginning with No.573, ex works 25th May 1946, what was known as a pressed joint ring was introduced. It was of smaller diameter and welded to the front plate. It was U-shaped in section, into which asbestos packing was placed. A more dished door had a rim which pressed into the ring, instead of the flat contact made hitherto. Eighteen are known to have had this type but eight, Nos.9373, 9375, E9376, 9383, 69385, 69394, 9397, and 9399, kept the flat flange.

Until August 1940, the normal whistle gear was two bell shape types on the cab roof with the larger one on the right hand – the drivers – side.

During the early 1930s at least nine had the drivers whistle changed to the organ pipe type. So noted were Nos.212, 218, 346, 348, 445, 509, 515, 961, and 1124.

No.1091's whistles were a curiosity. Even when two bell-shaped were fitted (*see* page 12, top), they were opposite of normal, the larger one being on the left side. In September 1933 that changed to organ pipe and the reversed positions were kept until September 1943.

When No.864 was ex works on 2nd August 1940 it had been fitted with new whistle gear of only one small bell-shape but still positioned above the cab roof. By November 1944 another nineteen, all still with Diagram 67 boilers, had this style of whistle: Nos.74, 76, 136, 210, 212, 219, 267, 271, 293, 348, 515, 573, 780, 862, 863, 1072, 1091, 1105 and 1127.

683 cont./
Dar. 10—23/9/36.**N/C.**
Dar. 12/7/39. *Not repaired.*

BOILERS:
 D659.
 G379 ?/6/98.
 G748 ?/1/10.
 2090 *(new)* 27/11/28.
D1089 *(ex185)* 5/4/34.

SHED:
Dairycoates.

RENUMBERED:
863ᴅ 9/10/23.

CONDEMNED: 15/7/39.
Cut up at Darlington.

_____

346

Darlington 66.

To traffic 2/1889.

REPAIRS:
 ??. ?/?—?/2/05.**G.**
Rebuilt to simple with p.v. 7/08.
Dar. 1/2—31/3/24.**G.**
Dar. 14/12/26—21/3/27.**G.**
Dar. 24/5—30/7/29.**G.**
Dar. 11/5—9/6/32.**G.**
Dar. 22/8—4/10/34.**G.**
Dar. 16/8—29/9/37.**G.**
Dar. 22/4—21/6/39.**L.**
Dar. 20/5—13/6/40.**G.**
Dar. 24/9—23/10/43.**G.**
Dar. 22/5—12/6/45.**L.**
Dar. 24/10—30/11/46.**G.**

BOILERS:
 D660.
D1868 ?/2/05.
D1518 *(new)* 31/3/24.
D1506 *(new, sup)* 21/3/27.
 D755 *(exJ21 314)* 13/6/40.
 3413 *(new, sat)* 23/10/43#.
 3436 *(ex9375)* 30/11/46#.

SHED:
Dairycoates.

RENUMBERED:
9383 1/9/46.

CONDEMNED: 29/8/49.
Cut up at Darlington.

_____

348

Darlington 67.

To traffic 2/1889.

REPAIRS:
 ??. ?/?—?/2/05.**G.**
Rebuilt to simple with p.v. 5/07.
 ??. ?/?—?/8/13.**G.**
 ??. ?/?—?/2/19.**G.**
 ??. ?/?—?/11/21.**G.**
Ghd. 7/1—30/3/25.**H.**
Dar. 28/8—16/11/28.**G.**
Dar. 17/2—7/3/30.**N/C.**
Vacuum ejector fitted.
Dar. 24/6—21/8/31.**G.**
Dar. 12/12/33—20/1/34.**G.**
Dar. 29/4—27/6/36.**G.**
Dar. 7/12/38—18/1/39.**G.**
Dar. 7—17/3/39.**N/C.**
Dar. 1—23/10/40.**N/C.**
Dar. 25/7—12/9/42.**G.**
Dar. 28/6—17/8/46.**G.**
Changed from Westinghouse to steam brake, still with VE.

BOILERS:
 D661.
D1862 ?/2/05.
 G893 ?/8/13.
 D747 *(new, sup)* ?/2/19.
 D760 *(ex1072)* 30/3/25.
D1489 *(ex74)* 20/1/34.
D1387 *(ex210)* 18/1/39.
 2575 *(exJ21 5109)* 17/8/46.

SHEDS:
Blaydon.
Starbeck 18/2/26.
Springhead 28/3/43.
Borough Gardens 12/3/45.
Sunderland 6/9/46.
Consett 20/1/47.

RENUMBERED:
9384 22/12/46.

CONDEMNED: 14/3/49.
Cut up at Darlington.

_____

349

Darlington 68.

To traffic 2/1889.

REPAIRS:
 ??. ?/?—?/12/07.**G.**
Rebuilt to simple with p.v.
 ??. ?/?—?/3/18.**G.**
 ??. ?/?—?/9/21.**.?.**
Ghd. 23/12/26—7/4/27.**G.**
Ghd. 14/10—19/11/30.**G.**

Dar. 31/5—26/6/34.**L.**
Dar. 11—26/3/35.**L.**
Dar. 23/3—20/5/36.**H.**

BOILERS:
 D662.
 G640 ?/12/07.
 D672 *(new, sup)* ?/3/18.

SHED:
Bowes Bridge.

CONDEMNED: 26/6/37.
Into Dar. for cut up 14/8/37.

_____

350

Darlington 69.

To traffic 3/1889.

REPAIRS:
 ??. ?/?—?/9/05.**G.**
Rebuilt to simple with p.v.
 ??. ?/?—?/7/22.**G.**
Ghd. 11/11/26—2/2/27.**G.**
Ghd. 20/8—20/9/28.**L.**
Ghd. 1/6—17/7/31.**G.**
Dar. 26/11/36. *Not repaired.*

BOILERS:
 D663.
 G465 ?/9/05.
D1265 *(new)* ?/7/22.
D1509 *(new, sup)* 2/2/27.

SHED:
Waskerley.

CONDEMNED: 12/12/36.
Cut up at Darlington.

_____

351

Darlington 70.

To traffic 3/1889.

REPAIRS:
 ??. ?/?—?/12/04.**G.**
Rebuilt to simple 3/11.
 ??. ?/?—?/7/20.**G.**
Dar. 2/10—23/12/25.**G.**
Dar. 18/10—7/12/28.**G.**

BOILERS:
 D664.
D1864 ?/12/04.
D1092 *(new)* ?/7/20.

SHEDS:
Springhead.
Dairycoates ?/9/25.

Shildon 27/5/27.
Dairycoates 27/8/27.

CONDEMNED: 17/9/30.
Cut up at Darlington.

_____

373

Darlington 71.

To traffic 4/1889.

REPAIRS:
 ??. ?/?—?/12/05.**G.**
Rebuilt to simple with p.v.
 ??. ?/?—?/10/15.**G.**
Dar. 25/10/22—24/1/23.**G.**
Dar. 25/9—16/12/25.**G.**
Dar. 13/6—27/8/28.**G.**
Dar. 27/6—10/9/30.**G.**

BOILERS:
 D689.
 G872 ?/12/05.
 D439 *(new, sup)* ?/10/15.

SHEDS:
Dairycoates.
Shildon 27/5/27.
Dairycoates 27/8/27.

CONDEMNED: 20/4/33.
Cut up at Darlington.

_____

1124

Darlington 72.

To traffic 4/1889.

REPAIRS:
 ??. ?/?—?/10/03.**G.**
Rebuilt to simple with p.v. 2/04.
 ??. ?/?—?/10/20.**G.**
Dar. 19/4—26/7/23.**G.**
Dar. 1/9—29/11/25.**G.**
Dar. 2/6—2/8/28.**G.**
Dar. 12/4—15/7/30.**G.**
Dar. 28/7—1/9/33.**G.**
Dar. 7/4—26/5/36.**G.**
Dar. 17/3—25/5/37.**H.**
Dar. 12/7/39. *Not repaired.*

BOILERS:
D1775 ?/10/03.
 D786 *(new, sup)* ?/10/20.
 D411 *(exJ25 2037)* 26/7/23.
 D441 *(ex218)* 15/7/30.
 D788 *(exJ25 2067)* 26/5/36.

SHED:
Dairycoates.

On the Diagram 67A boiler, the whistle was mounted over an isolating valve and fitted on the firebox between the safety valves and the cab.

The cylinder and valves of superheated engines were lubricated by a NER type mechanical device mounted on the left hand running plate and driven off the crosshead. When the superheater was removed the mechanical lubricator was usually left in place – *see* bottom illustration.

Only a few survived Grouping still fitted with parallel shank buffers housing a hollow spindle.

Alteration to taper shank with solid spindle was still being made in 1923 – *see* page 34, bottom of No.213. None of this class acquired Group Standard buffers.

Quite late in its life No.69390 had circular wooden pads put behind its front buffers although it had a wood sandwich type bufferbeam. Note the prominent inner rim to the chimney which, as centre photograph on page 15 shows, was not a windjabber. These wooden pads were also fitted to No.69394.

On the engines fitted for working passenger trains, wood sandwich front buffer beams was normal, and only Nos.210, 863 and 961 had single steel plate beams – *see* page 33, bottom.

(below) On the other hand, at least nine of those fitted only with steam brake, had the wood sandwich buffer beam at the front end. These were Nos.287, 346, 445, 503, 509, 573, 857, 1091 and 1127.

1124 cont./
CONDEMNED: 15/7/39.
Laid aside and cut up at
Darlington November/December
1939.

_____

1145

Darlington 73.

To traffic 4/1889.

REPAIRS:
  ??. ?/?—?/2/06.**G**.
Rebuilt to simple with p.v.
  ??. ?/?—?/10/11.**G**.
Ghd. 5/1—29/3/23.**G**.
Ghd. 25/1—23/4/26.**G**.
Ghd. 14/10—2/12/29.**G**.
Ghd. 20/5—4/7/32.**G**.
Dar. 26/11/36. *Not repaired.*

BOILERS:
D1112 ?/2/06.
 G824 ?/10/11.
D2177 *(new)* 2/12/29.

SHED:
Sunderland.

CONDEMNED: 12/12/36.
Cut up at Darlington.

_____

1152

Darlington 74.

To traffic 4/1889.

REPAIRS:
  ??. ?/?—?/2/06.**G**.
Rebuilt to simple 1/12.
Piston valves fitted 5/22.
Dar. 12/8—20/10/24.**G**.
Dar. 29/10—18/11/24.**L**.
Dar. 12/12/24—8/1/25.**L**.
Dar. 13/9—28/11/27.**G**.
Ghd. 2/6—14/7/32.**G**.
Dar. 4/4—22/5/34.**H**.
Dar. 17/8—17/9/37.**G**.
Dar. 15/7—23/8/40.**G**.
Dar. 29/9—28/10/43.**G**.
Dar. 20/3—19/4/47.**G**.
Ghd. 1/10—11/11/47.**L**.
Dar. 7/10—1/11/49.**G**.
Dar. 19/6—8/7/50.**C/L**.
After collision.
Dar. 15/11—11/12/51.**G**.

BOILERS:
 G481 ?/2/06.
D1490 *(new, sup)* 20/10/24.
 D551 *(ex531)* 17/9/37.

3416 *(new, sat)* 28/10/43#.
3268 *(exJ25 5695)* 19/4/47#.
3413 *(ex9397)* 1/11/49#.
25072 *(ex??)* 11/12/51#.

SHEDS:
Selby.
Consett 22/7/29.
Waskerley 30/12/35.
Consett 7/2/38.
Dairycoates 8/6/39.

RENUMBERED:
  9385 3/3/46.
69385 1/11/49.

CONDEMNED: 27/10/54.
Cut up at Darlington.

_____

1127

Darlington 78.

To traffic 5/1889.

REPAIRS:
  ??. ?/?—?/4/98.**G**.
Rebuilt to simple with p.v. 2/06.
  ??. ?/?—?/3/15.**G**.
Ghd. 18/7—24/9/24.**G**.
Ghd. 28/9—5/11/25.**L**.
Ghd. 6/11—23/12/29.**G**.
Dar. 22/6—18/7/34.**G**.
Dar. 28/3—22/6/38.**G**.
Dar. 27/3—1/5/41.**G**.
Dar. 20/3—15/4/44.**G**.
Dar. 12/5—14/6/47.**G**.
Dar. 2—16/1/48.**L**.
Dar. 30/9—22/10/49.**G**.
Dar. 4—22/3/52.**G**.
Ghd. 24/10—14/11/52.**C/L**.

BOILERS:
 D696.
 G377 ?/4/98.
 D427 *(new, sup)* ?/3/15.
D1197 *(ex959)* 18/7/34.
D1490 *(ex1152)* 22/6/38.
 2572 *(exJ21 1550)* 15/4/44.
 2491 *(ex9398)* 14/6/47.
 2650 *(exJ21 5078)* 22/10/49.
25085 *(ex??)* 22/3/52#.

SHEDS:
Gateshead.
Blaydon 14/8/29.
Sunderland 7/10/31.
Bowes Bridge 24/6/37.
Tyne Dock 28/10/37.
Borough Gardens 6/9/38.
Dairycoates 10/7/39.

RENUMBERED:
  9386 27/1/46.

69386 22/10/49.

CONDEMNED: 28/2/55.
Cut up at Darlington.

_____

136

Darlington 75.

To traffic 5/1889.

REPAIRS:
  ??. ?/?—?/6/02.**G**.
Rebuilt to simple with p.v. 8/08.
  ??. ?/?—?/12/20.**G**.
Ghd. 17/1—4/3/24.**G**.
Ghd. 10/12/26—11/7/27.**G**.
Ghd. 7—24/9/28.**L**.
After derailment.
Ghd. 4/6—25/7/30.**G**.
Vacuum ejector fitted.
Dar. 31/10—30/11/34.**G**.
Dar. 31/5—15/7/37.**H**.
New 19in. cylinders.
Dar. 4/8—8/9/39.**G**.
Dar. 28/9—14/10/39.**N/C**.
Dar. 18/3—10/4/41.**L**.
Dar. 3/2—1/4/43.**G**.
Dar. 24/10/45—10/1/46.**G**.
Changed from Westinghouse to
steam brake, still with VE.
Dar. 21/6—10/8/46.**L**.
Ghd. 9/7—9/10/47.**L**.
Dar. 24/5—18/6/49.**G**.

BOILERS:
 D693.
 G172 ?/6/02.
D1142 *(new)* ?/12/20.
D1098 *(exJ25 2126)* 30/11/34.
D1260 *(exJ25 2050)* 8/9/39.
 2082 *(ex445)* 10/1/46.
 3738 *(ex74)* 18/6/49#.

SHEDS:
Waskerley.
Consett 30/12/35.
Waskerley 7/2/38.
Heaton 24/11/39.
Dairycoates 28/3/43.
Heaton 14/12/47.

RENUMBERED:
  9387 8/12/46.
69387 18/6/49.

CONDEMNED: 7/7/52.
Cut up at Darlington.

_____

445

Darlington 76.

To traffic 5/1889.

REPAIRS:
  ??. ?/?—?/4/02.**G**.
Rebuilt to simple 4/10.
  ??. ?/?—?/3/21.**G**.
Piston valves fitted.
Dar. 29/2—6/5/24.**G**.
Dar. 28/1—16/5/27.**G**.
Dar. 19/8—9/10/29.**G**.
Dar. 17/11—23/12/31.**G**.
Dar. 4/5—14/6/35.**G**.
Dar. 17—21/6/35.**N/C**.
Dar. 20/1—18/2/38.**G**.
Dar. 17/1—13/3/40.**G**.
Dar. 30/1—13/3/43.**G**.
Dar. 27/10/45. *Not repaired.*

BOILERS:
 D694.
 G161 ?/4/02.
 G609 ?/3/21.
D1934 *(new)* 16/5/27.
D1518 *(ex346)* 23/12/31.
 2363 *(ex219)* 14/6/35.
D1238 *(exJ21 665)* 18/2/38.
 2082 *(exJ25 2051)* 13/3/40.

SHEDS:
Starbeck.
Selby 8/10/24.
Springhead 28/3/43.

RENUMBERED:
9388 allocated.

CONDEMNED: 8/12/45.
Cut up at Darlington.

_____

523

Darlington 77.

To traffic 5/1889.

REPAIRS:
  ??. ?/?—?/5/06.**G**.
Rebuilt to simple with p.v. 2/07.
Dar. 4/12/23—28/2/24.**G**.
Dar. 30/11/26—25/2/27.**G**.
Dar. 8/8—28/9/29.**G**.
Dar. 18/5—27/6/32.**G**.
Dar. 30/7—31/8/34.**G**.

BOILERS:
 D695
 G501 ?/5/06.
D1511 *(new)* 28/2/24.
D1428 *(new, sup)* 25/2/27.

(above) The nineteen fitted for passenger working, with the exception of No.216, had screw coupling and carriage heating apparatus with connecting hose at both ends.

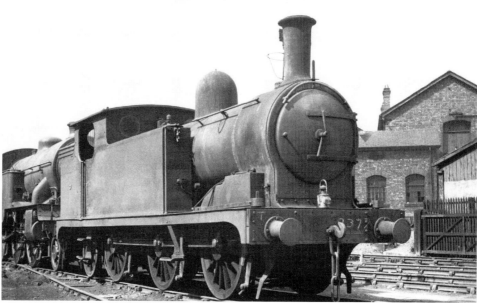

The other forty-three were always rated as goods engines and had three-link loose couplings and no train braking facility.

From 1909 plating had been fitted behind the bunker rails to help prevent coal being spilled. At first two rails were the normal fitment.

(above) **By 1923 a start had been made on adding a third rail, but that process was never completed.**

No.69372 at its 27th November 1950 withdrawal still had only two rails on the bunker, as did No.69385 to 27th October 1954 withdrawal – *see* page 39, bottom.

The fitting of superheaters did not change the status as to goods or passenger type and twenty-four superheated engines still had only steam brakes and no train braking facility. These were Nos.74, 219, 284, 293, 346, 349, 350, 373, 503, 504, 515, 523, 531, 535, 780, 859, 862, 959, 1072, 1091, 1124, 1127, 1152, and 1165.

523 cont./
SHED:
Dairycoates.

CONDEMNED: 15/5/37.
Into Dar. for cut up 31/7/37.

509

Darlington 79.

To traffic 6/1889.

REPAIRS:
Dar. ?/3/08—?/12/10.**G**.
Rebuilt to simple.
Dar. 3/5—13/7/24.**G**.
Dar. 13/7—29/11/27.**G**.
Dar. 1/10—19/11/29.**G**.
Dar. 1/2—3/3/32.**G**.
Dar. 29/5—23/6/34.**G**.
Dar. 19/12/36. *Not repaired.*

BOILERS:
  D697.
  G823 ?/12/10.
D1936 *(new)* 29/11/27.
  2090 *(ex683)* 23/6/34.

SHED:
Dairycoates.

CONDEMNED: 9/1/37.
Cut up at Darlington.

1105

Darlington 80.

To traffic 6/1889.

REPAIRS:
  ??. ?/?—?/4/08.**G**.
Rebuilt to simple 1/11.
  ??. ?/?—?/7/18.**G**.
  ??. ?/?—17/3/22.**?**.
Ghd. 12/4—5/8/26.**G**.
Ghd. 1/8—10/9/30.**G**.
Ghd. 4/8—6/9/32.**H**.
Dar. 28/5—28/8/34.**L**.
Dar. 12/6—16/7/35.**H**.
Dar. 22/11/37—4/1/38.**G**.
Dar. 13/2—21/3/41.**G**.
Dar. 1/7—17/8/43.**G**.
Dar. 19/10—21/11/46.**G**.
Dar. 9/9—1/10/49.**G**.

BOILERS:
  D698.
  G644 ?/4/08.
D1818 *(new)* 5/8/26.
  3390 *(new)* 17/8/43#.
  3748 *(exJ25 5687)* 1/10/49#.

SHEDS:
Waskerley.
Borough Gardens 2/12/38.
Dairycoates 30/6/39.

RENUMBERED:
  9389 27/1/46.
  69389 1/10/49.

CONDEMNED: 7/7/52.
Cut up at Darlington.

215

Darlington 92.

To traffic 10/1889.

REPAIRS:
Dar. ?/?—11/05.**G**.
Rebuilt to simple 12/10.
Dar. 20/12/22—10/4/23.**G**.
Dar. 22/5—5/6/24.**L**.
Dar. 25/6—13/8/24.**L**.
Dar. 13/9—22/12/26.**G**.
Dar. 10/12/28—31/1/29.**G**.
Dar. 18/8—22/9/31.**G**.
Dar. 27/4—26/5/34.**G**.
Dar. 19/12/36. *Not repaired.*

BOILERS:
  D770.
D1867 ?/11/05.
D1474 *(new)* 10/4/23.
D1261 *(ex287)* 26/5/34.

SHED:
Dairycoates.

CONDEMNED: 9/1/37.
Cut up at Darlington.

216

Darlington 91.

To traffic 10/1889.

REPAIRS:
  ??. ?/?—?/10/01.**G**.
Rebuilt to simple 6/09.
  ??. ?/?—?/6/17.**G**.
  ??. ?/?—?/9/21.**G**.
Dar. 4/12/23—28/2/24.**G**.
Dar. 21/3—11/4/24.**L**.
Dar. 16/5—30/7/27.**G**.
Dar. 16/12/29—8/2/30.**G**.
Vacuum ejector fitted.

BOILERS:
  D769.
  G96 ?/10/01.
  G473 ?/6/17.

D1268 *(new)* ?/9/21.

SHED:
Dairycoates.

CONDEMNED: 12/12/31.
Cut up at Darlington.

218

Darlington 93.

To traffic 11/1889.

REPAIRS:
  ??. ?/?—?/3/02.**G**.
Rebuilt to simple with p.v. 9/04.
  ??. ?/?—?/11/16.**G**.
  ??. ?/?—?/12/20.**G**.
Dar. 29/10/24—26/1/25.**G**.
Dar. 28/8—19/10/28.**G**.
Dar. 14/10—27/11/29.**N/C**.
Vacuum ejector fitted.
Dar. 30/5—31/8/32.**G**.
Dar. 9/1—20/2/33.**L**.
Dar. 6/2—20/3/35.**G**.
Dar. 6/10—12/11/37.**G**.
Dar. 8/7—17/8/40.**G**.
Dar. 26/7/43. *Not repaired.*

BOILERS:
  D771.
  G163 ?/3/02.
  D441 *(new, sup)* ?/11/16.
  D437 *(ex861)* 19/10/28.
  2364 *(new, sat)* 31/8/32.
D1089 *(ex683)* 17/8/40.

SHEDS:
Starbeck.
Pickering 9/10/34.
Dairycoates 19/11/34.

CONDEMNED: 4/9/43.
Cut up at Darlington.

238

Darlington 94.

To traffic 11/1889.

REPAIRS:
  ??. ?/?—?/10/02.**G**.
Rebuilt to simple 7/11.
  ??. ?/?—?/12/16.**G**.
Ghd. 6/8—1/10/24.**G**.
Ghd. 7/6—3/7/29. *Not repaired
and sent to Dar. for scrapping.*

BOILERS:
  D772.
D1767 ?/10/02.

G895 ?/12/16.

SHED:
Consett.

CONDEMNED: 8/7/29.
Cut up at Darlington.

345

Darlington 95.

To traffic 11/1889.

REPAIRS:
  ??. ?/?—?/6/02.**G**.
Rebuilt to simple with p.v. 7/07.
  ??. ?/?—?/2/19.**G**.
Ghd. ?/?—28/7/22.**G**.
Ghd. 16/3—3/5/23.**L**.
Ghd. 6—25/7/23.**L**.
*Changed from steam to
Westinghouse brake.*
Ghd. 12/10—30/12/25.**G**.
Dar. 4/5—20/7/28.**G**.
Dar. 10/3—17/4/30.**N/C**.
Vacuum ejector fitted.
Dar. 4/12/30—30/1/31.**G**.
Dar. 30/12/31—15/1/32.**N/C**.
Dar. 5/9—17/10/32.**H**.
Dar. 13/7—28/8/33.**G**.
Dar. 25/11/35—17/1/36.**G**.
Dar. 2/4—20/5/36.**H**.
Dar. 20/6—4/8/38.**G**.
Dar. 5—10/8/38.**N/C**.
Dar. 12/3—9/6/41.**G**.
Dar. 6/9—23/10/44.**G**.
*Changed from Westinghouse to
steam brake, still with VE.*
Dar. 10/5—7/6/47.**G**.
Dar. 10—19/6/47.**N/C**.
Ghd. 26/1—10/3/48.**L**.
Dar. 25/5—17/6/50.**G**.
Dar. 19—20/6/50.**N/C**.
Ghd. 1—3/5/51.**C/L**.
Ghd. 11/5—12/6/53.**G**.
Ghd. 15—18/6/53.**N/C**.

BOILERS:
  D773.
  G162 ?/6/02.
  D692 *(new, sup)* ?/2/19.
  2491 *(new)* 28/8/33.
  D746 *(ex504)* 4/8/38.
  3204 *(new)* 9/6/41#.
D1197 *(ex9379)* 7/6/47.
  2494 *(ex9373)* 17/6/50.
25051 *(ex??)* 12/6/53#.

SHEDS:
East Hartlepool.
Starbeck 18/2/26.
Neville Hill 27/7/37.
Dairycoates 28/3/43.

(above) There were also nineteen not superheated which were only ever steam braked. These being Nos.14, 185, 215, 238, 271, 287, 351, 371, 428, 445, 509, 528, 573, 683, 857, 858, 1105, 1145, and 1168.

(left) Between December 1899 and 1902, fifteen engines Nos.76, 136, 210, 212, 213, 216, 218, 267, 348, 855, 856, 860, 864, 961 and 1104, were fitted with Westinghouse brakes for engine and train working. Four more were similarly fitted late: Nos.861 in March 1906, 863 in June 1922, 345 and 809 in June 1923.

Under the 1928 Unification of Brakes programme nineteen had vacuum ejectors and train pipes added from January 1929 to November 1930. Nine remained dual fitted to withdrawal.

The last N8 to retain Westinghouse equipment was No.69378 which kept it to its 26th September 1955 withdrawal.

The vacuum ejector exhaust pipe did not have a condensing drain pipe fitted until after August 1935 and for some years there was no external evidence of it but by January 1939 No.348 – *see* page 22, second from top – had one emerging from the right hand side of the smokebox.

The other ten which had Westinghouse equipment had it taken off from March 1944 to November 1947. The vacuum was then combined with an automatic steam brake.

345 cont./
Heaton 14/12/47.
Consett 14/9/52.
Sunderland 14/2/54.
Tyne Dock 23/10/55.

RENUMBERED:
 9390 15/12/46.
 69390 17/6/50.

CONDEMNED: 18/10/56.
Cut up at Darlington.

_____

515

Darlington 96.

To traffic 11/1889.

REPAIRS:
Dar. ?/?—?/3/01.**G.**
Reb. to simple with p.v. 10/08.
Dar. ?/?—?/5/19.**G.**
Dar. 12/6—11/9/23.**G.**
Dar. 9/7—10/11/26.**G.**
Dar. 7/2—27/3/29.**G.**
Dar. 14/7– 31/10/31.**G.**
Dar. 21/9—24/10/33.**G.**
Dar. 3/6—11/7/36.**G.**
Dar. 11/1—15/2/39.**G.**
Dar. 30/4—5/7/41.**G.**
Dar. 22/3—20/4/44.**G.**
Dar. 28/9—21/11/46.**G.**
Dar. 15/3—9/4/49.**G.**
Ghd. 20/2—13/3/52.**C/L.**
After collision.
Dar. 3/2/53. *Not repaired.*

BOILERS:
 D774.
  G61 ?/3/01.
 D755 *(new, sup)* ?/5/19.
 D786 *(ex1124)* 11/9/23.
 D1192 *(ex535)* 24/10/33.
  2490 *(ex267)* 20/4/44.
  2575 *(ex348)* 9/4/49.

SHEDS:
Dairycoates.
Borough Gardens 22/1/50.
Heaton 24/12/50.

RENUMBERED:
 9391 19/5/46.
 69391 9/4/49.

CONDEMNED: 16/2/53.
Cut up at Darlington.

_____

573

Darlington 97.

To traffic 12/1889.

REPAIRS:
 ??. ?/?—?/6/05.**G.**
Rebuilt to simple 3/11.
 ??. ?/?—?/2/22.**G.**
Dar. 1/1—20/3/24.**G.**
Dar. 17/3—28/5/27.**G.**
Dar. 9/4—30/5/29.**G.**
Dar. 29/6—24/8/31.**G.**
Dar. 13/6—13/7/34.**G.**
Dar. 20/4—24/5/37.**G.**
Dar. 14/2—9/4/40.**G.**
Dar. 1/7—18/8/43.**G.**
Dar. 30/4—25/5/46.**G.**
Dar. 3—29/10/48.**G.**
Dar. 1—24/11/51.**G.**
Dar. 26—27/11/51.**N/C.**
Dar. 11—15/12/51.**N/C.**

BOILERS:
 D775.
D1865 ?/6/05.
D1260 *(new)* ?/2/22.
D1936 *(ex509)* 13/7/34.
 D923 *(exJ25 1994)* 9/4/40.
  3697 *(new)* 25/5/46#.
  3682 *(exJ21 5118)* 29/10/48#.
 25063 *(ex??)* 24/11/51#.

SHEDS:
Dairycoates.
Tyne Dock 1/3/53.
Sunderland 8/3/53.

RENUMBERED:
 9392 1/9/46.
 69392 29/10/48.

CONDEMNED: 4/5/55.
Cut up at Darlington.

_____

809

Darlington 98.

To traffic 12/1889.

REPAIRS:
 ??. ?/?—?/7/01.**G.**
Reb. to simple with p.v. 12/07.
 ??. ?/?—?/10/18.**G.**
Ghd. ?/?—31/3/22.**G.**
Ghd. 24/4—4/6/23.**L.**
Changed from steam to
Westinghouse brake.
Ghd. 16/11/25—23/2/26.**G.**
Ghd. 5—25/1/28.**L.**
Ghd. 29/9—7/11/30.**G.**
Vacuum ejector fitted.

Dar. 23/1—23/2/34.**G.**
Dar. 9/3/37. *Not repaired.*

BOILERS:
 D776.
  G87 ?/7/01.
  G534 ?/10/18.
D1217 *(new, sup)* 31/3/22.
 D760 *(ex348)* 23/2/34.

SHEDS:
East Hartlepool.
West Hartlepool 9/7/31.

CONDEMNED: 27/3/37.
Cut up at Darlington.

_____

1072

Darlington 99.

To traffic 12/1889.

REPAIRS:
 ??. ?/?—?/8/01.**G.**
Reb. to simple with p.v. 10/06.
 ??. ?/?—?/12/19.**G.**
 ??. ?/?—2/6/22.**?.**
Ghd. 23/6—2/10/24.**G.**
Ghd. 5/5—13/7/28.**G.**
Ghd. 14—25/4/30.**L.**
Dar. 8/6—8/8/36.**G.**
Dar. 1—29/5/40.**G.**
Dar. 20/8—21/9/43.**G.**
Dar. 4/9—9/10/46.**G.**
Dar. 30/11—24/12/46.**L.**
Dar. 16/6—15/7/49.**G.**
Ghd. 22/8—12/9/49.**C/L.**
Dar. 25/10/52. *Not repaired.*

BOILERS:
 D777.
  G88 ?/8/01.
 D760 *(new, sup)* ?/12/19.
 D768 *(ex855)* 2/10/24.
  2185 *(exJ21 1590)* 21/9/43.
 D1387 *(ex348)* 9/10/46.
  2490 *(ex9391)* 15/7/49.

SHEDS:
Blaydon.
Tweedmouth 16/9/35.
Dairycoates 5/10/39.

RENUMBERED:
 9393 17/2/46.
 69393 15/7/49.

CONDEMNED: 25/10/52.
Cut up at Darlington.

_____

1168

Darlington 100.

To traffic 12/1889.

REPAIRS:
 ??. ?/?—?/5/97.**G.**
Rebuilt to simple 5/04.
 ??. ?/?—?/9/10.**G.**
Ghd. 26/10/23—9/1/24.**G.**
Ghd. 2/11—2/12/25.**L.**
Ghd. 26/11/26—18/5/27.**G.**

BOILERS:
D778.
G373 ?/5/97.
G822 ?/9/10.

SHED:
Waskerley.

RENUMBERED:
1168ᴅ 9/1/24.

CONDEMNED: 15/1/31.
Cut up at Darlington.

_____

76

Darlington 101.

To traffic 2/1890.

REPAIRS:
Rebuilt to simple 8/02.
 ??. ?/?—11/04.**G.**
 ??. ?/?—?/9/18.**G.**
Piston valves fitted.
Dar. 6/2—14/4/24.**G.**
Dar. 15/10/26—24/3/27.**G.**
Dar. 13/3—11/7/29.**G.**
Vacuum ejector fitted.
Dar. 8/12/31—1/2/32.**G.**
Dar. 6/3—9/4/34.**G.**
Dar. 20/1—26/2/36.**G.**
Dar. 17/8—16/9/38.**G.**
Dar. 20/1—24/2/41.**L.**
Dar. 4/11—6/12/41.**G.**
Dar. 10/3—15/4/44.**G.**
Changed from Westinghouse to
steam brake , still with VE.
Dar. 16/6—12/7/47.**G.**
Dar. 6—14/10/47.**N/C.**
Dar. 8/1—10/3/50.**G.**
Dar. 14—16/3/50.**N/C.**
Ghd. 28/4—23/5/53.**L/I.**
Dar. 27—29/5/53.**N/C.**

BOILERS:
 D779.
D1870 ?/11/04.
 D679 *(new, sup)* ?/9/18.
  2494 *(new)* 9/4/34.

No.69387 (ex 136) was never superheated and so did not get mechanical lubrication. The cylinders and valves were fed from Globe displacement lubricators on the sides of the smokebox.

Although the Globe lubricator was antiquated it was effective and No.69381 still had that type to its 29th June 1955 withdrawal when it was the last of the engines which had never carried a superheater.

Passenger workings took some of the class on lines for which they had to be fitted with Raven fog signalling apparatus. The striker for it can be seen between the leading and middle coupled wheels.

At Grouping, standard painting was unlined black, even for passenger engines. Note the 24in. brass numberplate had already been superseded by the $8^5/_8$in. wide plate, which the LNER adopted as standard.

To June 1928 it is believed they had single red lining but thereafter were plain black until the 1950s. Only two seem to have had L.&N.E.R., Nos.215 (10th April 1923), and 293 (29th May 1923) but seven got the area suffix D, Nos.515ᴅ (11th September 1923), 683ᴅ (9th October 1923), 213ᴅ (20th October 1923), 780ᴅ (23rd November 1923), 185ᴅ (17th December 1923), 1168ᴅ (9th January 1924), and 267ᴅ (4th February 1924).

76 cont./
2572 (ex9386) 12/7/47.
3268 (ex9385, sat) 10/3/50#.
3268 reno.25111 23/5/53.

SHEDS:
Dairycoates.
Malton 4/2/25.
Dairycoates 10/7/25.
Pickering 19/11/34.
York 22/1/38.
Pickering 30/1/39.
York 16/11/40.
Heaton 7/12/40.
Consett 14/12/42.
Tyne Dock 14/3/54.

RENUMBERED:
  9394 21/6/46.
69394 10/3/50.

CONDEMNED: 3/10/55.
Cut up at Darlington.

267

Darlington 102.

To traffic 2/1890.

REPAIRS:
  ??. ?/?—?/7/01.**G**.
Rebuilt to simple with p.v. 6/07.
  ??. ?/?—?/2/21.**G**.
Dar. 1/11/23—4/2/24.**G**.
Dar. 19/6—12/7/24.**L**.
Dar. 26/4—16/9/26.**G**.
Dar. 5/7—17/9/28.**G**.
Dar. 11/11—20/12/29.**G**.
Vacuum ejector fitted.
Dar. 29/9—16/10/31.**L**.
Dar. 21/6—9/8/32.**G**.
Dar. 15/3—18/4/35.**G**.
Dar. 22/2—6/4/38.**G**.
Dar. 21/9—12/10/39.**L**.
Dar. 1/10—7/11/40.**G**.
Dar. 11/3—7/4/44.**G**.
Changed from Westinghouse to steam brake, still with VE.
Dar. 4/1—22/2/47.**G**.
Dar. 20/9—27/10/49.**G**.
Dar. 12/8/52. *Not repaired.*

BOILERS:
 D780.
  G89 ?/7/01.
D1185 (new, sup) ?/2/21.
  2648 (new) 18/4/35.
  2490 (ex1091) 7/11/40.
  2477 (exJ21 1562) 7/4/44.
  3088 (exJ25 1991) 22/2/47#.
  3333 (exJ21 5088) 27/10/49#.

SHEDS:
Starbeck.
West Hartlepool 22/8/41.
Northallerton 28/2/42.
Springhead 28/3/43.
Borough Gardens 12/3/45.
Sunderland 16/6/45.
Tyne Dock 27/9/45.
Consett 3/4/49.

RENUMBERED:
  267ᴅ 4/2/24.
  9395 7/7/46.
69395 27/10/49.

CONDEMNED: 18/8/52.
Cut up at Darlington.

271

Darlington 103.

To traffic 3/1890.

REPAIRS:
  ??. ?/?—?/4/01.**G**.
Rebuilt to simple 12/08.
  ??. ?/?—?/3/14.**G**.
  ??. ?/?—?/10/18.**G**.
  ??. ?/?—?/8/21.**G**.
Ghd. 27/1—28/3/25.**G**.
Ghd. 18/2—11/4/29.**G**.
Dar. 28/3—28/4/34.**G**.
Dar. 14/10—2/12/38.**G**.
Dar. 19/12/40—25/1/41.**G**.
Dar. 7/2—8/3/44.**G**.
Dar. 9/1—15/2/47.**G**.
Dar. 26/8/49. *Not repaired.*

BOILERS:
 D781.
  G65 ?/4/01.
D1798 ?/3/14.
D1863 (ex780) ?/10/18.
  G641 ?/8/21.
D1688 (new) 28/3/25.
  2366 (new) 28/4/34.
  3303 (exJ21 5056) 15/2/47#.

SHEDS:
Heaton.
Dairycoates 23/4/37.

RENUMBERED:
9396 1/9/46.

CONDEMNED: 29/8/49.
Cut up at Darlington.

287

Darlington 104.

To traffic 3/1890.

REPAIRS:
  ??. ?/?—?/10/05.**G**.
Rebuilt to simple 3/10.
  ??. ?/?—?/6/22.**G**.
Dar. 22/4—12/7/24.**G**.
Dar. 3/5—16/7/27.**G**.
Dar. 19/8—2/10/29.**G**.
Dar. 23/11/31—8/1/32.**G**.
Dar. 9/3—6/4/34.**G**.
Dar. 10—20/4/34.**N/C**.
Dar. 23/12/36. *Not repaired.*

BOILERS:
 D782.
D1871 ?/10/05.
D1261 (new) ?/6/22.
D1256 (ex528) 6/4/34.

SHED:
Dairycoates.

CONDEMNED: 9/1/37.
Cut up at Darlington.

780

Darlington 105.

To traffic 3/1890.

REPAIRS:
  ??. ?/?—?/5/05.**G**.
Rebuilt to simple with p.v. 4/07.
  ??. ?/?—?/12/18.**G**.
Ghd. 12/9—23/11/23.**G**.
Ghd. 18/2—28/3/25.**L**.
Ghd. 5/5—2/9/27.**G**.
Ghd. 19/9—5/11/30.**G**.
Dar. 7/4—6/6/36.**G**.
Dar. 4/1—22/2/38.**L**.
Dar. 21/3—17/5/39.**H**.
Dar. 31/10—27/11/40.**G**.
Dar. 8/1—2/2/44.**G**.
Dar. 15/11—14/12/46.**G**.
Dar. 8/8/49. *Not repaired.*

BOILERS:
 D783.
D1863 ?/5/05.
  D688 (new, sup) ?/12/18.
  D441 (ex1124) 6/6/36.
  3435 (new, sat) 2/2/44#.
  3413 (ex9383) 14/12/46#.

SHEDS:
Sunderland.
Borough Gardens 27/9/35.
Waskerley 2/12/38.

Dairycoates 4/8/39.

RENUMBERED:
  780ᴅ 23/11/23.
  9397 14/12/46.

CONDEMNED: 8/8/49.
Cut up at Darlington.

959

Darlington 106.

To traffic 3/1890.

REPAIRS:
Dar. ?/?—?/4/05.**G**.
Dar. ?/?—?/12/08.**G**.
Rebuilt to simple with p.v.
Dar. ?/?—?/4/21.**G**.
Dar. 25/3—27/7/23.**G**.
Dar. 13/11/25—15/2/26.**G**.
Dar. 3/9—25/10/28.**G**.
Dar. 26/8—5/10/31.**G**.
Dar. 11/5/34. *Not repaired.*

BOILERS:
 D784.
D779 (ex76) ?/4/05.
G745 ?/12/08.
D1197 (new, sup) ?/4/21.

SHED:
Dairycoates.

CONDEMNED: 25/5/34.
Cut up at Darlington.

961

Darlington 107.

To traffic 4/1890.

REPAIRS:
  ??. ?/?—?/10/01.**G**.
Rebuilt to simple with p.v. 9/07.
  ??. ?/?—?/11/17.**G**.
Ghd. 4/11/24—19/1/25.**G**.
Ghd. 3/10—22/11/29.**G**.
Vacuum ejector fitted.
Dar. 6/12/34—13/2/35.**G**.
Dar. 29/11/38—4/1/39.**H**.
Dar. 18/11—16/12/39.**G**.
Dar. 18—21/12/39.**N/C**.
Dar. 6—31/3/44.**G**.
Changed from Westinghouse to steam brake, still with VE.
Dar. 20/10—17/11/45.**L**.
After collision.
Dar. 14/4—10/5/47.**G**.
Dar. 8/12/49—18/1/50.**G**.

The North Eastern Area continued to put NER classification on the front bufferbeam in 2in. white letters and until 1932 did not change to the LNER equivalent.

From 1932 Class B was then shown as N8 and from March 1938 the other workshops applied this style of classification.

Starting in July 1942, only NE replaced LNER but in 12in. instead of 7½in. shaded transfers.

(above) In January 1946 LNER was restored and again in 7½in. shaded transfers. From 1943 to 1946 Darlington showed the month and year of General repair in 1°in. white figures just above the shaded numerals.

(right) During 1946 the thirty-one engines in stock when the scheme was formulated in 1943 were re-numbered from 9371 to 9401, and only 9388 (ex 445) failed to take its new number. Although No.9393, ex works 9th October 1946, had the usual shaded transfers (see page 21, bottom) by 14th December 1946 when No.9397 was ex works (see page 15, top), yellow painted and unshaded characters were being applied. As many as seventeen got this style, Nos.9371, 9373, 9377, 9378, 9379, 9380, 9381, 9382, 9385, 9386, 9390, 9394, 9395, 9396, 9397, 9398, and 9400.

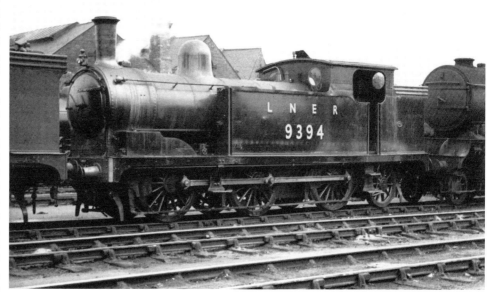

During the two months that numbers had the British Railways regional prefix put on, only one N8 got it, No.e9376, ex works 6th February 1948.

961 cont./
BOILERS:
 D785.
 G107 ?/10/01.
 D549 *(new, sup)* ?/11/17.
 D693 *(ex863)* 13/2/35.
 D1200 *(ex862)* 16/12/39.
  2491 *(exJ21 1613)* 31/3/44.
  2477 *(ex9395)* 10/5/47.
  2991 *(exN10 9094, sat)*
 18/1/50#.

SHEDS:
East Hartlepool.
West Hartlepool 28/3/38.
Dairycoates 24/4/39.
Neville Hill 22/6/39.
Dairycoates 28/3/43.
Neville Hill 15/8/48.
Dairycoates 17/10/48.

RENUMBERED:
 9398 27/10/46.
 69398 18/1/50.

CONDEMNED: 17/10/51.
Cut up at Darlington.

1091

Darlington 109.

To traffic 4/1890.

REPAIRS:
 ??. ?/?—?/2/99.**G.**
Rebuilt to simple with p.v. 1/07.
 ??. ?/?—?/5/12.**G.**
 ??. ?/?—?/3/17.**G.**
Ghd. 15/12/22—9/3/23.**G.**
Ghd. 20—26/9/23.**N/C.**
Ghd. 29/9/26—14/1/27.**G.**
Ghd. 1/11—20/12/29.**G.**
Ghd. 25/11—23/12/31.**L.**
Dar. 25/8—26/9/33.**G.**
Dar. 19/8—1/10/37.**G.**

Dar. 12/6—6/7/40.**G.**
Dar. 8/9—14/10/43.**G.**
Dar. 24/12/45—1/2/46.**G.**
Dar. 18/9/48. *Not repaired.*

BOILERS:
 D787.
 G890 ?/2/99.
 G895 ?/5/12.
 D543 *(new, sup)* ?/3/17.
  2490 *(new)* 26/9/33.
 D1498 *(exJ21 93)* 6/7/40.
  3398 *(new, sat)* 14/10/43#.

SHEDS:
Tweedmouth.
Dairycoates 9/11/39.
RENUMBERED:
9399 24/2/46.

CONDEMNED: 7/10/48.
Cut up at Darlington.

1104

Darlington 110.

To traffic 4/1890.

REPAIRS:
 ??. ?/5/04—?/12/05.**G.**
Rebuilt to simple with p.v.
 ??. ?/?—?/3/09.**G.**
Dar. 26/8—15/11/24.**G.**
Dar. 8/8—28/9/28.**G.**
Dar. 15/4—17/5/29.**H.**
Vacuum ejector fitted.
Dar. 16/7—2/8/29.**L.**
Dar. 31/3—14/5/31.**G.**
Dar. 29/2—31/3/32.**H.**
Dar. 7/12/34—21/4/35.**L.**
Dar. 13/9—21/10/38.**G.**
Dar. 22/10—18/11/43.**G.**
Dar. 12/9—17/10/47.**G.**
Altered to steam brake (date not confirmed).

Dar. 18/10/51. *Not repaired.*

BOILERS:
 D788.
D1120 ?/12/05.
 G747 ?/3/09.
D1511 *(ex523)* 28/9/28.
D1696 *(exJ21 511)* 21/10/38.
  2651 *(exJ25 2134)* 18/11/43.
  3198 *(exN9 9412)* 17/10/47#.

SHEDS:
Stockton.
Dairycoates 3/3/26.
Stockton 10/6/26.
Haverton Hill 25/3/29.
Stockton 18/1/37.
York 13/9/37.
Selby 31/1/38.
York 5/6/39.
Starbeck 9/12/40.
Springhead 28/3/43.
Borough Gardens 12/3/45.
Sunderland 2/11/47.
Tyne Dock 31/10/48.

RENUMBERED:
9400 20/1/46.

CONDEMNED: 22/10/51.
Cut up at Darlington.

293

Darlington 108.

To traffic 5/1890.

REPAIRS:
Rebuilt to simple with p.v. 7/05.
 ??. ?/?—?/4/08.**G.**
 ??. ?/?—?/6/17.**G.**
Ghd. 15/3—29/5/23.**G.**
Ghd. 26/4—1/9/26.**G.**
Ghd. 21/6—15/8/29.**G.**

Ghd. 29/4—18/7/32.**G.**
Dar. 13/2—11/3/35.**L.**
Dar. 25/5—9/7/38.**G.**
Dar. 17/9—18/10/41.**G.**
Dar. 1—27/4/44.**G.**
Dar. 5/10—2/11/46.**G.**
Dar. 15/2—12/3/49.**G.**
Dar. 17—21/3/49.**N/C.**

BOILERS:
 D786.
 G643 ?/4/08.
 D551 *(new, sup)* ?/6/17.
 D753 *(ex504)* 15/8/29.
D1197 *(ex1127)* 9/7/38.
  2192 *(exJ21 1575)* 18/10/41.
D1490 *(ex1127)* 27/4/44.
  2185 *(ex1072)* 2/11/46.
D1676 *(ex9371)* 12/3/49.

SHEDS:
Sunderland.
Borough Gardens 15/2/35.
Blaydon 17/4/39.
Waskerley 13/5/39.
Dairycoates 22/6/39.

RENUMBERED:
 9401 2/11/46.
 69401 12/3/49.

CONDEMNED: 25/8/51.
Cut up at Darlington.

The first to get full BR number did so combined with LNER. After repair to rear end collision damage No.69371 was ex Gateshead works on 19th April 1948 with 12in. number still on the tanks.

By the time the first N8 got BR painting, the settled style had been attained with 10in. letters and figures, with numbers on the bunker on the same level as lettering on the tank. Correct Gill sans was used, both painted and on the cast smokebox number plate. Seven got this style thus: Nos.69372 (15th October 1948), 69392 (29th October 1948), 69401 (12th March 1949), 69391 (9th April 1949), 69387 (18th June 1949), 69377 (2nd July 1949), and 69393 (15th July 1949). Only No.69392 had further change.

Lettering was discarded and the emblem took its place, still on unlined black. Ten of the N8 were so done: Nos. 69389 (1st October 1949), 69381 (20th October 1949), 69386 (22nd October 1949), 69395 (27th October 1949), 69385 (1st November 1949), 69379 (23rd November 1949), 69382 (23rd November 1949), 69398 (18th January 1950), 69394 (10th March 1950), 69390 (17th June 1950).

Finally, those getting heavy repairs from November 1951 acquired full BR lining of red, cream, and grey. Five were so treated: Nos. 69392 (24th November 1951), 69385 (11th December 1951), 69378 (15th December 1951), 69377 (8th March 1952), 69390 (12th June 1953). Two of these could qualify as mixed traffic locomotives but Nos.69377, 69385 and 69392 had been just steam braked goods types throughout their lives.

The three at Grouping still with smaller coal and water capacity were Nos.1645, 1648 and 1652. By then also, all except four, Nos.1642, 1647, 1650 and 1653 had had the well tank removed.

The LNER did not change any of the smaller tanks so that Nos.1645 (15th June 1946), 9420 (11th July 1949), and 69424 (27th June 1955), still had them to withdrawal on the dates shown.

(below) This view shows the absence of a well tank below the bunker and No.1618 was one of two which kept only the two coal rails first fitted; No.9413 (1641) was the other (*see* page 43, top).

CLASS N 9

Diagram 67A boiler.

1617

Darlington 216.

To traffic 5/1893.

REPAIRS:
??. ?/?—?/3/06.**G.**
??. ?/?—?/1/21.**G.**
Hls. ?/?—?/5/24.**G.**
Dar. 3/7—10/9/28.**G.**
Dar. 4/8—30/9/30.**G.**
Dar. 1/9—6/10/33.**G.**
Dar. 3/6—28/7/36.**G.**
Dar. 20/6—9/8/39.**G.**
Dar. 27/4—17/8/43.**G.**
Dar. 19/12/46—1/2/47.**G.**
Dar. 8—11/2/47.**N/C.**
Dar. 27/2—7/3/47.**N/C.**

BOILERS:
D1107.
 G494 ?/3/06.
 G816 ?/1/21.
 2084 *(new)* 10/9/28.
D1259 *(ex1643)* 9/8/39.
 2183 *(exJ25 5712)* 1/2/47.

SHEDS:
Springhead.
Dairycoates 31/5/27.
Starbeck 28/3/43.
Darlington 28/7/46.
Tyne Dock 2/11/47.

RENUMBERED:
9410 3/2/46.

CONDEMNED: 19/10/50.
Cut up at Darlington.

_____

1618

Darlington 217.

To traffic 6/1893.

REPAIRS:
??. ?/?—?/11/06.**G.**
??. ?/?—?/6/18.**G.**
??. ?/?—?/1/21.**G.**
Dar. 11/5—28/8/25.**G.**
Ghd. 7/1—4/3/29.**G.**

Dar. 13/4—9/5/34.**G.**
Dar. 14/11—23/12/38.**G.**
Dar. 25/2—3/4/42.**G.**
Dar. 28/7—30/8/44.**G.**
Dar. 22/8—23/10/47.**G.**

BOILERS:
D1108.
 G521 ?/11/06.
D1870 ?/6/18.
D1194 *(new)* ?/1/21.
 2369 *(new)* 9/5/34.

SHEDS:
Darlington.
Blaydon 14/3/28.
Borough Gardens 7/11/31.
Blaydon 26/11/31.
Tweedmouth 7/9/36.
Tyne Dock 7/9/38.
Consett 14/10/40.

RENUMBERED:
9411 25/8/46.

CONDEMNED: 3/11/49.
Cut up at Darlington.

_____

1640

Darlington 218.

To traffic 6/1893.

REPAIRS:
 ??. ?/?—?/11/09.**G.**
Ghd. ?/?—13/9/22.**G.**
Ghd. 13—30/11/23.**L.**
Ghd. 15/3—19/5/27.**G.**
Ghd. 12/3—21/4/31.**G.**
Vacuum ejector added to
Westinghouse brake.
Ghd. 29/5—5/6/31.**N/C.**
Dar. 30/4—20/6/36.**G.**
Dar. 25/6—28/8/40.**G.**
Dar. 8/9—9/10/41.**L.**
Dar. 6/9—13/10/44.**G.**
Westinghouse changed to steam
brake.
Dar. 1/7/46. *Not repaired.*

BOILERS:
D1109.
 G814 ?/11/09.
D1914 *(new)* 19/5/27.

2089 *(ex1650)* 20/6/36.
3198 *(exJ25 2048)* 13/10/44#.

SHEDS:
East Hartlepool.
Hexham 22/10/28.
Gateshead 1/5/33.
Bowes Bridge 12/12/35.
Sunderland 24/6/37.
Borough Gardens 7/7/39.
Sunderland 6/5/40.
Heaton 14/12/42.
Tyne Dock 28/3/43.

RENUMBERED:
9412 7/7/46.

CONDEMNED: 2/8/47.
Cut up at Darlington.

_____

1641

Darlington 219.

To traffic 6/1893.

REPAIRS:
 ??. ?/?—4/10.**G.**
 ??. ?/?—?/11/20.**G.**
Dar. 8/10—22/12/24.**G.**
Dar. 9/12/27—27/2/28.**G.**
Dar. 19/5—29/6/33.**G.**
Dar. 2/9—14/10/36.**G.**
Dar. 20/2—28/3/39.**G.**
Dar. 4/3—16/5/42.**G.**
Dar. 8/11—6/12/44.**G.**
Dar. 25/11—19/12/47.**G.**

BOILERS:
D1110.
 G816 ?/4/10.
 G744 ?/11/20.
D1938 *(new)* 27/2/28.
 3429 *(exJ25 5690)* 19/12/47#.

SHEDS:
Barnard Castle.
Darlington 4/6/28.
Ferryhill 29/11/28.
Sunderland 2/6/32.
Darlington 12/7/39.
Sunderland 15/4/40.

RENUMBERED:
9413 7/7/46.

CONDEMNED: 14/12/50.
Cut up at Darlington.

_____

1642

Darlington 220.

To traffic 7/1893.

REPAIRS:
??. ?/?—?/9/06.**G.**
??. ?/?—?/5/17.**G.**
??. ?/?—?/12/19.**G.**
Dar. 28/11/24—26/2/25.**G.**
Dar. 7/9—31/10/28.**G.**
Dar. 20/9—7/11/32.**G.**
Dar. 7/11/32—21/7/34.**G.**
In store at the Paint shop.
Dar. 29/8—30/9/35.**L.**
After collision.
Dar. 4—30/3/40.**G.**
Dar. 28/5—19/9/42.**G.**
Dar. 7/12/44—17/1/45.**G.**
Dar. 24/9—31/10/47.**G.**

BOILERS:
D1111.
 G519 ?/9/06.
 G163 ?/5/17.
D892 *(new)* ?/12/19.
 D84 *(ex1649)* 31/10/28.
D1291 *(exJ25 2047)* 30/3/40.
 3300 *(new)* 19/9/42#.
 3823 *(new)* 31/10/47#.

SHEDS:
Barnard Castle.
Darlington 4/6/28.
East Hartlepool 16/7/34.
West Hartlepool 28/3/38.
Darlington 14/11/38.
Stockton 4/12/39.
Consett 28/3/43.

RENUMBERED:
9414 25/8/46.

CONDEMNED: 5/7/50.
Cut up at Darlington.

_____

WORKS CODES:- Cow - Cowlairs. Dar - Darlington. Don - Doncaster. Ghd - Gateshead. Gor - Gorton. Hls – Hull Springhead. Inv - Inverurie. Str - Stratford. Yk - York.
REPAIR CODES:- **C/H** - Casual Heavy. **C/L** - Casual Light. **G** - General. **H**- Heavy. **H/I** - Heavy Intermediate. **L** - Light. **L/I** - Light Intermediate. **N/C** - Non-Classified.

41

No.1653 was one of the four to keep a well tank to withdrawal. It was also one to which a third coal rail had been added before Grouping.

The boilers used by Class N9 were to Diagram 67 and interchangeable with classes J21, J25, N8 and N10 but only the non-superheated type was used by N9 class.

Between September 1942 and January 1949 ten of the class received Diagram 67A boilers in which the dome was 1ft 9in. further back and the whistle was on the firebox. Again only the non-superheated variety was carried.

By Grouping at least thirteen of the class had a third rail on the coal bunker and the LNER later added a third rail to four others: Nos.1643, 1650, 1651 and 1655.

Not all got the third rail; No.9413 (ex 1641) still had only two at its 14th December 1950 withdrawal.

(below) Until September 1928 all twenty had boilers with Ramsbottom safety valves in the shaped brass casing.

No.1647, ex works 29th September 1928 with a new boiler, was the first one fitted with Ross 'pop' safety valves and they had a circular casing around the base.

1643

Darlington 221.

To traffic 8/1893.

REPAIRS:
 ??. ?/?—?/10/04.**G.**
 ??. ?/?—?/11/07.**G.**
 ??. ?/?—?/9/18.**G.**
 Dar. 16/10/23—6/2/24.**G.**
 Dar. 4/1—23/3/27.**G.**
 Dar. 22/4—20/6/30.**G.**
 Vacuum ejector added to
 Westinghouse brake.
 Dar. 23/1—23/2/34.**G.**
 Dar. 12/6—26/7/39.**G.**
 Dar. 13/5—9/7/43.**G.**
 Dar. 15—29/9/43.**L.**
 Dar. 30/10—7/12/46.**G.**
 Westinghouse changed to steam
 brake.

BOILERS:
D1112.
 G51 ?/10/04.
 G609 ?/11/07.
 G521 ?/9/18.
 D1894 *(new)* 23/3/27.
 D1259 *(exN8 212)* 23/2/34.
 D1894 *(ex1645)* 26/7/39.
 D1309 *(ex1648)* 7/12/46.

SHEDS:
Darlington.
Ferryhill 4/6/28.
West Hartlepool 7/6/33.
Gateshead 2/3/35.
Darlington 7/11/38.

RENUMBERED:
1643D 6/2/24.
9415 14/7/46.

CONDEMNED: 24/10/49.
Cut up at Darlington.

1644

Darlington 222.

To traffic 8/1893.

REPAIRS:
 ??. ?/?—?/5/08.**G.**
 Ghd. ?/?—2/11/22.**G.**
 Ghd. 8—28/11/23.**L.**
 Ghd. 24/3—27/5/27.**G.**
 Ghd. 2/4—20/5/30.**G.**
 Vacuum ejector added to
 Westinghouse brake.
 Dar. 14/12/34—25/1/35.**G.**
 Dar. 18/2—3/4/39.**G.**
 Dar. 9/12/43—15/1/44.**G.**

Dar. 28/12/46—16/1/47.**L.**
Dar. 11/12/47. *Not repaired.*

BOILERS:
D1113.
 G642 ?/5/08.
D1898 *(new)* 27/5/27.
 D756 *(exJ25 2073)* 25/1/35.
 D879 *(exN10 1317)* 3/4/39.
 2367 *(exN10 1683)* 15/1/44.

SHEDS:
East Hartlepool.
Darlington 5/7/34.
Tyne Dock 11/11/37.
Borough Gardens 7/9/40.
Sunderland 21/3/42.

RENUMBERED:
9416 17/11/46.

CONDEMNED: 31/12/47.
Cut up at Darlington.

1645

Darlington 223.

To traffic 8/1893.

REPAIRS:
 ??. ?/?—?/5/11.**G.**
 Dar. 6/2—7/5/23.**G.**
 Changed from steam to
 Westinghouse brake.
 Ghd. 12/1—31/3/26.**G.**
 Ghd. 27/9—12/12/28.**G.**
 Vacuum ejector fitted.
 Ghd. 22/5—10/7/31.**G.**
 Dar. 1—29/3/34.**G.**
 Dar. 4/4—16/5/39.**G.**
 Dar. 26/6—12/8/42.**G.**
 Dar. 15/5/46. *Not repaired.*

BOILERS:
D1114.
 G897 ?/5/11.
 D1265 *(exN8 350)* 12/12/28.
 D1894 *(ex1643)* 29/3/34.
 D1279 *(exN10 1697)* 16/5/39.

SHEDS:
Blaydon.
Alnmouth 9/10/26.
Blaydon 11/12/26.
Hexham 6/6/29.
Gateshead 1/5/33.
Tweedmouth 2/7/37.
Pickering 22/1/38.
York (DVLR) 30/1/39.
Dairycoates 12/6/39.
Sunderland 28/3/43.
Borough Gardens 28/8/44.
Darlington 12/3/45.

RENUMBERED:
9417 allocated.

CONDEMNED: 15/6/46.
Cut up at Darlington.

1646

Darlington 224.

To traffic 9/1893.

REPAIRS:
 ??. ?/?—?/11/09.**G.**
 Dar. 18/10/23—5/1/24.**G.**
 Dar. 29/4—10/9/26.**G.**
 Dar. 19/11—7/12/26.**L.**
 Dar. 28/12/28—18/2/29.**G.**
 Vacuum ejector added to
 Westinghouse brake.
 Dar. 3—12/12/29.**N/C.**
 Dar. 5/7—18/8/33.**G.**
 Dar. 14/12/36—2/2/37.**G.**
 Dar. 6/4—3/5/37.**H.**
 Dar. 1/7—16/8/41.**G.**
 Dar. 27/1—27/2/42.**L.**
 Dar. 26/5—12/8/44.**G.**
 Westinghouse changed to steam
 brake.
 Dar. 16/11—7/12/46.**L.**
 Dar. 27/2—16/4/48.**G.**

BOILERS:
D1115.
 G815 *(new)* ?/11/09.
 D892 *(ex1642)* 18/2/29.
 D1256 *(exN8 287)* 2/2/37.
 2357 *(exJ21 1576)* 12/8/44.

SHEDS:
West Auckland.
Wear Valley Jct. 11/4/31.
Sunderland 2/6/32.
Dairycoates 18/7/39.
York 6/7/40.
Heaton 7/12/40.
Dairycoates 18/6/42.
Sunderland 28/3/43.
Borough Gardens 28/8/44.
Darlington 12/3/45.
Sunderland 17/7/49.
Tyne Dock 24/7/49.
Sunderland 27/8/50.

RENUMBERED:
 1646D 5/1/24.
 9418 7/12/46.
69418 16/4/48.

CONDEMNED: 1/1/51.
Cut up at Darlington.

1647

Darlington 225.

To traffic 9/1893.

REPAIRS:
 ??. ?/?—?/12/08.**G.**
 ??. ?/?—?/9/20.**G.**
 Dar. 9/11/22—14/2/23.**G.**
 Dar. 11/5—14/6/23.**L.**
 Dar. 19/8—10/11/25.**G.**
 Dar. 12/7—29/9/28.**G.**
 Dar. 15/4—21/5/31.**G.**
 Dar. 3—30/4/34.**G.**
 Dar. 17/3—21/4/37.**G.**
 Dar. 31/10—2/12/39.**G.**
 Dar. 14/1—21/2/42.**G.**
 Dar. 19/8—29/9/44.**G.**
 Dar. 9/10—8/11/44.**N/C.**
 Dar. 4/2/48. *Not repaired.*

BOILERS:
D1116.
 G744 ?/12/08.
 G896 ?/9/20.
 2117 *(new)* 29/9/28.
 2370 *(new)* 30/4/34.
 D1098 *(exN8 136)* 2/12/39.
 2363 *(exN10 1138)* 21/2/42.

SHEDS:
Dairycoates.
Starbeck 28/3/43.
Darlington 28/7/46.
Haverton Hill 4/5/47.

RENUMBERED:
9419 12/1/47.

CONDEMNED: 14/2/48.
Cut up at Darlington.

1648

Darlington 226.

To traffic 10/1893.

REPAIRS:
 ??. ?/?—?/5/11.**G.**
 Ghd. 27/11/24—29/1/25.**G.**
 Ghd. 2/4—9/5/28.**L.**
 Ghd. 31/10—14/11/28.**L.**
 Ghd. 22/3—9/5/30.**G.**
 Ghd. 14—24/5/32.**L.**
 Dar. 25/4—4/6/35.**G.**
 Dar. 9/10—10/11/39.**G.**
 Dar. 19/11—27/12/41.**H.**
 After collision.
 Dar. 8/6—29/7/43.**G.**
 Dar. 31/10—6/12/46.**G.**

Ramsbottom valves did survive to the end of the class because the last one, No.69429, withdrawn 4th July 1955, had them on a boiler which had been built in 1924.

Most had two handles for fastening the smokebox door although No.1644 did have a wheel and handle at least to December 1934. The door with a flat flange mating with a riveted ring also served most of them through to withdrawal.

(below) Two had their smokebox doors changed to pressed joint ring type, Nos.9425 (12th July 1947), and 9414 (31st October 1947).

Until 1940 the standard whistle gear was above the cab roof with a large bell-shape on the driver's side and a smaller bell-shape on the left hand side.

Only one, No.1649, was noted with its driver's whistle changed to the organ-pipe type.

Beginning with No.1653, ex works 27th July 1940, a new whistle arrangement was used, with only one small bell shape, but still on the cab roof with Diagram 67 boilers.

(*above*) **Diagram 67A boilers had a similar whistle mounted over an isolating valve but positioned on the firebox.**

The original buffers were the parallel shank type with hollow spindle and could still be seen on No.9418 (ex 1646) to at least November 1946 (*see* page 51, top).

Many of the class changed to buffers with a taper shank and solid spindle, at least seven being so noted.

Ex works 3rd December 1937, No.1651 had Group Standard buffers and drawhook. Others so fitted were Nos.1617 (9th August 1939), 1644 (3rd April 1939), 1645 (16th May 1939), 9413, and 9429.

(below) Until it went out of use in October 1933, some of the class were fitted with the Raven fog signalling apparatus and the striker for this can be seen below the forward footstep on No.1647.

Originally intended only for mineral work, just steam brakes on the engine was provided and no change was made on Nos.1617, 1618, 1641, 1642, 1647, 1648, 1649, 1650, 1652 and 1653.

1648 cont./
BOILERS:
D1117.
 G898 ?/5/11.
 2359 *(new)* 9/5/30.
D1309 *(exJ25 2000)* 10/11/39.
 3512 *(exJ25 1726)* 6/12/46#.

SHEDS:
Annfield Plain.
Tyne Dock 18/2/39.

RENUMBERED:
9420 9/11/46.

CONDEMNED: 11/7/49.
Cut up at Darlington.

1649

Darlington 227.

To traffic 11/1893.

REPAIRS:
 ??. ?/?—?/11/12.**G**.
Dar. 14/2—30/4/24.**G**.
Dar. 15/11/27—26/1/28.**G**.
Dar. 31/12/29—17/2/30.**G**.
Dar. 13/8—23/9/32.**G**.
Dar. 31/10—27/11/34.**G**.
Dar. 3/11—16/12/37.**G**.
Dar. 1—27/6/40.**G**.
Dar. 9/9—2/10/43.**G**.
Dar. 28/8—28/9/46.**G**.

BOILERS:
D1118.
 D84 *(new)* ?/11/12.
 G523 *(ex??)* 30/4/24.
D1915 *(new)* 26/1/28.
D1936 *(exN8 573)* 27/6/40.
 2618 *(exN10 89)* 2/10/43.
D1935 *(exN10 1699)* 28/9/46.

SHEDS:
Springhead.
Dairycoates 31/5/27.
Sunderland 28/3/43.

RENUMBERED:
9421 28/9/46.

CONDEMNED: 24/8/49.
Cut up at Darlington.

1650

Darlington 228.

To traffic 11/1893.

REPAIRS:
 ??. ?/?—?/9/09.**G**.
Dar. 5/9—29/11/23.**G**.
Dar. 26/11—23/12/24.**L**.
Dar. 9—14/1/25.**N/C**.
Dar. 16/3—15/5/28.**G**.
Dar. 21/2—10/4/30.**G**.
Dar. 22/12/32—3/2/33.**G**.
Dar. 3/2—16/3/36.**G**.
Dar. 23/1—25/2/39.**G**.
Dar. 15/11—19/12/41.**G**.
Dar. 22/5—17/6/44.**G**.
Dar. 26/6—3/7/44.**N/C**.
After collision.
Dar. 25/1—1/3/47.**G**.
Dar. 23/1—13/2/48.**L**.
Ghd. 16—24/11/49.**C/L**.

BOILERS:
D1119.
 G793 ?/9/09.
 2089 *(new)* 15/5/28.
D1275 *(ex1654)* 16/3/36.

SHEDS:
Springhead.
Dairycoates 31/5/27.
York (DVLR) 25/10/38.
Darlington 26/6/39.
West Auckland 8/10/45.
Sunderland 4/1/48.
West Auckland 11/1/48.
Consett 27/11/49.

RENUMBERED:
1650D 29/11/23.
9422 27/10/46.

CONDEMNED: 28/4/50.
Cut up at Darlington.

1651

Darlington 229.

To traffic 12/1893.

REPAIRS:
 ??. ?/?—?/9/04.**G**.
 ??. ?/?—?/8/07.**G**.
 ??. ?/?—?/4/11.**G**.
 ??. ?/?—?/6/20.**G**.
Dar. 1/11/22—31/1/23.**G**.
Dar. 3—6/10/24.**N/C**.
Dar. 21/10/25—9/2/26.**G**.
Dar. 26/11/26—2/6/27.**L**.
Dar. 3—24/5/28.**N/C**.
Dar. 7/10—6/12/29.**G**.
Vacuum ejector added to Westinghouse brake.
Dar. 7—12/5/31.**N/C**.
Raven FSA fitted.
Dar. 16/5—29/6/33.**G**.

Dar. 21/9—19/10/34.**L**.
After collision.
Dar. 11/10—3/12/37.**G**.
Dar. 24/10—5/12/41.**G**.
Dar. 15—23/4/43.**L**.
Dar. 21/2—29/3/45.**G**.
Westinghouse changed to steam brake.
Dar. 25/10—5/12/47.**G**.
Dar. 11—17/12/47.**N/C**.

BOILERS:
D1120.
 D843 ?/9/04.
D1111 *(ex1642)* ?/8/07.
 G896 *(ex??)* ?/4/11.
D1105 *(new)* ?/6/20.
 2973 *(exJ25 2047)* 29/3/45.
 3410 *(exJ25 5720)* 5/12/47#.

SHEDS:
West Auckland.
Shildon 1/4/28.
West Auckland 25/3/29.
Darlington 14/4/31.
Ferryhill 31/12/36.
Darlington 7/11/38.
Northallerton 4/5/47.
Sunderland 23/1/48.

RENUMBERED:
9423 14/7/46.

CONDEMNED: 9/7/51.
Cut up at Darlington.

1652

Darlington 230.

To traffic 12/1893.

REPAIRS:
 ??. ?/?—?/9/11.**G**.
 ??. ?/?—?/5/21.**G**.
Ghd. 14/7—13/10/25.**G**.
Ghd. 16/7—29/8/30.**G**.
Dar. 30/7—14/9/37.**G**.
Dar. 23/7—5/9/40.**G**.
Dar. 8/10—6/11/43.**G**.
Dar. 29/5—5/7/47.**G**.
Dar. 12—17/7/47.**N/C**.
Dar. 30/1—23/2/52.**G**.

BOILERS:
D1121.
 G900 ?/9/11.
 2368 *(new)* 29/8/30.
 2955 *(exJ25 5664)* 5/7/47#.
 25079 *(ex??)* 23/2/52#.

SHEDS:
Annfield Plain.

Gateshead 12/12/35.
Pelton Level 26/10/37.
Sunderland 31/10/48.
Tyne Dock 17/11/51.

RENUMBERED:
9424 1/12/46.
69424 23/2/52.

CONDEMNED: 27/6/55.
Cut up at Darlington.

1653

Darlington 231.

To traffic 12/1893.

REPAIRS:
 ??. ?/?—?/2/07.**G**.
 ??. ?/?—?/11/12.**G**.
 ??. ?/?—?/8/21.**G**.
Hls. ?/?—?/2/24.**G**.
Dar. 15/6—28/9/27.**G**.
Dar. 27/8—16/10/29.**G**.
Dar. 21/7—13/9/32.**G**.
Dar. 1/11—1/12/34.**G**.
Dar. 18/1—17/2/38.**G**.
Dar. 18/6—27/7/40.**G**.
Dar. 7/7—30/8/43.**G**.
Dar. 9/6—12/7/47.**G**.

BOILERS:
D1122.
D1108 *(ex1618)* ?/2/07.
 D85 *(new)* ?/11/12.
 2175 *(new)* 16/10/29.
D1884 *(exJ21 1566)* 1/12/34.
D1914 *(exN10 1707)* 27/7/40.
 3531 *(exJ25 5667)* 12/7/47#.

SHEDS:
Springhead.
Dairycoates 7/4/25.
Sunderland 28/3/43.

RENUMBERED:
9425 27/10/46.

CONDEMNED: 29/11/50.
Cut up at Darlington.

1654

Darlington 232.

To traffic 12/1893.

REPAIRS:
 ??. ?/?—?/8/09.**G**.
 ??. ?/?—?/4/22.**G**.
Ghd. 15/1—31/3/26.**G**.

So that they could move fish vans and other piped vehicles, the other ten were altered to Westinghouse brake for engine and train as follows: Nos.1654 and 1655 in December 1900, six more in 1911/12, No.383 in January 1922 and 1645 on 7th May 1923. They also got train heating connections at both ends, although only as late as March 1927 on No.1643.

(above) Included in the Unification of Brakes programme, the ten Westinghouse fitted engines had vacuum ejectors added for train braking on the following dates: Nos.1640 (21st April 1931), 1643 (20th June 1930), 1644 (20th May 1930), 1645 (12th December 1928), 1646 (18th February 1929), 1651 (6th December 1929), 1654 (15th March 1930), 1655 (2nd May 1930), 383 (15th January 1929), and 1705 (16th April 1930).

From 1946 the condensate drain pipe from the vacuum ejector exhaust pipe was brought outside the smokebox to discharge on to the tracks.

Four of the class remained dual brake fitted to withdrawal but the other six had the Westinghouse equipment taken off and had combined steam and vacuum brakes. These were Nos.1646 (12th August 1944), 1640 (13th October 1944), 1651 (29th March 1945), 1654 (21st June 1946), 9415 (7th December 1946), and 9428 (26th April 1947). Note also that No.9418 (ex 1646) had the train heating connection taken off and coupling changed to loose 3-link type.

Until after 1917 the number was carried on the 24in. wide brass plate on the bunker.

By Grouping all had the number on the tank in 12in. shaded transfers with only an $8^{5}/_{8}$in. wide plate on the bunker. Painting was unlined black.

Only one, No.1645 ex works 7th May 1923, got L.& N.E.R. but three got area suffix D as follows: Nos.1650D (29th November 1923), 1646D (5th January 1924), and 1643D (6th February 1924). The LNER accorded them single red lining.

1654 cont./
Ghd. 1/2—15/3/30.**G.**
Vacuum ejector added to
Westinghouse brake.
Ghd. 27/5—17/7/30.**H.**
Ghd. 1—15/6/32.**L.**
Dar. 6/3—20/4/35.**G.**
Dar. 23/2—23/3/40.**G.**
Dar. 26/8—13/10/43.**G.**
Dar. 21/5—21/6/46.**G.**
Westinghouse changed to steam
brake.
Dar. 16/12/48—15/1/49.**G.**
Dar. 19/2/53. *Not repaired.*

BOILERS:
D1123.
 G791 ?/8/09.
D1275 *(new)* ?/4/22.
 2621 *(new)* 20/4/35.
 2628 *(exJ25 25)* 21/6/46.
 2957 *(exN10 9102)* 15/1/49#.

SHEDS:
East Hartlepool.
West Hartlepool 9/7/31.
Sunderland 5/2/37.
Borough Gardens 28/6/39.
Darlington 15/4/40.
Northallerton 11/3/44.
Darlington 25/6/45.
Sunderland 4/2/51.
Tyne Dock 17/11/51.

RENUMBERED:
 9426 27/10/46.
 69426 15/1/49.

CONDEMNED: 23/2/53.
Cut up at Darlington.

1655

Darlington 233.

To traffic 12/1893.

REPAIRS:
 ??. ?/?—?/5/11.**G.**
Ghd. 21/3—3/6/24.**G.**
Ghd. 13/6—22/8/28.**G.**
Ghd. 10/4—2/5/30.**L.**
Vacuum ejector added to
Westinghouse brake.
Ghd. 4/8—27/9/32.**G.**
Dar. 21/1—16/3/37.**G.**
Dar. 8/8—12/9/40.**G.**
Dar. 25/1—22/2/44.**G.**
Dar. 10/3—7/4/44.**N/C.**
Dar. 11/9—23/10/47.**G.**
Dar. 1—26/1/52.**G.**
Dar. 28/1—1/2/52.**N/C.**

BOILERS:
D1124.
 G899 ?/5/11.
D1524 *(new)* 3/6/24.
D2076 *(exJ21 1802)* 16/3/37.
D1884 *(ex1653)* 12/9/40.
 3504 *(exJ21 5095)* 23/10/47#.
 25077 *(ex??)* 26/1/52#.

SHEDS:
East Hartlepool.
West Hartlepool 9/7/31.
Darlington 7/11/38.
Dairycoates 28/6/39.
York 29/5/40.
Sunderland 28/3/43.
Tyne Dock 8/3/53.

RENUMBERED:
 9427 27/10/46.
 69427 26/1/52.

CONDEMNED: 27/6/55.
Cut up at Darlington.

383

Darlington 234.

To traffic 2/1894.

REPAIRS:
 ??. ?/?—?/3/10.**G.**
 ??. ?/?—?/1/22.**G.**
Ghd. 3/3—6/5/25.**G.**
Ghd. 22/11/28—15/1/29.**G.**
Vacuum ejector added to
Westinghouse brake.
Ghd. 5/4—11/5/32.**G.**
Dar. 21/7—26/8/38.**G.**
Dar. 15/11—19/12/40.**G.**
Dar. 2/3—10/5/43.**G.**
Dar. 28/3—26/4/47.**G.**
Westinghouse changed to steam
brake.

BOILERS:
D1126.
 G750 ?/3/10.
D1697 *(new)* 6/5/25.
D1296 *(exN10 1699)* 11/5/32.
 3761 *(new)* 26/4/47#.

SHEDS:
East Hartlepool.
Dairycoates 8/3/37.
Sunderland 28/3/43.

RENUMBERED:
 9428 17/11/46.

CONDEMNED: 9/8/50.
Cut up at Darlington.

1705

Darlington 235.

To traffic 2/1894.

REPAIRS:
 ??. ?/?—?/10/08.**G.**
 ??. ?/?—?/10/20.**G.**
Ghd. 26/4—15/5/23.**L.**
Ghd. 19/5—28/10/24.**G.**
Ghd. 28/11—22/12/24.**L.**
Ghd. 14/8—5/10/28.**G.**
Ghd. 26/3—16/4/30.**G.**
Vacuum ejector added to steam
brake.
Ghd. 19/2—23/3/32.**G.**
Ghd. 25/7—31/8/32.**L.**
Dar. 21/1—17/3/37.**G.**
Dar. 29/4—24/5/37.**N/C.**
Dar. 10/10—14/11/40.**G.**
Dar. 9/11—4/12/43.**G.**
Dar. 30/11—30/12/44.**L.**
After collision.
Dar. 12/11/47—16/1/48.**G.**
Dar. 14/2—14/3/52.**H/I.**

BOILERS:
D1125.
 G736 ?/10/08.
D1681 *(new)* 28/10/24.
 2072 *(exJ21 1568)* 17/3/37.
 2076 *(ex1655)* 14/11/40.
D1696 *(exN8 1104)* 4/12/43.
D1507 *(exN10 9096)* 16/1/48.
D1507 reno.25089 14/3/52.

SHEDS:
East Hartlepool.
West Hartlepool 9/7/31.
Darlington 14/11/38.
Dairycoates 26/6/39.
Sunderland 28/3/43.
Tyne Dock 3/4/49.

RENUMBERED:
 9429 17/11/46.
 69429 14/3/52.

CONDEMNED: 4/7/55.
Cut up at Darlington.

The other sixteen went straight to the style which the LNER adopted as standard, although it was 27th May 1927 before No.1644 completed the process.

Following the June 1928 painting economies, only unlined black was then applied to N9 class, a situation which continued through to their withdrawal.

All had single plate steel front bufferbeam (none getting the wood sandwich type), and this continued to be painted red. No.1650 only got LNER Class N9 from 3rd February 1933, hitherto carrying the NER Class N designation.

From July 1942 only NE was used but in 12in. shaded transfers instead of 7½in. LNER. No. 383 was so done when ex works 10th May 1943.

Allocated numbers 9410 to 9429 in the 1946 re-numbering, all except one duly changed; No.1645 (to have been 9417) was withdrawn as such 15th June 1946. No.1640 went to Darlington works for repair 1st July 1946 and on Sunday 7th July 1946 became No.9412 but was not repaired and stood out of service until withdrawn, more than a year later, on 2nd August 1947.

Ex works 21st June 1946, No.1654 had 7½in. LNER restored with that and the number in shaded transfers. On Sunday 27th October 1946, at Darlington shed, it was re-numbered 9426 by a works painter in unshaded figures in Gill sans style but with modified 6 and 9.

Between 6th December 1946 and 16th January 1948, no less than thirteen were ex works with Gill sans style lettering and numbers thus: Nos.9420 (6th December 1946), 9415 (7th December 1946), 9410 (1st February 1947), 9422 (1st March 1947), 9428 (26th April 1947), 9424 (5th July 1947), 9425 (12th July 1947), 9411 and 9427 (23rd October 1947), 9414 (31st October 1947), 9423 (5th December 1947), 9413 (19th December 1947), and 9429 (16th January 1948).

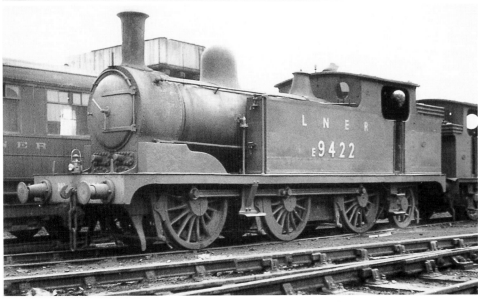

From a Darlington light repair on 13th February 1948, No.9422 was ex works still with LNER but with an E prefix to its number.

(above) When No.69418 was ex works 16th April 1948, its BR number was in 12in. figures but moved to the bunker. This allowed 10in. lettering to be centred on the tanks. At the front, the number was still on the buffer beam.

When No.69426 was ex works 15th January 1949, it had the same style lettering but the numerals were also 10in. tall to match and they included the correct Gill sans 6 and 9. At the front a smokebox numberplate had been fitted.

Only three others got evidence of BR ownership, all having small emblems: Nos.69427 (26th January 1952), 69424 (23rd February 1952), and 69429 (14th March 1952).

(above) **From 1917 the number had been put on the tank in 12in. shaded transfers and when this was done, the 24in. original brass numberplate was normally replaced by one which was only 8⅝in. wide. No.1317 escaped this change at its April 1920 repair and may even have done so when ex Darlington works on 31st January 1923.**

(left) **This class was designed to use the same boiler as J21, J25, N8 and N9 classes and which became LNER Diagram 67, but none of the N10 ever carried a superheater.**

Until 1939, the only change on boilers put on N10 class was that new ones built from January 1930 were fitted with Ross 'pop' safety valves instead of the Ramsbottom type.

Beginning with No.1697, ex works 17th February 1939, the Diagram 67A boiler was introduced to this class and except for No.9103 (ex 1706) withdrawn in 1948; all the other nineteen carried at least two of the modern 67A type. This one was put on No.1317 when ex works 7th March 1939. Note the dome is 1ft 9in. further back and the whistle is mounted on the firebox.

CLASS N 10

Diagram 67A boiler.

1321

Darlington 448.

To traffic 10/1902.

REPAIRS:
??. ?/?—?/12/20.**G.**
??. ?/?—2/6/22.**G.**
Ghd. 26/8—2/11/26.**G.**
Ghd. 28/8—18/10/29.**G.**
Vacuum ejector fitted.
Ghd. 26/11/31—12/1/32.**L.**
Dar. 10/3—20/4/33.**G.**
Dar. 19/5—2/7/37.**G.**
Dar. 20/8—24/9/41.**G.**
Dar. 13/1—25/2/43.**L.**
Damaged by fire.
Dar. 30/11—21/12/44.**L.**
Dar. 3/8—6/10/45.**G.**
Westinghouse brake replaced by steam. Vacuum ejector removed.
Ghd. 16/2—11/3/49.**C/L.**
After rear end collision.
Dar. 31/8—23/9/49.**G.**
Ghd. 6—12/10/49.**N/C.**
Ghd. 13—30/4/51.**C/L.**
After rear end collision.
Dar. 17/3—5/4/52.**G.**
Ghd. 4—7/1/54.**N/C.**
Ghd. 12—19/2/54.**C/L.**
Dar. 9/4—6/5/54.**C/L.**

BOILERS:
D1734.
D1150 *(new)* ?/12/20.
D1109 *(ex89)* 20/4/33.
D1076 *(exJ25 1974)* 2/7/37.
 2133 *(exJ21 965)* 24/9/41.
 2969 *(ex9106)* 23/9/49#.
 25090 *(ex??)* 5/4/52#.

SHEDS:
Gateshead.
Tweedmouth 31/1/27.
Gateshead 2/7/37.

RENUMBERED:
 9090 17/3/46.
69090 27/1/49.

CONDEMNED: 19/11/56.
Cut up at Darlington.

1667

Darlington 449.

To traffic 10/1902.

REPAIRS:
 ??. ?/?—?/9/19.**G.**
 ??. ?/?—18/7/22.**G.**
Ghd. 14/1—24/3/25.**G.**
Ghd. 29/11/27—8/2/28.**G.**
Ghd. 23/5—15/6/28.**L.**
Ghd. 9—22/5/30.**L.**
Vacuum ejector fitted.
Ghd. 14/4—3/6/31.**G.**
Dar. 27/11/34—21/1/35.**G.**
Dar. 22/3—5/5/38.**G.**
Dar. 24/8—20/9/38.**N/C.**
Dar. 29/8—8/10/42.**G.**
Dar. 27/1—12/2/44.**L.**
After collision.
Dar. 14/2—29/3/46.**G.**
Westinghouse replaced by steam brake. Vacuum ejector removed.
Ghd. 10/7—29/8/47.**N/C.**
Ghd. 24/11—24/12/48.**L.**
Dar. 14/10—12/11/49.**G.**
Ghd. 15—28/2/52.**N/C.**
Ghd. 11/11—4/12/52.**G.**
Ghd. 20/4—13/5/54.**C/L.**
Dar. 26/11/56. *Not repaired.*

BOILERS:
D1735.
 D885 *(new)* ?/9/19.
D1092 *(exJ25 1982)* 21/1/35.
 3304 *(new)* 8/10/42#.
 3416 *(exN8 9381)* 12/11/49#.
 25101 *(ex??)* 4/12/52#.

SHEDS:
Alnmouth.
Percy Main 22/1/40.
Blaydon 6/7/40.
Heaton 20/1/43.
Gateshead 13/11/43.

RENUMBERED:
 9091 29/3/46.
69091 24/12/48.

CONDEMNED: 26/11/56.
Cut up at Darlington.

1683

Darlington 450.

To traffic 11/1902.

REPAIRS:
 ??. ?/?—?/9/14.**G.**
Ghd. 29/11/22—6/2/23.**G.**
Ghd. 22/5—23/7/28.**G.**
Ghd. 19/5—26/7/32.**G.**
Vacuum ejector fitted.
Ghd. 11/10—9/11/32.**L.**
Dar. 13/11/34—11/1/35.**H.**
Dar. 14/7—26/8/38.**G.**
Dar. 27/1—14/3/41.**G.**
Dar. 24/6—3/7/42.**N/C.**
Dar. 10/11—11/12/43.**G.**
Dar. 19/10—9/11/46.
Not repaired.
Ghd. 12/11/46—6/1/47.**L.**
After rear end collision.
Dar. 10/7—6/9/47.**G.**
Westinghouse brake replaced by steam brake.
Dar. 22/11—23/12/50.**G.**
Dar. 27—28/12/50.**N/C.**
Ghd. 29/5—23/6/52.**N/C.**
Ghd. 26/5—11/6/53.**C/L.**
Ghd. 30/8—1/10/54.**G.**
Ghd. 9/4—4/5/56.**C/H.**
Dar. 31/3/59. *Not repaired.*

BOILERS:
D1737.
 D357 *(new)* ?/9/14.
 2367 *(new)* 26/7/32.
 2076 *(exN9 1705)* 11/12/43.
 2368 *(exN9 9424)* 6/9/47.
 25031 *(exJ25 5689)* 23/12/50#.
 25076 *(ex??)* 1/10/54#.

SHEDS:
Bowes Bridge.
East Hartlepool 22/10/28.
Dairycoates 2/12/36.
Waskerley 17/7/39.
Consett 9/9/40.
Heaton 26/10/40.
Gateshead 14/12/47.
Borough Gardens 4/12/49.
Gateshead 22/1/50.

RENUMBERED:
 9092 24/4/46.
69092 23/12/50.

CONDEMNED: 6/4/59.
Cut up at Darlington.

1697

Darlington 452.

To traffic 11/1902.

REPAIRS:
 ??. ?/?—?/2/15.**G.**
 ??. ?/?—?/8/21.**G.**
Dar. 6/2—24/4/25.**G.**
Dar. 14/4—11/6/28.**G.**
Dar. 18/4—9/5/30.**N/C.**
Vacuum ejector fitted.
Dar. 14/7—14/9/31.**G.**
Dar. 28/12/33—1/2/34.**G.**
Dar. 5/5—25/6/36.**G.**
Dar. 11/1—17/2/39.**G.**
Dar. 14/5—18/6/40.**L.**
Dar. 24/2—27/4/43.**G.**
Dar. 1/9—3/10/44.**L.**
Dar. 18/10—14/12/45.**G.**
Westinghouse brake replaced by steam. Vacuum ejector removed.
Dar. 9/2—3/3/49.**G.**
Ghd. 25/4—24/5/49.**C/L.**
After rear end collision.
Dar. 19/11—8/12/51.**G.**
Dar. 29/7—9/9/54.**G.**
Ghd. 23/4—25/5/56.**C/L.**

BOILERS:
D1738.
D1742 *(ex89)* ?/2/15.
D1266 *(new)* ?/8/21.
D1279 *(ex1711)* 1/2/34.
 2961 *(new)* 17/2/39#.
 2628 *(exN9 9426)* 3/3/49.
 25076 *(ex??)* 8/12/51.

SHEDS:
Dairycoates.
Consett 17/7/39.
Tyne Dock 14/10/40.
Gateshead 28/3/43.
Dairycoates 18/9/49.
Tyne Dock 3/7/55.

RENUMBERED:
 9093 5/5/46.
69093 3/3/49.

CONDEMNED: 23/12/57.
Cut up at Darlington.

Although the normal chimney had a plain top, when No.1710 was ex works 8th July 1926, it had one with the windjabber but by March 1946 (*see* opposite, centre) it had the customary type. Only one other N10 was so fitted – No.89 in the period 1935 to 1938 (*see* page 56, second from bottom). The last one noted still with Ramsbottom safety valves was No.69100 (*see* page 70, bottom) until it went for repair on 30th October 1950.

Boilers built from 1930 and fitted with 'pop' valves did not usually have any casing around the base of the valves. Just one example of a casing was noted – on No.9104 (ex 1710) from March 1946 – *see* opposite, centre.

(below) This engine never carried a Diagram 67A boiler and was withdrawn 8th November 1948 with a Diagram 67 type that had begun life on Class N9 No.1644 in May 1927.

Until 25th October 1940 when No.89 was the first to be changed, the normal whistle gear was one large and one small bell-shape above the cab roof.

Where a Diagram 67 boiler was concerned, from October 1940, new whistle gear had a single small bell-shaped whistle but still above the cab roof. All Diagram 67A boilers had the whistle on the firebox as shown in the photograph on page 56, bottom.

One exception to the two-whistle arrangement was recorded. No.1148 at some time in the 1930s not only had the small bell-shape moved to the drivers' side but it was replaced by an organ pipe on the left hand side.

No.1706 was an odd one with regard to its whistles. It was like No.1148 – see above – in changing to organ pipe on the left hand side but on the drivers' side it kept the larger bell-shaped whistle.

A wheel and handle was used in many cases for fastening the smokebox door until during the 1930s. No.1683 to July 1938 was the last to have a wheel.

Two handles became the accepted method for fastening the door and from 1938 all had them thereafter. Note door with flat flange for sealing.

(below) No.1707 from May 1946 was the first to get the more dished door with the pressed joint ring to give an improved seal. At least nine – 69093, 69095, 69096, 69098, 69099, 69101, 69105, 69106 and 69108 – got this type.

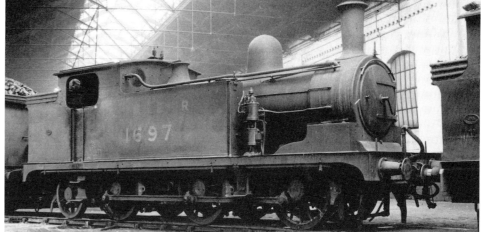

There was variation in the type of buffers, the most common being those with taper shank and solid spindle.

Changes did take place because some time in the 1930s No.1697 acquired parallel shank type with hollow spindles at the front end, although keeping taper shank type at the rear end.

In their later years, at least three, Nos.69099, 69101 and 69104, had circular wood pads inserted behind the front buffers to provide extra resilience, and in No.69099's case for the extra length of the Group Standard drawhook, but not the fitting of GS buffers of corresponding length.

Starting with No.1112, ex works 16th May 1934, Group Standard buffers were fitted when replacement was needed. No.1716 got them 9th November 1936 and 1706 on 17th February 1942. In BR days Nos.69095 and 69096 were also fitted.

1774

Darlington 451.

To traffic 11/1902.

REPAIRS:
Dar. ?/?—?/3/20.**G.**
Dar. 4/4—17/6/24.**G.**
Dar. 6/1—22/3/27.**G.**
Dar. 11/4—30/5/29.**G.**
Vacuum ejector fitted.
Dar. 15/2—22/3/32.**G.**
Dar. 18/10—7/11/32.**H.**
Dar. 7/7—23/8/34.**G.**
Dar. 20/7—3/9/37.**G.**
Dar. 24/6—1/8/40.**G.**
Dar. 8—22/1/43.**L.**
Dar. 29/4—15/5/43.**L.**
Dar. 1/12/43—4/1/44.**G.**
Dar. 10/8—11/9/46.**G.**
Westinghouse brake replaced by steam. Vacuum ejector removed.
Dar. 7/10—2/11/49.**G.**
Dar. 27/1—16/2/50.**C/L.**
Dar. 2—12/8/50.**C/L.**
Dar. 12/1—6/2/52.**G.**
Ghd. 1—27/3/54.**G.**
Dar. 27/6/57. *Not repaired.*

BOILERS:
D1736.
 D891 *(new)* ?/3/20.
 2117 *(exN9 1647)* 23/8/34.
D1265 *(ex1148)* 3/9/37.
 3425 *(new)* 4/1/44#.
 2991 *(exJ25 1972)* 11/9/46#.
 3510 *(exJ25 5683)* 2/11/49#.
 25078 *(ex??)* 6/2/52#.
 25033 *(ex??)* 27/3/54#.

SHEDS:
Dairycoates.
Consett 12/6/39.
Heaton 28/3/43.
Dairycoates 14/12/47.

RENUMBERED:
 9094 10/11/46.
69094 2/11/49.
CONDEMNED: 1/7/57.
Cut up at Darlington.

89

Darlington 456.

To traffic 12/1902.

REPAIRS:
Dar. ?/?—?/12/14.**G.**
Dar. ?/?—?/11/20.**G.**
Dar. 1/7—15/9/24.**G.**
Dar. 21/3—13/6/27.**G.**

Dar. 2/7—28/8/29.**G.**
Vacuum ejector fitted.
Dar. 2/5—3/6/32.**G.**
Dar. 4/3—13/4/35.**G.**
Dar. 4/10—16/11/38.**G.**
Dar. 18/9—25/10/40.**G.**
Dar. 31/12/40—27/1/41.**L.**
After collision.
Dar. 29/12/42—16/1/43.**L.**
After collision.
Dar. 26/8—25/9/43.**G.**
Dar. 9/8—25/9/44.**L.**
Dar. 15/10—21/11/47.**G.**
Westinghouse brake replace by steam brake.
Dar. 4—28/10/50.**G.**
Dar. 3/7—15/8/53.**G.**
Dar. 24/10/55. *Not repaired.*

BOILERS:
D1742.
D1740 *(ex1710)* ?/12/14.
D1109 *(new)* ?/11/20.
D1268 *(exN8 216)* 3/6/32.
 2618 *(new)* 13/4/35.
 3397 *(new)* 25/9/43#.
 3300 *(exN9 9414)* 21/11/47#.
 25011 *(exN8 9376)* 28/10/50#.
 25021 *(ex??)* 15/8/53#.

SHEDS:
Dairycoates.
Heaton 10/4/37.
Blaydon 2/11/44.
Gateshead 6/7/52.

RENUMBERED:
 9095 18/8/46.
69095 28/10/50.

CONDEMNED: 25/10/55.
Cut up at Darlington.

429

Darlington 457.

To traffic 12/1902.

REPAIRS:
Dar. ?/?—?/10/13.**G.**
Dar. ?/?—?/2/22.**G.**
Dar. 12/6—28/8/24.**G.**
Dar. 12/1—31/3/27.**G.**
Dar. 30/7—16/9/29.**G.**
Vacuum ejector fitted.
Dar. 13/3—7/10/32.**G.**
Dar. 11/9—18/10/35.**G.**
Dar. 18/11/38—10/2/39.**G.**
Dar. 13—17/2/39.**N/C.**
Dar. 13/1—28/2/42.**G.**
Dar. 22/9—21/10/44.**G.**
Westinghouse brake replaced by steam. Vacuum ejector removed.

Dar. 18/10—10/11/45.**L.**
Dar. 10/10—14/11/47.**G.**
Dar. 3—27/5/50.**G.**
Vacuum ejector refitted.
Dar. 19/11—24/12/53.**G.**
Ghd. 27/8—21/9/56.**G.**

BOILERS:
D1743.
D1862 ?/10/13.
D1277 *(new)* ?/2/22.
D1898 *(exN9 1644)* 18/10/35.
D1507 *(ex1716)* 21/10/44.
D1884 *(exN9 9427)* 14/11/47.
 3301 *(exJ21 5079)* 27/5/50#.
 25093 *(ex??)* 24/12/53#.
 25027 *(ex??)* 21/9/56#.

SHEDS:
Neville Hill.
Dairycoates 1-4/28.
Heaton 23/4/37.
Blaydon 20/1/43.
Heaton 2/11/44.
Dairycoates 14/12/47.

RENUMBERED:
 9096 24/11/46.
69096 27/5/50.

CONDEMNED: 27/12/57.
Cut up at Darlington.

1109

Darlington 458.

To traffic 12/1902.

REPAIRS:
 ??. ?/?—?/11/19.**G.**
 ??. ?/?—?/12/21.**G.**
Ghd. 13/6—25/7/24.**L.**
Ghd. 30/11/25—29/1/26.**G.**
Ghd. 29/3—19/4/26.**L.**
Ghd. 21/10—6/11/29.**L.**
Ghd. 11/11—24/12/30.**G.**
Vacuum ejector fitted.
Dar. 21/4—30/6/36.**G.**
Dar. 18/11—12/12/39.**L.**
Dar. 30/1—20/3/41.**G.**
Dar. 4/8—16/9/44.**G.**
Westinghouse brake replaced by steam. Vacuum ejector removed.
Dar. 31/12/47—6/2/48.**G.**
Ghd. 4/5—8/6/49.**C/L.**
After rear end collision.
Ghd. 11—19/12/50.**N/C.**
Dar. 22/1—17/2/51.**G.**
Ghd. 1/9—15/10/53.**C/H.**
Ghd. 24/10—18/11/55.**G.**
Ghd. 23—29/11/55.**N/C.**
Dar. 17/9—24/10/58.**C/H.**

BOILERS:
D1744.
 D888 *(new)* ?/11/19.
 3188 *(new)* 20/3/41#.
 25023 *(ex??)* 17/2/51#.
 25072 *(ex??)* 18/11/55#.

SHEDS:
Blaydon.
Bowes Bridge 14/8/29.

RENUMBERED:
 9097 10/2/46.
ᴇ**9097** 6/2/48.
69097 7/3/50.

CONDEMNED: 9/4/62.
Into Dar. for cut up 29/6/62.

1112

Darlington 446.

To traffic 10/1902.

REPAIRS:
Dar. ?/?—?/7/19.**G.**
Dar. 1/11/23—21/1/24.**G.**
Dar. 5/10/26—14/1/27.**G.**
Dar. 7/12/28—30/1/29.**G.**
Vacuum ejector fitted.
Dar. 30/10—9/12/31.**G.**
Dar. 17/4—16/5/34.**G.**
Dar. 26/5—1/6/34.**N/C.**
Dar. 9/2—14/4/37.**G.**
Dar. 27/11/39—27/1/40.**G.**
Dar. 1/6—28/7/43.**G.**
Dar. 8—24/12/43.**L.**
After collision.
Dar. 24/5—22/6/46.**G.**
Westinghouse brake replaced by steam. Vacuum ejector removed.
Dar. 23/4—26/5/49.**G.**
Dar. 6—22/12/51.**G.**
Dar. 29/9—22/10/54.**G.**
Dar. 24/9/57. *Not repaired.*

BOILERS:
D1732.
 D875 *(new)* ?/7/19.
 D887 *(ex1317)* 16/5/34.
D1353 *(exJ21 538)* 14/4/37.
 2364 *(exN8 219)* 28/7/43.
 3432 *(exN8 503)* 22/6/46#.
 3394 *(exN8 9374)* 26/5/49#.
 25075 *(ex??)* 22/12/51#.
 25031 *(ex69092)* 22/10/54#.

SHEDS:
Dairycoates.
Sunderland 12/6/39.
Heaton 28/3/43.
Dairycoates 14/12/47.
Neville Hill 9/1/55.

From new, the bunker was topped by three open coal rails. From 1909 plating was fixed behind them.

There was just one odd example as by 1930 No.1132 had acquired a fourth rail, which as No.69099 it then carried to 10th February 1958 withdrawal – *see* page 61.

Until August 1928 all had Westinghouse equipment, for both engine and train braking. The large cylinder under the bunker – *see* previous illustration – was the air reservoir.

In the Unification of Brakes programme all twenty had vacuum ejector added for train braking. No.1785, ex works 28th August 1928, was the first, and No.1683, out 26th July 1932, completed this process.

Ex works 5th February 1942, No.1138 had been fitted with external drain pipe for the ejector exhaust. Note that it still kept the screw coupling until its January 1947 brake change.

By 1944 Westinghouse was no longer required and removals began with No.1699, ex works 12th February 1944. All except Nos.9092 and 9095 also had the vacuum brake removed at the same time, so that by January 1947 eighteen simply had steam brake on the engine. At brake change those still with screw couplings had them changed to three-link except for the two in 1947 which kept the vacuum brake.

The last two engines to lose the Westinghouse equipment – Nos.9092 (6th September 1947) and 9095 (21st November 1947) – retained the vacuum brake combined with automatic steam brake. This proved useful so BR changed three more to that arrangement: Nos.69096 (27th May 1950), 69100 (8th May 1954), and 69108 (17th December 1954). These five were also fitted with screw couplings and train heating apparatus so that they could be used for station carriage pilots – three at Newcastle and two at Hull.

1112 cont./
RENUMBERED:
 1112ᴅ 21/1/24.
 9098 17/2/46.
69098 26/5/49.

CONDEMNED: 24/9/57.
Cut up at Darlington.

1132

Darlington 459.

To traffic 12/1902.

REPAIRS:
Dar. ?/?—?/6/19.**G**.
Dar. 11/12/22—28/3/23.**G**.
Dar. 29/9—17/12/25.**G**.
Dar. 23/6—28/8/28.**G**.
Dar. 21/12/28—16/1/29.**N/C**.
Vacuum ejector fitted.
Dar. 17/8—3/10/33.**G**.
Dar. 16/9—21/10/37.**G**.
Dar. 21/9—23/10/39.**L**.
Dar. 28/11/40—21/1/41.**G**.
Dar. 14/4—8/6/45.**G**.
*Westinghouse brake replaced by
steam. Vacuum ejector removed.*
Ghd. 17/1—22/3/48.**L**.
Dar. 1—19/11/48.**G**.
Dar. 27/11—1/12/48.**N/C**.
After derailment.
Ghd. 24/5—17/6/49.**L**.
Dar. 6/11—1/12/51.**G**.
Ghd. 7/7—7/8/54.**G**.
Dar. 10/2/58. *Not repaired.*

BOILERS:
D1745.
 D874 *(new)* ?/6/19.
D1519 *(ex1138)* 3/10/33.
 2117 *(ex1774)* 21/10/37.
 2370 *(ex1706)* 8/6/45.
 3697 *(exN8 9392)* 19/11/48#.
 25071 *(ex??)* 1/12/51#.
 25022 *(ex??)* 7/8/54#.

SHEDS:
Neville Hill.
Tweedmouth 14/8/39.
Gateshead 3/6/44.
Dairycoates 18/9/49.

RENUMBERED:
 9099 10/3/46.
69099 19/11/48.

CONDEMNED: 10/2/58.
Cut up at Darlington.

1138

Darlington 447.

To traffic 10/1902.

REPAIRS:
 ??. ?/?—?/5/17.**G**.
Ghd. 18/1—5/4/23.**H**.
Ghd. 8/10/23—4/1/24.**L**.
Ghd. 28/4—31/8/26.**G**.
Ghd. 5/7—2/8/29.**L**.
Vacuum ejector fitted.
Ghd. 29/11/32—6/1/33.**L**.
Dar. 23/5—3/7/33.**G**.
Dar. 19/1—9/3/38.**G**.
Dar. 3/1—5/2/42.**G**.
Dar. 27/7—13/8/42.**L**.
Dar. 13/1—24/2/43.**L**.
Damaged by fire.
Dar. 4—23/10/44.**N/C**.
Dar. 26/10/46—25/1/47.**G**.
*Westinghouse brake replaced by
steam. Vacuum ejector removed.*
Ghd. 12/4—9/5/50.**C/L**.
After collision.
Dar. 30/10—25/11/50.**G**.
Ghd. 5—26/5/52.**C/L**.
After collision.
Ghd. 27/10—14/11/52.**C/H**.
Ghd. 6/4—8/5/54.**G**.
Vacuum ejector refitted.
Dar. 18/11/57. *Not repaired.*

BOILERS:
D1733.
 G489 ?/5/17.
D1519 *(new)* 4/1/24.
D1150 *(ex1321)* 3/7/33.
 2363 *(exN8 445)* 9/3/38.
D1211 *(exJ21 139)* 5/2/42.
D1894 *(exN9 9415)* 25/1/47.
 25015 *(ex??)* 25/11/50#.
 25078 *(ex69094)* 8/5/54#.

SHED:
Bowes Bridge.

RENUMBERED:
 9100 27/1/46.
69100 9/5/50.

CONDEMNED: 25/11/57.
Cut up at Darlington.

1148

Darlington 460.

To traffic 12/1902.

REPAIRS:
 ??. ?/?—5/21.**G**.
Ghd. 28/7—3/10/23.**G**.

Dar. 3/9—17/12/26.**G**.
Dar. 9/7—4/9/29.**G**.
Vacuum ejector fitted.
Dar. 24/2—1/4/32.**G**.
Dar. 19/7—7/9/34.**G**.
Dar. 30/6—19/8/37.**G**.
Dar. 24/8—5/10/37.**N/C**.
Dar. 16/7—23/8/40.**G**.
Dar. 27/3—23/4/43.**L**.
Dar. 3/2—6/3/44.**G**.
*Westinghouse brake replaced by
steam. Vacuum ejector removed.*
Dar. 3/10/46—4/1/47.**G**.
Dar. 11/10—3/11/49.**G**.
Dar. 7—10/11/49.**N/C**.
Dar. 28/10—15/11/52.**G**.
Dar. 17—18/11/52.**N/C**.
Dar. 7/12/55—11/1/56.**G**.
Dar. 1/12/59—8/1/60.**G**.

BOILERS:
D1746.
 G515 ?/5/21.
D1911 *(new)* 17/12/26.
D1265 *(exN9 1645)* 7/9/34.
D1109 *(ex1321)* 19/8/37.
D1150 *(ex1699)* 6/3/44.
D1937 *(ex9108)* 4/1/47.
 3418 *(exJ21 5107)* 3/11/49#.
 25099 *(ex??)* 15/11/52#.
 25023 *(ex69097)* 11/1/56#.
 25015 *(ex69109)* 8/1/60#.

SHEDS:
Selby.
Dairycoates 12/2/25.
Waskerley 17/7/39.
Consett 9/9/40.
Sunderland 14/12/42.
Northallerton 28/3/43.
Darlington 11/3/44.
Northallerton 25/6/45.
Sunderland 28/1/51.
Tyne Dock 29/6/58.
Gateshead 16/4/59.

RENUMBERED:
 1148ᴅ 3/10/23.
 9101 10/2/46.
69101 3/11/49.

CONDEMNED: 9/4/62.
Into Dar. for cut up 28/6/62.

1317

Darlington 455.

To traffic 12/1902.

REPAIRS:
Dar. ?/?—?/4/20.**G**.
Dar. 8/11/22—31/1/23.**G**.
Dar. 16/7—14/10/25.**G**.

Dar. 23/3—31/5/28.**G**.
Dar. 20/12/28—15/1/29.**N/C**.
Vacuum ejector fitted.
Dar. 17/9—29/10/30.**G**.
Dar. 21/2—23/3/34.**G**.
Dar. 26/1—7/3/39.**G**.
Dar. 27/2—14/4/42.**G**.
Dar. 19/7—15/9/45.**G**.
*Westinghouse brake replaced by
steam. Vacuum ejector removed.*
Dar. 4—28/12/48.**G**.
Ghd. 14/3—1/4/49.**L**.
After collision.
Dar. 4/2—1/3/52.**G**.
Ghd. 10/8—24/9/54.**G**.
Ghd. 14/6—13/7/56.**C/L**.
After collision.
Dar. 3/2/59. *Not repaired.*

BOILERS:
D1741.
 D887 *(new)* ?/4/20.
 D879 *(ex1785)* 23/3/34.
 2957 *(new)* 7/3/39#.
 2370 *(ex9099)* 28/12/48.
 25083 *(ex??)* 1/3/52#.
 25070 *(ex69107)* 24/9/54#.

SHEDS:
Neville Hill.
Tweedmouth 24/7/39.
Gateshead 3/6/44.
Dairycoates 18/9/49.
Tyne Dock 10/7/55.
Bowes Bridge 24/11/57.

RENUMBERED:
 9102 7/4/46.
69102 28/12/48.

CONDEMNED: 9/2/59.
Cut up at Darlington.

1706

Darlington 453.

To traffic 12/1902.

REPAIRS:
Dar. ?/?—?/9/18.**G**.
Dar. 3/1—13/3/24.**G**.
Dar. 23/2—16/5/27.**G**.
Dar. 8/8—24/9/29.**G**.
Vacuum ejector fitted.
Dar. 21/9—27/10/32.**G**.
Dar. 23/10—28/11/36.**G**.
Dar. 2/3—5/4/40.**G**.
Dar. 6—11/4/40.**N/C**.
Dar. 20/11/41—17/2/42.**G**.
Dar. 5—30/3/45.**G**.
*Westinghouse brake replaced by
steam brake. Vacuum brake
removed.*

Quite a number had their screw coupling replaced by the three-link loose type long before they lost train brakes, No.1711 – *see* opposite, top – as early as 1933, and No.1109 probably in June 1936. This 1940 photograph shows a cab with ARP screen and the white patch on the bufferbeam aided visibility in blackout.

Apart from No.1317 (*see* page 56, top) the LNER took over the class in this style of painting and it could still be seen until No.1683 went to works 22nd May 1928. It was ex Gateshead works 6th February 1923 still as N.1683 E., as was N.1785 E. from Darlington on 24th March 1923 until 19th August 1925.

Along with the new company initials, red lining was used until discarded in the June 1928 painting economies. The first with it were Nos.1132 (28th March 1923) and 1710 (20th May 1923), both as L.&N.E.R. There were also two which got the area suffix D, 1148D (3rd October 1923) and 1112D (21st January 1924). No.1711 still had red lining from a General repair 18th April 1928, the vacuum ejector being added on 1st February 1929 at a Non-Classified works visit.

From June 1928, and then right through to withdrawal, only plain black was applied.

1706 cont./
Ghd. 8/12/47—20/2/48.**L.**
After collision.
Dar. 6/10/48. *Not repaired.*

BOILERS:
D1739.
 G538 ?/9/18.
D1937 *(new)* 16/5/27.
 2370 *(exN9 1647)* 5/4/40.
D1898 *(ex429)* 30/3/45.

SHEDS:
Dairycoates.
Sunderland 12/7/39.
Percy Main 28/3/43.
Gateshead 3/6/44.

RENUMBERED:
9103 10/11/46.

CONDEMNED: 8/11/48.
Cut up at Darlington.

_____

1710

Darlington 454.

To traffic 12/1902.

REPAIRS:
 ??. ?/?—?/7/14.**G.**
 ??. ?/?—?/8/20.**G.**
Dar. 13/3—20/5/23.**G.**
Ghd. 6/4—8/7/26.**G.**
Ghd. 22/12/28—14/2/29.**G.**
Vacuum ejector fitted.
Ghd. 16/3—21/4/32.**G.**
Dar. 15/1—9/3/36.**G.**
Dar. 27/9—14/11/39.**G.**
Dar. 30/7—24/9/40.**L.**
Dar. 1/12/42—29/1/43.**G.**
Dar. 17/11—8/12/43.**L.**
Dar. 28/1—22/3/46.**G.**
Westinghouse brake replaced by steam. Vacuum ejector removed.
Dar. 6/4—3/5/49.**G.**
Dar. 31/10—23/11/51.**G.**
Ghd. 22/4—12/6/54.**G.**
Dar. 3/3/58. *Not repaired.*

BOILERS:
D1740.
D1743 *(ex429)* ?/7/14.
D1094 *(new)* ?/8/20.
D1277 *(ex429)* 9/3/36.
 2359 *(exN9 1648)* 14/11/39.
 3685 *(ex9107)* 3/5/49#.
 25028 *(ex??)* 23/11/51#.
 25012 *(ex??)* 12/6/54#.

SHEDS:
Neville Hill.

Tweedmouth 24/1/25.
Heaton 18/2/37.
Alnmouth 20/4/42.
Heaton 13/7/42.
Dairycoates 14/12/47.

RENUMBERED:
9104 17/11/46.
69104 3/5/49.

CONDEMNED: 17/3/58.
Cut up at Darlington.

_____

1699

Darlington 461.

To traffic 3/1903.

REPAIRS:
 ??. ?/?—?/4/18.**G.**
Ghd. ?/?—21/9/22.**G.**
Ghd. 8/6—6/10/26.**G.**
Ghd. 22/10—1/12/31.**G.**
Vacuum ejector fitted.
Dar. 16/11—17/12/36.**G.**
Dar. 15/10—13/11/40.**G.**
Dar. 15/1—12/2/44.**G.**
Westinghouse brake replaced by steam. Vacuum ejector removed.
Dar. 8/7—17/8/46.**G.**
Dar. 17/5—11/6/49.**G.**
Ghd. 4—28/6/52.**G.**
Ghd. 8—11/7/52.**N/C.**
Dar. 8/5—20/6/56.**G.**
Dar. 16/6/61. *Not repaired.*

BOILERS:
D1747.
 G519 ?/4/18.
D1296 *(new)* 21/9/22.
 D842 *(exJ21 56)* 1/12/31.
D1263 *(ex1716)* 17/12/36.
D1150 *(exJ21 582)* 13/11/40.
D1935 *(exJ25 2061)* 12/2/44.
 2364 *(ex9098)* 17/8/46.
 2359 *(ex9104)* 11/6/49.
 25092 *(ex??)* 26/8/52#.
 25095 *(ex??)* 20/6/56#.

SHEDS:
Sunderland.
Heaton 28/3/43.
Gateshead 3/6/44.
Dairycoates 19/9/48.
Gateshead 6/2/49.
Dairycoates 18/9/49.
Tyne Dock 3/12/50.
Gateshead 26/4/59.

RENUMBERED:
9105 27/9/46.
69105 11/6/49.

CONDEMNED: 16/6/61.
Cut up at Darlington.

_____

1707

Darlington 462.

To traffic 3/1903.

REPAIRS:
 ??. ?/?—?/12/13.**G.**
Ghd. 20/3—12/5/24.**G.**
Ghd. 19/6—17/8/28.**G.**
Ghd. 9—22/5/30.**N/C.**
Vacuum ejector fitted.
Ghd. 3—22/7/31.**L.**
Ghd. 23/10—8/12/31.**G.**
Dar. 5/6—11/7/36.**G.**
Dar. 7—24/10/38.**N/C.**
Dar. 10/6—11/7/40.**G.**
Dar. 26/5—23/8/41.**H.**
Dar. 2—26/2/44.**G.**
Westinghouse brake replaced by steam. Vacuum ejector removed.
Dar. 1—25/5/46.**G.**
Dar. 9/5—2/6/49.**G.**
Dar. 17/12/51—12/1/52.**G.**
Dar. 24—30/4/52.**N/C.**
Dar. 24/11—18/12/54.**G.**
Dar. 29/3—3/4/57.**N/C.**
Ghd. 20—31/5/57.**C/L.**
Dar. 3/3/58. *Not repaired.*

BOILERS:
D1748.
 D28 *(new)* ?/12/13.
D1302 *(new)* 12/5/24.
D1914 *(exN9 1640)* 11/7/36.
D1915 *(exN9 1649)* 11/7/40.
 2969 *(ex1711)* 25/5/46#.
 3432 *(ex9098)* 2/6/49#.
 25074 *(ex??)* 12/1/52#.
 25045 *(ex??)* 18/12/54#.

SHEDS:
Sunderland.
Heaton 28/3/43.
Gateshead 3/6/44.
Dairycoates 19/9/48.
Tyne Dock 3/7/55.

RENUMBERED:
9106 17/11/46.
69106 2/6/49.

CONDEMNED: 17/3/58.
Cut up at Darlington.

_____

1711

Darlington 463.

To traffic 3/1903.

REPAIRS:
Dar. ?/?—?/11/21.**G.**
Dar. 10/10—22/12/24.**G.**
Dar. 9/2—18/4/28.**G.**
Dar. 17/1—1/2/29.**N/C.**
Vacuum ejector fitted.
Dar. 27/6—8/9/30.**G.**
Dar. 11/10—10/11/33.**G.**
Dar. 24/6—23/9/36.**G.**
Dar. 23/2—31/3/39.**G.**
Dar. 16/4—30/5/40.**L.**
Dar. 29/9—29/10/42.**G.**
Dar. 15/3—13/4/46.**G.**
Westinghouse brake replaced by steam. vacuum ejector removed.
Ghd. 19/11/47—9/1/48.**L.**
Dar. 18/3—9/4/49.**G.**
Dar. 10/10/51—5/1/52.**G.**
Ghd. 17/6—17/7/54.**G.**
Ghd. 19—21/7/54.**N/C.**

BOILERS:
D1749.
D1279 *(new)* ?/11/21.
 D874 *(ex1132)* 10/11/33.
D1129 *(exJ21 26)* 23/9/36.
 2969 *(new)* 31/3/39#.
 3685 *(new)* 13/4/46#.
 2990 *(exJ25 5656)* 9/4/49#.
 2990 reno.25070 5/1/52.
 25015 *(ex69100)* 17/7/54#.

SHEDS:
Dairycoates.
Heaton 10/4/37.
Sunderland 15/2/41.
Percy Main 28/3/43.
Gateshead 3/6/44.
Dairycoates 18/9/49.

RENUMBERED:
9107 1/12/46.
69107 9/4/49.

CONDEMNED: 27/12/57.
Cut up at Darlington.

_____

1785

Darlington 465.

To traffic 4/1903.

REPAIRS:
Dar. ?/?—?/10/15.**G.**
Dar. ?/?—?/8/19.**G.**
Dar. 8/1—24/3/23.**G.**
Dar. 19/8—30/10/25.**G.**

Dar. 30/7—28/8/28.**G.**
Vacuum ejector fitted.
Dar. 19/8—25/9/31.**G.**
Dar. 30/1—23/2/34.**G.**
Dar. 4/5—12/8/37.**G.**
Dar. 13/8—2/9/37.**N/C.**
Dar. 6/5—5/6/40.**G.**
Dar. 20/12/43—18/1/44.**G.**
Dar. 14/11—14/12/46.**G.**
Westinghouse brake replaced by steam. Vacuum ejector removed.
Dar. 14/9—22/10/49.**G.**
Dar. 4—27/3/52.**G.**
Ghd. 16/11—17/12/54.**G.**
Vacuum ejector refitted.

BOILERS:
D1751.
D1738 *(ex1697)* ?/10/15.
 D879 *(new)* ?/8/19.
D1266 *(ex1697)* 23/2/34.
D1937 *(ex1706)* 5/6/40.
 2090 *(exJ21 30)* 14/12/46.
 3390 *(exN8 9389)* 22/10/49#.
 25086 *(ex??)* 27/3/52#.
 25083 *(ex69102)* 17/12/54#.

SHEDS:
Dairycoates.
Sunderland 12/6/39.
Heaton 28/3/43.
Dairycoates 14/12/47.

RENUMBERED:
 9108 10/2/46.
 69108 22/10/49.

CONDEMNED: 30/7/57.
Cut up at Darlington.

1716

Darlington 464.

To traffic 4/1903.

REPAIRS:
 ??. ?/?—?/8/21.**G.**
Ghd. 16/11/26—28/1/27.**G.**
Ghd. 21/7—14/8/30.**L.**
Vacuum ejector fitted.
Ghd. 23/5—15/7/31.**G.**
Ghd. 24/9—8/10/31.**L.**
Dar. 10/9—9/11/36.**G.**
Dar. 13/12/40—14/1/41.**G.**
Dar. 11/9—17/10/44.**G.**
Westinghouse brake replaced by steam. Vacuum ejector removed.
Ghd. 30/12/46—13/3/47.**L.**
After collision.
Dar. 23/6—9/7/48.**G.**
Ghd. 4—23/6/51.**H/I.**
Ghd. 6—19/3/52.**C/L.**
Ghd. 25/1—20/2/54.**G.**

Ghd. 30/7—4/9/56.**C/H.**
Dar. 24/9—31/10/59.**G.**

BOILERS:
D1750.
D1263 *(new)* ?/8/21.
D1507 *(exJ25 2053)* 9/11/36.
 2089 *(exN9 1640)* 17/10/44.
 3189 *(exJ25 2051)* 9/7/48#.
 3189 reno.25054 23/6/51.
 25118 *(ex??)* 20/2/54#.
 25027 *(ex??)* 31/10/59#.

SHED:
Gateshead.

RENUMBERED:
 9109 25/8/46.
 69109 9/7/48.

CONDEMNED: 9/4/62.
Into Dar. for cut up 28/6/62.

(below) **War conditions caused initials to be limited to NE from July 1942 but they were in 12in. shaded transfers. No.1774 acquired them when ex works 4th January 1944. Fourteen were re-numbered in 1946 whilst still only NE.**

(bottom) **When ex works 11th September 1946, No.1774 had 7½in. LNER again, this having been restored from January 1946. Six others, Nos.9091, 9094, 9104, 9105, 9106, and 9107 had LNER restored before they were re-numbered in 1946.**

When Darlington's stock of shaded transfers was exhausted, lettering and numerals were put on in yellow painted and unshaded Gill sans but with modified 6 and 9. Six N10 got that style: 9092 (6th September 1947), 9095 (21st November 1947), 9096 (14th November 1947), 9100 (25th January 1947), 9101 (4th January 1947), and 9108 (14th December 1946).

Only one got the first BR style with an E prefix. Ex works 6th February 1948, No.ᴇ9097 had 12in. figures but moved to the bunker. On the tank BRITISH RAILWAYS was centred but only in 8in. letters. Note the prefix has also been applied to the buffer beam number.

There were two examples where the BR number was combined with LNER, with both still on the tank as a result of Light repairs. On 24th December 1948 No.69091 was ex Gateshead works with LNER in shaded transfers from its 29th March 1946 General repair. See left side of top illustration on this page for the bufferbeam number. On 9th May 1950 No.69100 got that number in correct Gill sans figures but on the front bufferbeam Gateshead had still put the modified 6 and 9.

10in. matching letters and numbers became standard until August 1949 and nine were put into this style: 69093 (3rd March 1949), 69098 (26th May 1949), 69099 (19th November 1948), 69102 (28th December 1948), 69104 (3rd May 1949), 69105 (11th June 1949), 69106 (2nd June 1949), 69107 (9th April 1949), and 69109 (9th July 1948).

When the 15½in. size emblem replaced BRITISH RAILWAYS in September 1949, all except the scrapped No.9103 got it.

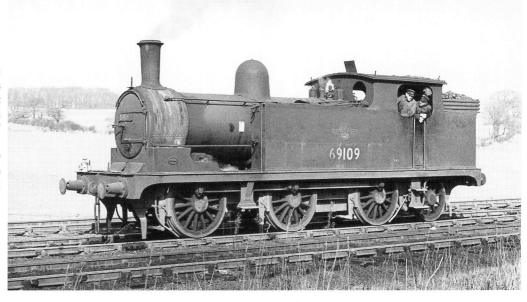

When BR changed from emblem to crest in 1957, N10 class was already on withdrawal lists, but three did have repairs at which the crest was put on: Nos.69097 (24th October 1958), 69101 (8th January 1960), and 69109 (31st October 1959). All three were withdrawn on 9th April 1962 and N10 class was then extinct.

Before the North Eastern Railway take-over on 1st April 1922, more significant alterations had been made. The vacuum brakes had been removed and steam brakes fitted, smokebox doors had been made flush fitting, with two dog clips at the base, and an H&B type cast chimney replaced the built-up Kitson design. All the class had new fireboxes fitted thus (Nos.97 [May 1911], 98 [May 1911], 99 [June 1916], 100 [July 1913], and 101 [November 1911]) and on which the safety valves were mounted directly and the whistle moved to a separate mounting – see page 75, top. Nos.100 and 101 had also acquired two more coal rails.

The NER numbered them 3097 to 3101 – see page 75 – but from 26th February 1924 they became LNER 2478 to 2482. From June 1923 they began to go to Darlington for repair and to be fitted with new boilers because all five still had those put on in 1901. Darlington built five new boilers for them and they were put on as follows: 3099D (17th September 1923), 3097D (28th September 1923), 2482 (26th February 1924), 2479 (17th September 1924), and 2481 (14th November 1924). These had NER type smokebox doors with wheel and handle for fastening, Ross 'pop' safety valves and two whistles on the cab roof. The engines were supplied equipped with a re-railing jack carried on the running plate alongside the right hand front sandbox and they survived each engine's first visit to Darlington. By 1930 all had had the re-railing jack taken off, its purpose being served by other means.

(left) At reboilering Nos.2479, 2480 and 2481 kept the H&B chimney but Nos.2478 and 2482 got a NER design but with a plain top. This type was fitted to the other three in 1923/24, Darlington also plating behind the coal rails.

From its final repair, ex works 20th January 1939, No.2478 had a chimney with windjabber, the only one so fitted. From the 1923/24 re-boilering, all carried organ-pipe whistles on the right hand side and a small bell shape whistle on the left hand side; these were retained to withdrawal.

CLASS N 11

3097/2478

Kitson 3964.

To traffic 2/1901.

REPAIRS:
Hls.. ?/?—?/3/22.**G.**
Dar. 6/7—28/9/23.**G.**
Dar. 31/8/27—24/2/28.**G.**
Dar. 7/7—28/8/31.**G.**
Dar. 3/7—19/9/34.**G.**
Dar. 24/3—4/5/36.**L.**
Dar. 29/11/38—20/1/39.**G.**
Dar. 16/11/42. *Not repaired.*

BOILERS:
D1560 *(new)* 28/9/23.

SHEDS:
Springhead.
Dairycoates 22/5/30.
Springhead 12/6/39.

RENUMBERED:
3097ᴅ 28/9/23.
2478 23/5/24.

CONDEMNED: 9/1/43.
Cut up at Darlington.

3098/2479

Kitson 3965.

To traffic 2/1901.

REPAIRS:
Hls. ?/?—?/8/19.**G.**
Dar. 5/6—17/9/24.**G.**
Dar. 27/8—29/10/29.**G.**
Dar. 11/2—23/3/35.**G.**
Dar. 16/1—17/2/41.**G.**

Dar. 23/11/44. *Not repaired.*

BOILERS:
D1562 *(new)* 17/9/24.

SHEDS:
Springhead.
Dairycoates 26/1/29.
West Hartlepool 12/11/30.
Dairycoates 21/12/36.
Springhead 12/6/39.

RENUMBERED:
2479 15/9/24.
9085 allocated.

CONDEMNED: 30/12/44.
Cut up at Darlington.

3099/2480

Kitson 3966.

To traffic 2/1901.

REPAIRS:
Hls. ?/?—?/3/22.**G.**
Dar. 19/6—17/9/23.**G.**
Dar. 14/8—5/10/28.**G.**
Dar. 2/10—9/11/33.**G.**
Dar. 21/9—7/11/34.**H.**
Dar. 15/12/38—27/1/39.**G.**
Dar. 30/1—3/2/39.**N/C.**
Dar. 17/2—20/3/43.**G.**
Dar. 12/4/46. *Not repaired.*

BOILERS:
D1548 *(new)* 17/9/23.

D1560 *(ex2478)* 20/3/43.

SHEDS:
Springhead.
Dairycoates 15/9/27.
Springhead 3/7/39.

RENUMBERED:
3099ᴅ 17/9/23.
2480 19/7/24.
9086 allocated.

CONDEMNED: 18/5/46.
Cut up at Darlington.

3100/2481

Darlington 3967.

To traffic 2/1901.

REPAIRS:
Hls. ?/?—?/3/21.**G.**
Dar. 26/8—14/11/24.**G.**
Dar. 21/1—7/3/30.**G.**
Dar. 28/8—11/11/36.**G.**
Dar. 7/8—20/9/41.**G.**
Dar. 15/11/45. *Not repaired.*

BOILERS:
D1563 *(new)* 14/11/24.

SHEDS:
Cudworth.
Springhead 28/3/43.

RENUMBERED:
2481 13/11/24.

9087 allocated.

CONDEMNED: 22/12/45.
Cut up at Darlington.

3101/2482

Darlington 3968.

To traffic 2/1901.

REPAIRS:
Hls. ?/?—?/4/21.**G.**
Dar. 20/11/23—26/2/24.**G.**
Dar. 16/10—10/12/28.**G.**
Dar. 19/3—21/4/34.**G.**
Dar. 23/9—27/10/39.**G.**
Dar. 14/5—26/8/42.**H.**
Dar. 30/6/44. *Not repaired.*

BOILERS:
D1565 *(new)* 26/2/24.

SHEDS:
Springhead.
Dairycoates 15/9/27.
Springhead 7/7/33.
Cudworth 2/8/37.
Springhead 28/3/43.

RENUMBERED:
2482 26/2/24.
9088 allocated.

CONDEMNED: 5/8/44.
Cut up at Darlington.

Until about 1933 the smokebox door still had the wheel and handle fastening (*see* page 74, centre), but by 1936 the wheel was no longer to be seen and had been replaced by a second handle. Ex works 20th September 1941, No.2481 had a white painted front bufferbeam to be more easily seen in the blackout.

The first three engines had only two coal rails and other than Darlington putting plating behind them in 1923/24, no alteration was made to them. Under the H&B these three normally worked at Hull.

(below) On the other two, which in their earlier years worked from Cudworth shed, the H&B had fitted two extra coal rails. Other than the plating which Darlington added in 1924, they remained in that form to the 1944/45 withdrawals.

A curiosity which stemmed from their LD&EC ancestry was the lamp irons on the front of the sandbox. Only Nos.2478 and 2479 had them because these two had been completed when the original order for them fell through. For the H&B the irons were put on in the normal positions but Nos.2478 and 2479 retained the redundant irons to their 1943/44 withdrawal.

This was the livery in which the North Eastern took them over on 1st April 1922 with blue and vermillion lining on invisible green which was equal parts of Brunswick green and Drop black. Numbers and letters were 6in. high in light gold leaf shaded on the right hand side.

By 1922 lining was almost unseen due to reduced standards from the 1914-18 war. Numbers were now 9in. and during 1922 they had a three thousand addition to avoid duplication of the NER numbers. None of this class got NER painting.

As shown by the illustration on page 74, centre, Darlington put their classification style on the front bufferbeam using Class F1 (HB). Not until No.2480 was ex works 9th November 1933 did they go over to the LNER Class N11. From 1923/24 to withdrawal they were only in unlined black.

Only one changed to the post-July 1942 war economy lettering of just NE, but in 12in. size. No.2480 had this ex works 20th March 1943 when it got the boiler from No.2478 which was withdrawn on 9th January 1943. Their Diagram 66 boilers built in 1923 were not usable on any other class. When the 1943 renumbering scheme was drawn up the four survivors were allocated 9085 to 9088 but they were never applied. When No.2480 was withdrawn on 18th May 1946 Class N11 was extinct.

The NER and the LNER needed to make immediate boiler renewals and as a first step, Darlington sent a 1917 built '901' class boiler which Springhead put on No.3104 ex works 11th June 1923. It was of course domed, and was fed by clack boxes on the front ring. Other changes were removal of vacuum brake, replaced by steam on the engine, addition of a fourth more substantial coal rail, and black paint with single red lining.

Meanwhile Springhead works had been preparing material for five domeless boilers and this was sent to Darlington for completion. One was used for J75 class and three were put on Nos.3110D (30th November 1923), 3109D (19th December 1923), and 2486 (30th April 1924). The other boiler was sent to Springhead for fitting there. All three changed to NER smokebox doors with wheel and handle. No.3110D kept the H&B chimney but the other two got the NER type. No.3109D kept three coal rails as did No.2486 whilst 3110D got the additional stronger one. Only 2486 lost its vacuum brake.

The other domeless boiler was used by Springhead for No.2489, ex works 29th February 1924. They kept the H&B chimney but fitted a H&B smokebox which had a flat base and was 8in. longer than on any of the others. No.2489 also got the stronger extra coal rail and changed from vacuum to steam brake. On to these domeless boilers, Darlington fitted Ross 'pop' valves with a casing around their base.

CLASS N 12

^ Diagram 69 boiler.
* Diagram 71a boiler.
# Diagram 71B boiler.

3102/2483

Kitson 4070.

To traffic 11/1901.

REPAIRS:
Hls. ?/?—?/7/21.**G.**
Dar. 21/6—20/9/24.**G.**
Changed from vacuum to steam brake.
Dar. 8/10—5/12/29.**G.**
Dar. 16/12/32—27/1/33.**H.**
Dar. 25/10—23/11/34.**G.**
Dar. 29/6/38. *Not repaired.*

BOILERS:
D1596 *(new, domed)* 20/9/24#.
D1599 *(ex2484)* 23/11/34#.

SHEDS:
Cudworth.
York (DVLR) 19/10/36.

RENUMBERED:
2483 20/9/24.

CONDEMNED: 30/7/38.
Cut up at Darlington.

3103/2484

Kitson 4071.

To traffic 12/1901.

REPAIRS:
Hls. ?/?—?/12/19.**G.**
Dar. 24/10/24—16/1/25.**G.**
Changed from vacuum to steam brake.
Dar. 15/1—3/3/30.**G.**
Dar. 12/5—12/6/30.**L.**
Dar. 28/8—17/10/34.**G.**
Dar. 4/12/36. *Not repaired.*

BOILERS:
D1599 *(new, domed)* 16/1/25#.
D1576 *(ex2486, domeless)* 17/10/34*.
D1576 marked as sold April 1939 in Darlington's 'Boilers Condemned Register'.

SHEDS:
Cudworth.
Woodford 17/1/35.
Cudworth 21/2/35.
Ardsley 22/1/36.

RENUMBERED:
2484 1/10/24.

CONDEMNED: 26/12/36.
Cut up at Darlington.

3104/2485

Kitson 4072.

To traffic 12/1901.

REPAIRS:
Hls. ?/?—?/5/19.**G.**
Hls. ?/?—11/6/23.**G.**
Changed from vacuum to steam brake.
Dar. 25/10—21/12/28.**G.**
Dar. 9/5—21/6/33.**G.**
Dar. 25/2/37. *Not repaired.*

BOILERS:
D669 *(ex '901' 156, domed)* 11/6/23^.

SHEDS:
Springhead.
Cudworth 1-5/24.
York (DVLR) 28/1/29.
Cudworth 27/7/36.

RENUMBERED:
2485 2/6/24.

CONDEMNED: 4/3/37.
Cut up at Darlington.

3105/2486

Kitson 4073.

To traffic 12/1901.

REPAIRS:
Hls. ?/?—?/4/22.**G.**
Dar. 1/2—30/4/24.**G.**
Dar. 20/11/24—8/5/25.**L.**
Dar. 12/6—29/8/29.**G.**
Dar. 9/7—25/8/34.**G.**
Dar. 1/3—25/6/38. *Not repaired and returned to Doncaster.*
Don. 18/7—12/8/38.**G.**

Dar. 27/3—23/4/42.**G.**
Dar. 23/11/44—4/1/45.**G.**
Dar. 14/8/48. *Not repaired.*

BOILERS:
D1576 *(new)* 30/4/24*.
2389 *(exN13 2419, domed)* 25/8/34#.
2581 *(exN13 2537)* 23/4/42#.
2400 *(exN13 2415)* 4/1/45#.

SHEDS:
Cudworth.
Bullcroft Jct. ?/11/24.
Springhead 5/12/31.
Ardsley 16/2/37.
Tuxford 16/11/38.
Springhead 29/1/42.

RENUMBERED:
2486 23/4/24.
9089 1/12/46.

CONDEMNED: 30/8/48.
Cut up at Darlington.

3106/2487

Kitson 4074.

To traffic 12/1901.

REPAIRS:
Hls. ?/?—?/12/20.**G.**
Dar. 5/4—15/9/24.**G.**
Changed from vacuum to steam brake.
Dar. 20/11/29—15/1/30.**G.**
Dar. 10/8—13/10/34.**G.**

BOILERS:
D1590 *(new, domed)* 15/9/24#.
D642 *(exJ80 2449)* 13/10/34^.

SHEDS:
Cudworth.
Ardsley 24/1/36.

RENUMBERED:
2487 15/9/24.

CONDEMNED: 28/9/38.
Cut up at Doncaster.

3107/2488

Kitson 4075.

To traffic 12/1901.

REPAIRS:
Hls. ?/?—?/4/21.**G.**
Dar. 2/7—6/10/24.**G.**
Changed from vacuum to steam brake.
Dar. 9/12/29—31/1/30.**G.**
Dar. 19/10/38. *Not repaired.*

BOILERS:
D1600 *(new, domed)* 6/10/24#.

SHEDS:
Cudworth.
Dairycoates 7/6/27.
West Hartlepool 17/11/27.
Ferryhill 20/12/27.
Cudworth 18/6/35.
Dairycoates 15/7/35.
Cudworth 30/10/36.
Springhead 2/8/37.
York (DVLR) 12/7/38.

RENUMBERED:
2488 1/10/24.

CONDEMNED: 22/10/38.
Cut up at Darlington.

3108/2489

Kitson 4076.

To traffic 12/1901.

REPAIRS:
Hls. ?/?—?/9/21.**G.**
Hls. ?/11/23—29/2/24.**G.**
Changed from vacuum to steam brake.
Dar. 17/6—5/9/29.**G.**
Dar. 24/11—13/12/32.**L.**
Dar. 1/2/37. *Not repaired.*

BOILERS:
D1574 *(new)* 29/2/24*.

SHEDS:
Cudworth.
Denaby ?/11/24.
Dairycoates 28/5/27.
East Hartlepool 17/11/27.
Cudworth 23/4/28.

Nos.2483, 2484, 2487 and 2488 completed the re-boilering by getting similar boilers built by Darlington but fitted with a dome. They were ex works as follows: 2483 (20th September 1924), 2484 (16th January 1925), 2487 (15th September 1924), 2488 (6th October 1924). All four changed to NER type smokebox doors with wheel and handle but only No.2488 kept its H&B chimney. The others got the NER type; No.2487's chimney was complete with a windjabber. All were altered to steam brake but only No.2483 and 2487 got the fourth coal rail.

Ex works 17th October 1934, No.2484 had the domeless boiler from No.2486. It was the only H&B locomotive to revert after getting a domed boiler. No.2486 got a domed replacement from N13 class. Note style of boiler handrails also reverted to three portions

There was one more boiler type change. Ex works on 13th October 1934, No.2487 had a spare '901' class boiler from scrapped J80 class No.2449. This made it similar to No.2485 except that No.2487 kept the brass casing to its Ramsbottom safety valves.

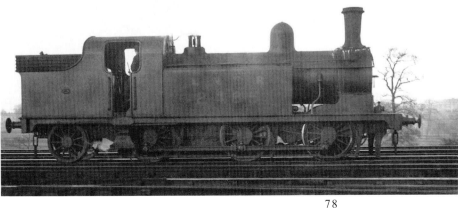

The H&B chimney proved very durable and Nos.2485 and 2488 kept that type to withdrawal on 4th March 1937 and 22nd October 1938 respectively. No.2489 – *see* page 76, bottom – is also believed to have kept the H&B type to its 5th February 1937 withdrawal. At re-boilering, a Worsdell type NER chimney with a plain rim was put on Nos.2483, 2484, 2486 and 2490, and this type remained on 2486 (9089) to its 30th August 1948 withdrawal (*see* page 83, bottom).

2489 cont./
RENUMBERED:
2489 29/2/24.

CONDEMNED: 5/2/37.
Cut up at Darlington.

3109/2490

Kitson 4077.

To traffic 12/1901.

REPAIRS:
Hls. ?/?—?/3/22.**H**.
Dar. 3/7—19/12/23.**G**.
Dar. 2/7—12/9/29.**G**.
Dar. 3—27/1/33.**L**.
Dar. 18/11/36. *Not repaired.*

BOILERS:
D1561 (new) 19/12/23*.

SHEDS:
Cudworth.
York (DVLR) 27/7/36.
Cudworth 19/10/36.
Dairycoates 30/10/36.

RENUMBERED:
3109ᴅ 19/12/23.
2490 22/10/24.

CONDEMNED: 26/12/36.
Cut up at Darlington.

3110/2491

Kitson 4078.

To traffic 12/1901.

REPAIRS:
Hls. ?/?—?/4/21.**G**.
Dar. 28/8—30/11/23.**G**.
Dar. 4/2—12/4/29.**G**.
Dar. 25/10—30/11/32.**G**.

BOILERS:
D1567 (new) 30/11/23*.

SHEDS:
Cudworth.
Dairycoates 24/5/27.
Springhead 7/6/27.

RENUMBERED:
3110ᴅ 30/11/23.
2491 4/11/24.

CONDEMNED: 9/10/36.
Cut up at Darlington.

When No.2487 got a domed boiler, its NER chimney was one with a windjabber. By October 1934 – *see* page 78 – the chimney had a plain top. It is not known if this was a change of chimney or only a turning off of a corroded windjabber. In this 1926 photograph No.2487 still carried a re-railing jack, the only one then so equipped, and that was taken off by 15th January 1930 shopping.

When No.3110ᴅ got its new boiler – *see* page 84, centre – it kept its H&B type chimney and it became No.2491 from 4th November 1924. Ex works 12th April 1929 the chimney was changed to NER type with windjabber which it then kept to 9th October 1936 withdrawal. Note the ventilator on the cab roof. This engine was the only one so equipped.

Until 1933 the Ramsbottom safety valves on No.2485 (which carried a '901' class boiler) were open, but had a circular casing around the base of the same style as used for Ross 'pop' valves. Ex works 21st June 1933 from its final 'General', No.2485 had been provided with a bras trumpet shaped casing to its safety valves.

All the boilers which Darlington built to Diagram 71A (domeless) and 71B (domed) were fitted with Ross 'pop' safety valves, and they had NER style twin whistles, one organ pipe and one bell shape.

Despite getting a pure NER type boiler No.2485 continued the H&B style of having a single whistle although this was an organ pipe whereas the H&B used a bell-shape.

At its final repair, ex works 23rd November 1934, No.2483 changed from twin to a single bell shape whistle. Its smokebox door still had a wheel and handle, this one and No.2490 being the only ones to keep that style of fastening to withdrawal. The other seven all had twin handles on the smokebox door when withdrawn, which was how they had been in H&B days.

Until the 1923 reboilering, the boiler handrails were in three sections. From the front of each tank a continuous rail curved over the top of the smokebox door, and above each tank was a separate rail.

The new domeless boiler kept to the same arrangement of handrails, as did No.3104 (*see* page 76, top) with its NER boiler although that one had a separate blower control added on the right hand side.

(*below*) Those which got new domed boilers had altered handrails; the front portion was lifted to the same level as those on the tank tops, and on the left side was cut so that a blower control could be inserted.

Until 1923 the normal addition to the bunker was three open coal rails (*see* Introduction illustration). When Springhead changed the boiler on No.3104/2485 and on 2489 they added a fourth – and stronger – rail but still left the rails open.

(below) Only at the first Darlington repair, starting with No.3110D/2491 in November 1923 was plating put behind the coal rails. Not until 21st December 1928 and 5th September 1929 were 2485 and 2489 given plating. The other seven had it by January 1925. Only on Nos.2483, 2485, 2487, 2489 and 2491 was the fourth rail added.

In January 1936 Nos.2484 and 2487 were transferred from Cudworth to Ardsley to take over the working of coal trains on the Newmarket Colliery branch of the East & West Yorkshire Union Railways line. To give them extra working time, the workshop at Ardsley shed built up the plated coal rails to a total of six, from three on No.2484 and from four on No.2487.

N12/26

Ardsley augmented the coal capacity of No.2487 to the same extent, but neither the additional amount, nor the extra weight, was notified in the yearly Diagram Book alterations. Both kept these rails to withdrawal. No.2484 was scrapped at Darlington, but No.2487 was broken up at Doncaster.

After only eleven months on the E&WYUR No.2484 went to Darlington for repair but was withdrawn and No.2486 from Springhead shed went on 16th February 1937 to replace it. Ardsley shed built up its coal capacity to the same extent as on the other N12 but only added two rails to the existing three, using wider spacing. Although it left Ardsley in November 1938 (soon after No.2487 was scrapped) the enhanced coal capacity remained to withdrawal on 30th August 1948 as No.9089. When it was ex Darlington 23rd April 1942, No.2486 still had LNER. Note Southern area load class 2 put on at Doncaster when repaired there 18th July to 12th August 1938, when they put Class N12 below the front number.

When they were re-boilered in 1923-25, Nos.2483 to 2489 had their vacuum brakes taken off and became steam braked on the engine only. No.3109D (2490 from 22nd October 1924) retained its vacuum brake when re-boilered in December 1923 at Darlington, but at the front end its H&B style standpipe was taken off and replaced by a union under the bufferbeam as was NER practice.

(above) No.3110D (2491 from 4th November 1924) also kept its vacuum brake and the front end connection was altered from H&B to NER style as shown by the centre illustration opposite. From 1929 Darlington began to fit a vacuum standpipe which No.2491 acquired when ex works on 30th November 1932.

H&B style lined livery was still well in evidence when this class was taken over and had 3000 added to their numbers in 1922/23 as shown by this illustration.

Springhead's painting of No.3104 in June 1923 provided the only one of the class to get L.&N.E.R. and also the flat topped figure 3. It changed to black but had a single red lining panel on the tank and on the front sandbox.

(below) Only the first two to be repaired at Darlington got the area suffix, Nos.3110ᴅ (30ᵗʰ November 1923) and 3109ᴅ (19ᵗʰ December 1923). By 4ᵗʰ November 1924 all had been renumbered 2483 to 2491. Until the June 1928 painting economies they had single red lining but thereafter were just in plain black.

From its final repair, No.2486 was ex Darlington on 4ᵗʰ January 1945 with 12in. NE instead of 7¹/₂in. LNER. On Sunday 1ˢᵗ December 1946 it was re-numbered 9089 at Springhead shed in painted and unshaded figures on the same spacing as before. As shown it went to Darlington on 14ᵗʰ August 1948 but it was withdrawn on 30ᵗʰ August 1948 making Class N12 extinct. Note that NER twin whistles were fitted and they remained until ex works 4ᵗʰ January 1945. The twin mounting was retained with the left hand branch blanked off, the organ pipe removed and replaced by a small bell shape on the right hand side.

The other five were numbered 152 to 156 as being additions to the Capital stock. No alterations had been made to the ten engine when they were taken over by the NER on 1st April 1922, or by the LNER on 1st January 1923 except that between these dates their numbers had been increased by 3000.

Between 10th April and 9th October 1924 they were renumbered 2405, 2407, 2410, 2415, 2419 and 2533 to 2537, all by Springhead shed or works except No.2533 which was under repair at Darlington. Only at their first visit there were the coal rails plated.

(below) Although it had been decided by 1924 that when required their replacement boilers would be domed, it was not until No.2405 was ex works 8th September 1926 that the first domed boiler was put on Class N13. Even then it was done to provide a spare and not to cover for a condemned boiler.

CLASS N 13

3013/2405

H.Leslie 3008.

To traffic 11/1913.

REPAIRS:
Hls. ?/?—10/3/23.**G.**
Dar. 22/12/25—8/9/26.**G.**
Dar. 4/2—24/4/30.**G.**
Dar. 4/4—23/5/33.**G.**
Dar. 19/8—30/9/36.**G.**
Dar. 31/10—24/11/39.**G.**
Dar. 27—29/11/39.**N/C.**
Dar. 18/1—17/2/43.**G.**
Dar. 6/10—3/11/45.**G.**
Dar. 12/5/48. *Not repaired.*

BOILERS:
D1718 *(new, domed)* 8/9/26.
D1739 *(ex2523)* 23/5/33.
  2580 *(new)* 30/9/36.
D1739 *(ex2533)* 24/11/39.
  2391 *(ex2533)* 17/2/43.
  2008 *(ex2532)* 3/11/45.

SHEDS:
Springhead.
Selby 28/3/43.
Springhead 14/1/46.

RENUMBERED:
2405 27/5/24.
9110 7/7/46.

CONDEMNED: 26/6/48.
Cut up at Darlington.

3015/2407

H.Leslie 3009.

To traffic 12/1913.

REPAIRS:
Dar. 1/12/22—19/4/23.**G.**
Dar. 7/3—8/6/27.**G.**
Dar. 18/6/30—13/1/31.**G.**
Dar. 11/5—8/6/34.**G.**
Dar. 24/9—27/10/37.**G.**
Dar. 18/6—12/7/40.**G.**
Dar. 10/2—12/3/43.**G.**
Dar. 29/12/45—2/2/46.**G.**
Dar. 22/4—19/5/49.**G.**
Dar. 21/8/52. *Not repaired.*

BOILERS:
  2391 *(new, domed)* 13/1/31.
  2584 *(new)* 8/6/34.
  2400 *(ex2415)* 27/10/37.

D1718 *(ex2536)* 12/7/40.
D1739 *(ex2405)* 12/3/43.
  2452 *(ex2419)* 2/2/46.
  2400 *(ex9089)* 19/5/49.

SHEDS:
Springhead.
Newport 7/2/42.
Selby 28/3/43.
Dairycoates 28/7/46.
Springhead 19/8/46.
Alexandra Dock 22/5/49.
Springhead 26/11/50.

RENUMBERED:
2407 17/7/24.
9111 24/11/46.
69111 19/5/49.

CONDEMNED: 21/8/52.
Cut up at Darlington.

3018/2410

H.Leslie 3010.

To traffic 12/1913.

REPAIRS:
Hls. ?/?—21/2/23.**G.**
Dar. 9/7/26—19/1/27.**G.**
Dar. 5/8—27/9/29.**G.**
Dar. 15/8—15/9/33.**G.**
Dar. 4/11—18/12/36.**G.**
Dar. 21—31/12/36.**N/C.**
Dar. 23/3—26/4/40.**G.**
Dar. 29/4—28/5/43.**G.**
Dar. 25/5—27/6/46.**G.**
Dar. 7/12/49—11/1/50.**G.**
Ghd. 18/11/52. *Not repaired.*

BOILERS:
2452 *(new, domed)* 15/9/33.
2580 *(ex2405)* 26/4/40.
2451 *(ex2534)* 28/5/43.
2007 *(exJ75 2528)* 27/6/46.
2401 *(ex9113)* 11/1/50.

SHEDS:
Springhead.

RENUMBERED:
2410 10/4/24.
9112 27/6/46.
69112 11/1/50.

CONDEMNED: 24/11/52.
Cut up at Darlington 6/12/52.

3023/2415

H.Leslie 3011.

To traffic 12/1913.

REPAIRS:
Hls. ?/?—27/8/23.**G.**
Dar. 24/1—28/3/29.**G.**
Dar. 25/10—8/12/32.**G.**
Dar. 20/7—27/8/37.**G.**
Dar. 30/8—8/9/37.**N/C.**
Dar. 2/10—1/11/40.**G.**
Dar. 8/7—23/8/44.**G.**
Dar. 23/5—21/8/47.**G.**
Dar. 8/11—2/12/49.**G.**
Ghd. 13/4/53. *Not repaired.*

BOILERS:
2400 *(new, domed)* 8/12/32.
2401 *(ex2536)* 27/8/37.
2400 *(ex2407)* 1/11/40.
2401 *(ex2535)* 23/8/44.
2581 *(exJ75 8365)* 2/12/49.

SHEDS:
Cudworth.
Springhead 12/1/34.
Neville Hill 28/12/52.

RENUMBERED:
2415 9/10/24.
9113 24/11/46.
69113 2/12/49.

CONDEMNED: 4/5/53.
Cut up at Darlington.

3027/2419

H.Leslie 3012.

To traffic 1/1914.

REPAIRS:
Dar. 4/7—8/11/23.**G.**
Dar. 27/7—27/10/27.**G.**
Dar. 18/6—30/12/30.**G.**
Dar. 22/5—27/6/34.**G.**
Dar. 29/11/38—9/1/39.**G.**
Dar. 23/7—27/8/41.**G.**
Dar. 17/3—7/4/44.**G.**
Dar. 15/12/45—19/1/46.**G.**
Dar. 27/9/46—22/3/47.**L.**
Dar. 14/7—10/9/48.**G.**
Dar. 25/5—23/6/51.**G.**
Dar. 18/11—12/12/53.**G.**
Dar. 4—25/3/54.**N/C.**
Dar. 5/5—29/6/55.**C/L.**

BOILERS:
2389 *(new, domed)* 30/12/30.
2391 *(ex2407)* 27/6/34.
2454 *(ex2535)* 9/1/39.
2584 *(ex2535)* 27/8/41.
2452 *(ex2536)* 7/4/44.
2580 *(ex2535)* 19/1/46.
2580 reno.25511 23/6/51.
25515 *(ex??)* 12/12/53.

SHEDS:
Springhead.
Neville Hill 28/3/43.

RENUMBERED:
2419 14/8/24.
9114 19/1/46.
69114 10/9/48.

CONDEMNED: 22/10/56.
Cut up at Darlington.

3152/2533

H.Leslie 3013.

To traffic 1/1914.

REPAIRS:
Hls. ?/?—?/1/22.**G.**
Dar. 9/7—12/11/24.**G.**
Dar. 5/2—5/4/30.**G.**
New chimney.
Dar. 21/9—25/10/33.**G.**
Dar. 17/9—30/10/36.**G.**
Dar. 19/8—4/10/39.**G.**
Dar. 19/5—27/6/42.**G.**
Dar. 10/1—9/2/45.**G.**
Dar. 22/8—17/10/47.**G.**
Dar. 17/8—19/9/50.**G.**
Dar. 8/8—24/9/52.**G.**

BOILERS:
D1718 *(ex2405, domed)*
25/10/33.
D1739 *(ex2405)* 30/10/36.
  2391 *(ex2419)* 4/10/39.
  2389 *(exN12 2486)* 27/6/42.
  2584 *(ex2419)* 9/2/45.
  2454 *(ex2537)* 17/10/47.
  2454 reno.25510 19/9/50.

SHEDS:
Cudworth.
Springhead 22/5/30.
Neville Hill 28/3/43.

2533 cont./
RENUMBERED:
  2533 25/7/24.
  9115 3/11/46.
  69115 19/9/50.

CONDEMNED: 18/5/55.
Cut up at Darlington.

3153/2534

H.Leslie 3014.

To traffic 2/1914.

REPAIRS:
Hls. ?/?—6/10/22.**G**.
Dar. 14/8—17/12/24.**G**.
Dar. 23/1—14/3/29.**G**.
New chimney.
Dar. 3/4—18/5/33.**G**.
Dar. 5/11/35—20/1/36.**G**.
New cylinders.
Dar. 24/2—4/4/39.**G**.
Dar. 1—19/6/40.**N/C**.
Dar. 3—30/3/43.**G**.
Dar. 1—28/3/45.**G**.
Dar. 20/11—12/12/47.**G**.
Dar. 30/8—6/10/51.**G**.
Dar. 15/12/54. Not repaired.

BOILERS:
  2451 (new, domed) 18/5/33.
  D1599 (exN12 2483) 30/3/43.
  2389 (ex2533) 28/3/45.
  2584 (ex9115) 12/12/47.
  2584 reno.25512 6/10/51.

SHEDS:
Springhead.
Neville Hill 28/3/43.
Springhead 14/1/46.
Neville Hill 10/5/53.

RENUMBERED:
  2534 30/6/24.
  9116 24/11/46.
  69116 6/10/51.

CONDEMNED: 20/12/54.
Cut up at Darlington.

3154/2535

H.Leslie 3015.

To traffic 2/1914.

REPAIRS:
Hls. ?/?—?/11/21.**G**.
Hls. ?/?—13/8/24.**G**.
Dar. 2/6—24/8/27.**G**.
New cylinders.
Dar. 28/4—28/7/30.**G**.
New chimney.
Dar. 7/9—6/10/33.**G**.
Dar. 25/1—1/3/38.**G**.
Dar. 21/3—19/4/41.**G**.
Dar. 2/2—4/3/44.**G**.
Dar. 27/11/45—3/1/46.**G**.
Dar. 30/12/47—23/1/48.**G**.
Dar. 20/4—3/6/50.**G**.
Dar. 20/6—12/7/52.**G**.

BOILERS:
  2454 (new, domed) 6/10/33.
  2584 (ex2407) 1/3/38.
  2401 (ex2415) 19/4/41.
  2580 (ex2410) 4/3/44.
  2391 (ex2405) 3/1/46.
  2389 (ex9116) 23/1/48.
  25513 (ex??) 12/7/52.

SHEDS:
Springhead.
Neville Hill 28/3/43.

RENUMBERED:
  2535 13/8/24.
  9117 20/10/46.
  E**9117** 23/1/48.
  69117 3/6/50.

CONDEMNED: 5/7/55.
Cut up at Darlington.

3155/2536

H.Leslie 3016.

To traffic 3/1914.

REPAIRS:
Hls. ?/?—?/5/22.**G**.
Hls. ?/?—30/6/24.**G**.
Dar. 1/11/28—9/1/29.**G**.
New chimney.
Dar. 15/8—29/9/32.**G**.
Dar. 11/12/36—3/2/37.**G**.
Dar. 15/5—6/6/40.**G**.
Dar. 12/5—7/6/43.**G**.
Dar. 26/4—25/6/45.**G**.
Dar. 21/1—17/2/48.**G**.
Dar. 6/7—24/8/50.**G**.
Ghd. 7—26/1/52.**C/L**.
After collision.
Dar. 26/5/52. Not repaired.

BOILERS:
  2401 (new, domed) 29/9/32.
  D1718 (ex2533) 3/2/37.
  2452 (ex2410) 6/6/40.
  D1718 (ex2407) 7/6/43.
  D1600 (ex2532) 25/6/45.
  2391 (ex9117) 17/2/48.

SHEDS:
Springhead.
Neville Hill 28/3/43.

RENUMBERED:
  2536 9/7/24.
  9118 27/10/46.
  E**9118** 17/2/48.
  69118 24/8/50.

CONDEMNED: 26/5/52.
Cut up at Darlington.

3156/2537

H.Leslie 3017.

To traffic 3/1914.

REPAIRS:
Hls. ?/?—3/8/23.**G**.
Dar. 6/4—29/7/27.**G**.
Dar. 17/11/30—22/1/31.**G**.
Dar. 3/7—15/8/34.**G**.
New chimney.
Dar. 29/11/38—10/1/39.**G**.
Dar. 20/1—20/2/42.**G**.
Dar. 23/2—2/3/42.**N/C**.
Dar. 3/11—18/12/43.**G**.
Dar. 2/8—6/9/46.**G**.
Dar. 30/5—15/7/50.**G**.
Ghd. 24/11—24/12/52.**G**.
Ghd. 29—31/12/52.**N/C**.

BOILERS:
  2581 (new, domed) 15/8/34.
  2454 (ex2419) 20/2/42.
  2451 (ex2410) 6/9/46.
  25514 (ex69111) 24/12/52.

SHEDS:
Springhead.
Newport 31/1/42.
Selby 28/3/43.
Springhead 14/1/46.
Neville Hill 27/9/53.

RENUMBERED:
  2537 2/7/24.
  9119 6/9/46.
  69119 15/7/50.

CONDEMNED: 5/7/55.
Cut up at Darlington.

The original domeless boilers lasted well into the 1930s and were used by Nos.2533 and 2535 to September 1933 and by No.2537 to July 1934.

Starting with No.2419, ex works 30th December 1930, the other nine were fitted with a domed boiler, all except No.2533 getting a newly built one. Hitherto the 'pop' valves had been on mounting blocks but on the 1930 and later built boilers, the 'pops' were mounted directly on to the firebox, with the effect they looked shorter. No.2537, ex works 15th August 1934, completed this job.

The slightly higher pitch of the boiler was compensated by a shorter chimney, and all ten had the rear half of the chimney rim left off, in effect providing a capuchon.

At one of their early visits to Darlington a change was usually made to a Worsdell chimney with a plain rim, the extra height being of no consequence. No.2419 was changed ex works 27th October 1927.

No.2407 actually had the extra height of a windjabber on its Worsdell type chimney, probably fitted 8th June 1934.

No.2535 was the last one repaired at Springhead works being out 13th August 1924 and the works closed later that month. It had been fitted with a taller chimney with full and deep rim similar to those used on the H&B 2-4-0 engines scrapped in 1922. It also got an extended smokebox.

Ex Darlington 28th July 1930 from a General repair, No.2535 was recorded as having been fitted with a new chimney. Note that this 1931 photograph shows it was put on a H&B smokebox, but of the extended type.

From new until they were re-boilered, the safety valves were open Ramsbottom type.

(above) The boilers built from 1930 to 1934, which had 'pop' valves, were provided with a circular casing around the base of the valves. *(below)* Quite soon, these base casings were discarded from most of the class. Most continued to run to withdrawal without the casing at the base of the safety valves *(see page 99)*. Except from January 1946 to July 1948 – *see* page 95, middle – No.2419 retained its base casing to withdrawal as No.69114 *(see also* page 99, bottom). Another with base casing was No.69112 because from 27th June 1946 to 7th December 1949 it had a 1927 built boiler for J75 class which had its 'pops' on mounting blocks and these were retained for this boiler put on in January 1950 *(see again* page 95, middle).

No.2533's first domed boiler was the one used in 1926 for No.2405 – *see* page 86, bottom – and its safety valves were on mounting blocks. From 17th October 1947 to 18th May 1955 withdrawal, its boiler was one built in 1932 and first used on No.2535 that had safety valves then mounted direct, but No.2533 (9115 later) kept its mounting blocks through four repairs at which a boiler change was made.

When a domed boiler was put on, it was accompanied by NER type twin whistles, organ pipe on the driver's side and bell shaped on the left side.

Starting with No.2415, ex works 1st November 1940, only one whistle was fitted. The same mounting was used but the left hand branch was blanked off. At least three kept organ pipe, Nos.9112, 9114, and 9117 – *see* page 98, middle. No.69112 carried it's through to withdrawal but the rest changed to the small bell shape.

Five repaired at Springhead: H&B 27/2419 (June 1920), 3018/2410 (21st February 1923), 3156/2537 (3rd August 1923), 3023/2415 (27th August 1923), and 2535 (13th August 1924), were fitted with an 8in. circular extension to their smokeboxes but kept the flush-fitting door with its two dog clips.

When re-boilered, all got the same type of 2ft 8\!in. long smokebox. This was NER style with a flat flange and at first Nos.2405, 2407, 2419, 2534 and 2537 changed to wheel and handle fastening.

(above) The others had their doors fastened by two handles and before the 1939 war those with wheel had it replaced by a second handle. Springhead Shed Master George Gregory and author W.B.Yeadon can be seen in the cab in this 21st April 1934 photograph.

Originally, all buffers had square flange and a curved taper shank with end collar and solid spindle. The original style of buffers was retained to withdrawal by Nos.69112 and 69119 (see page 98, middle).

By 1932, probably at its 30th December 1930 repair, No.2419 had been changed to NER type buffers which had a circular flange and straight taper shank. It kept this style to withdrawal.

Two were fitted with Group Standard buffers and drawgear, both in 1943, Nos.2405 (9110 from 7th July 1946) ex works 17th February 1943, and No.2536 – *see* page 97, bottom – ex works 7th June 1943.

The first five arrived fitted with three open coal rails – *see* Introductory illustration – but the other five came with four open rails. By 1923 one change was the addition of a fourth rail to Nos.3013, 3015, 3018, and 3023 but not 3027, and reduction to three rails on No.3155 – later 2536. At their first Darlington works visit, plating was fitted behind the rails.

(below) No.3027 (later 69114) continued to carry only three rails to withdrawal. No.2536, and as 69118, never regained the fourth rail.

(above) The change of boiler from domeless to domed also coincided with a change to the handrails. When domeless there was a continuous rail from the front end of each tank, curved over the smokebox door.

(right) With the Darlington designed domed boiler the handrail was raised above the top of the tanks. On the left hand side it was extended to the cab and cut on the side of the smokebox so that it could house the rod controlling the blower valve.

(below) On the right hand side, the lifted rail only extended above the tank as far as the centre line of the dome.

The H&B lined livery was still apparent when the NER added 3000 to their number. When this was done the size of the figures became 9in. instead of 6in. At that stage, the maker's plate was still fitted on the front sandbox.

First repainted after Grouping were Nos.3018 (21st February 1923) and 3013 (10th March 1923), from Springhead works. They were black instead of invisible green and had N.E.R. on the tank but with the number still on the bunker, and in H&B style except for an increase in height. The makers' plates had been taken off by 1924.

From early February 1924 they were given LNER numbers 2405, 2407, 2410, 2415, 2419, 2533, 2534, 2535, 2536 and 2537, and these were applied as convenient. On 10th April 1924 Springhead altered N.E.R. 3018 to N. 2410 E. The number moved to the tank and was in 12in. shaded transfers whilst the bunker now carried standard 8⅝in. wide LNER numberplate.

Out from Springhead works 3rd August 1923, after a General repair, and as No.3156, the initials were in that works' unique style. No ampersand was included but the full points were. Single red lining had been put on the tank, sandbox and splasher, the maker's plate being discarded. On 2nd July 1924 the number 3156 was blacked over and replaced by 2537.

(above) **Following the painting economies of June 1928 no further lining was applied and through to withdrawal all were in plain black.**

(right) **The first LNER Diagram Book showed the state of stock as at the end of 1923 and accorded N13 to this class. However, it was not until into 1932 that Darlington accepted LNER classifications, hence Class F3 (HB) being seen in this 5th April 1933 photograph.**

(below) **From July 1942 only NE was used in place of LNER but the size of lettering went up from 7½in. to 12in. and shaded transfers were still put on. Small white figures above the number indicated the last shopping date – 6/45 – on 2536.**

From January 1946 LNER in 7½in. lettering was restored and No.2407, ex works 2nd February 1946, had it. During that year this class was re-numbered 9110 to 9119 and 2407 became 9111 on Sunday 24th November, at Springhead shed. Only Nos.9110, 9117 and 9118 did not have LNER restored.

(above) Ex Darlington on 27th June 1946, No.2410 had been changed to 9112 in pre-war style using shaded transfers. No.9119, ex works 6th September 1946, was the only other to have this style.

During 1947 the supply of shaded transfers ran out and they were regarded as being too expensive so in that year Nos.9113 (21st August), 9115 (17th October), and 9116 (12th December) had letters and numbers in yellow paint without shading. This style was Gill sans but with a modification to figures 6 and 9.

After Nationalisation No.E9117, ex works 23rd January 1948, showed the first sign of new ownership. It had the regional prefix E to its number, which was moved from tank to bunker. Only one other N13 got the prefix, E9118, ex works 17th February 1948.

Only two got this style – Nos.69114 (10th September 1948) and 69111 (19th May 1949). Note figures 6 and 9 were in true Gill sans and the reduction in number size to 10in. matched the letters.

(lower right) From August 1949 lettering was discarded and an emblem was introduced. Five went straight to this style from LNER: 69112 (11th January 1950), 69113 (2nd December 1949), 69115 (19th September 1950), 69116 (6th October 1951), 69119 (15th July 1950). Nos.69114 (23rd June 1951), 69117 (3rd June 1950), and 69118 (24th August 1950) joined them from carrying BRITISH RAILWAYS but No.69111 still had that lettering at its 21st August 1952 withdrawal.

(below) When No.69114 was withdrawn on Monday 22nd October 1956, the event not only made Class N13 extinct but it also saw the last Hull & Barnsley Railway locomotive condemned. As shown here it was still active only nine days before withdrawal from service. Note that it had acquired a Group Standard drawhook and to cope with its extra length, wood packing had been placed behind the buffer flanges.

As a result of interchange of boilers with N15 class, from January 1923 to July 1931 all six got a boiler which had lock-up safety valves on the firebox. Although none of the N14s ever again ran with a boiler that had safety valves on the dome, most of their original boilers saw further use on Class N15, the last one surviving on No.9096 until June 1946.

From 1923 all replacement boilers had Ross 'pop' safety valves on the firebox. The earlier ones had the valves on the same pitch as the lock-up type and with a circular casing around the base. Nos.9858 to 9862 were almost entirely used as Cowlairs incline bankers and as such were equipped with a slip coupling which could be operated by a wire from the cab.

(below) Replacement boilers built from December 1933 had the 'pops' wider apart and after the war, they commonly had a square casing at the base.

CLASS N 14

* - *Safety valves on dome.*

9858

N.B.Loco. 18862.

To traffic 9/1909.

REPAIRS:
Cow. ?/?—?/?/23.**G.**
Cow. ?/?—11/7/31.**G.**
Cow. ?/?—8/5/34.**G.**
Cow. ?/?—22/8/36.**G.**
Drop grate fitted.
Cow. ?/?—27/4/38.**L.**
Cow. ?/?—18/1/39.**G.**
Cow. ?/?—24/4/40.**L.**
Cow. ?/?—30/5/40.**L.**
Cow. 17/10—7/11/42.**G.**
Cow. ?/?—16/6/45.**L.**
Cow. 14/3—6/4/46.**H/I.**
Cow. ?/?—?/12/47.**L.**
Jay-Gee smoke eliminator fitted.
Cow. 2/3—2/4/49.**G.**
Jay-Gee smoke eliminator removed.
Cow. 15—19/5/51.**C/L.**
Cow. ?/?—?/5/53.**?.**
Inv. 12/3/54. *Not repaired.*

BOILERS:
309*.
228 *(ex859)* ?/?/23*.
256 *(exN15 9240)* 11/7/31.
1265 *(ex9862)* 22/8/36.
1892 *(new)* 7/11/42.
2048 *(new)* 2/4/49.
2048 reno.26473 ?/5/53.

SHED:
Eastfield.

RENUMBERED:
9858 *by* 17/4/26.
9120 13/10/46.
69120 2/4/49.

CONDEMNED: 25/3/54.
Cut up at Inverurie.

9859

N.B.Loco. 18863.

To traffic 9/1909.

REPAIRS:
Cow. ?/?—?/8/23.**G.**
Cow. ?/?—29/3/24.**L.**
Cow. ?/?—21/2/31.**G.**
Cow. ?/?—21/4/34.**G.**
Cow. ?/?—25/9/36.**G.**
Drop grate fitted.
Cow. ?/?—15/11/36.**L.**
Cow. ?/?—16/4/38.**L.**
Cow. ?/?—4/11/39.**H.**
Cow. ?/?—21/2/42.**G.**
Cow. ?/?—27/11/43.**H.**
Cow. ?/?—18/9/45.**L.**
Cow. 21/8/47. *Not repaired.*

BOILERS:
228*.
229 *(exN15 922)* ?/8/23.
231 *(ex9861)* 21/2/31.
1266 *(exN15 9055)* 21/4/34.
1280 *(exN15 9396)* 25/9/36.
1273 *(exN15 9230)* 21/2/42.

SHED:
Eastfield.

RENUMBERED:
9859 29/3/24.
9121 14/7/46.

CONDEMNED: 22/9/47.
Cut up at Cowlairs.

9860

N.B.Loco. 18864.

To traffic 9/1909.

REPAIRS:
Cow. ?/?—?/6/23.**G.**
Cow. 14/10/28—?/?/?.**?.**
Cow. ?/?—?/12/29.**?.**
Wakefield mech. lub. fitted.
Cow. ?/?—27/2/32.**G.**
Cow. ?/?—27/3/34.**G.**
Cow. 9—16/5/36.**G.**
Drop grate fitted.
Cow. ?/?—20/8/38.**L.**
Cow. ?/?—23/10/39.**L.**
Cow. ?/?—27/4/40.**H.**
Cow. ?/?—14/2/41.**L.**
Cow. ?/?—14/8/42.**L.**
Cow. 16—30/1/43.**G.**
Cow. ?/?—22/2/43.**L.**

Cow. ?/?—27/10/43.**L.**
Cow. ?/?—12/7/44.**L.**
Cow. ?/?—28/10/44.**L.**
Cow. ?/?—10/11/44.**L.**
Cow. ?/?—22/8/45.**L.**
Cow. ?/?—16/7/46.**L.**
Cow. ?/?—22/2/47.**N/C.**
Cow. 10/11/47. *Not repaired.*

BOILERS:
310*.
230 *(exN15 251)* ?/6/23.
1394 *(ex9862)* 27/2/32.
1269 *(exN15 9074)* 16/5/36.
1265 *(ex9858)* 30/1/43.

SHED:
Eastfield.

RENUMBERED:
9860 ?/8/26.
9122 25/8/46.

CONDEMNED: 28/11/47.
Cut up at Cowlairs.

9861

N.B.Loco. 18865.

To traffic 9/1909.

REPAIRS:
Cow. ?/?—?/4/25.**G.**
Cow. ?/?—19/4/30.**G.**
Cow. ?/?—18/5/35.**G.**
Drop grate fitted.
Cow. ?/?—16/7/36.**L.**
Cow. ?/?—14/3/38.**H.**
Cow. ?/?—29/6/40.**G.**
Cow. ?/?—23/9/44.**H.**
Cow. ?/?—28/4/45.**G.**

BOILERS:
291*.
231 *(exN15 9399)* ?/4/25.
250 *(exN15 9165)* 19/4/30.
237 *(exN15 9142)* 18/5/35.
275 *(exN15 9023)* 29/6/40.
1552 *(exN15 9389)* 28/4/45.

SHED:
Eastfield.

RENUMBERED:
9861 ?/4/25.
9123 13/10/46.

CONDEMNED: 31/12/47.
Cut up at Cowlairs.

9862

N.B.Loco. 18866.

To traffic 9/1909.

REPAIRS:
NBL. ?/?—9/11/20.**G.**
Cow. ?/?—?/1/26.**G.**
Cow. 6—28/11/31.**G.**
Cow. ?/?—23/3/33.**H.**
Cow. 20—29/12/33.**L.**
Cow. 15/8—5/9/36.**G.**
Drop grate fitted.
Cow. 4—8/4/39.**N/C.**
Anti glare screen fitted.
Cow. 2—4/11/39.**L.**
Cow. 12/4—4/5/40.**H.**
Cow. 4—23/1/43.**L.**
Cow. 9/10—6/11/43.**G.**
Cow. 13/6—11/7/47.**H/I.**
Cow. 24—27/12/47.**L.**
Jay-Gee smoke eliminator fitted.
Cow. 21—25/12/48.**L.**
Jay-Gee smoke eliminator removed.

BOILERS:
232*.
1394 *(new)* ?/1/26.
1265 *(exN15 9052)* 28/11/31.
234 *(exN15 9527)* 5/9/36.
1262 *(exN15 9915)* 6/11/43.

SHED:
Eastfield.

RENUMBERED:
9862 ?/1/26.
9124 2/6/46.
69124 25/12/48.

CONDEMNED: 3/11/50.
Cut up at Cowlairs.

WORKS CODES:- BGT – Bathgate shed. Cow - Cowlairs. Dar - Darlington. Daw – Dawsholm shed. DFU – Dunfermline shed. EFD – Eastfield shed. HAY – Haymarket shed. Inv - Inverurie. Kit - Kittybrewster. Klm – Kilmarnock. KPS – Kipps shed. RSH - Robert, Stephenson & Hawthorn. StM - St Margarets. THJ – Thornton Jct. shed. .
REPAIR CODES:- **C/H** - Casual Heavy. **C/L** - Casual Light. **G** - General. **H**- Heavy. **H/I** - Heavy Intermediate. **L** - Light. **L/I** - Light Intermediate. **N/C** - Non-Classified.

Until December 1929 axlebox lubrication was by siphon from oilboxes. Cylinders were fed from tallow cups on the front plate of the smokebox and a single feed hydrostatic in the cab supplied the steam chest, through a pipe along the right hand side.

(below) In December 1929 No.9860 had the siphon oilboxes taken off and replaced by a Wakefield mechanical lubricator mounted on the left hand front sandbox and with a most complicated drive from the front end coupling rod pin.

Four of the other five then had their oilboxes replaced by a Madison-Kipp mechanical lubricator on the left hand running plate. Nos.9858 (11th July 1931), 9859 (21st February 1931), 9861 (in 1932), and 9862 (28th November 1931). No.9863 had already transferred to the Northern Scottish Area and was not similarly altered.

9863

N.B.Loco. 18867.

To traffic 9/1909.

REPAIRS:
Cow. 10/11/24—25/2/25.**G.**
Vacuum ejector fitted.
Cow. ?/?—26/5/28.**G.**
Cow. ?/?—9/9/33.**G.**
Cow. ?/?—21/4/36.**G.**
Inv. ?/?—3/9/36.**L.**
Inv. ?/?—24/12/38.**H.**
Inv. ?/?—22/3/40.**L.**
Cow. ?/?—13/7/40.**G.**
Cow. ?/?—31/1/42.**H.**
Inv. ?/?—22/6/43.**L.**
Inv. ?/?—30/11/43.**L.**
Inv. ?/?—24/5/44.**L.**
Inv. 2—16/6/45.**G.**
Cow. 25/9—18/10/47.**G.**
Inv. 4—27/4/50.**H/I.**

BOILERS:
271*.
233 *(exN15 9924)* 25/2/25.
246 *(exN15 9106)* 26/5/28.
1281 *(exN15 9174)* 9/9/33.
277 *(exN15 9520)* 13/7/40.
1868 *(exN15 9107)* 16/6/45.
1399 *(exN15 9160)* 18/10/47.

SHEDS:
St Margarets.
Haymarket 27/2/25.
Kittybrewster 28/4/27.
Aberdeen 21/12/50.

RENUMBERED:
9863 25/2/25.
9125 27/10/46.
69125 27/4/50.

CONDEMNED: 25/3/54.
Cut up at Inverurie ???.

In December 1947 Nos.9120 and 9124 (ex9858 and 9862) had the tallow cups moved from the front to the side of the smokebox. This was to permit fitting a Jay-Gee smoke eliminator on these two. This device was removed from both these engines on the following dates: No.9124 (21st December 1948) and 9120 (2nd March 1949). The tallow cups then reverted to their former position at the front of the smokebox – *see* page 105, third from top.

Until 1935/36 the front sandbox had only one filler which was towards the rear of the top of the box. Note the coal rails now have plating – compare with the illustration at the top of page 100.

An additional filler, near the front, was put on the top of the sandbox as follows: Nos.9858 (22nd August 1936), 9859 (25th September 1936), 9860 (16th May 1936), 9861 (18th May 1935), 9862 (5th September 1936), and 9863 (21st April 1936). Sometime after 1928 Nos.9858, 9859 and 9863 were fitted with a raised ventilator on the cab roof, but the other three were not so equipped.

For use in connection with the wet ashpits put in at Eastfield shed, drop grates were fitted to the five Eastfield engines as follows on the dates shown. Nos.9858 (22nd August 1936), 9859 (25th September 1936), 9860 (16th May 1936), 9861 (18th May 1935), and 9862 (5th September 1936). The spring for the device can be seen between the middle and rear coupled wheels; the operating rod on the right hand side is visible in the third photograph from the top, opposite.

On No.9863 the exhaust from the Westinghouse pump entered the smokebox above the hand rail. All the others had it below. Note the handrail across the bunker, which the others did not have. At first No.9863 did not have shunters steps. The others never did had steps put on.

At Grouping the five Cowlairs bankers had Westinghouse brake and vacuum ejector – see Introduction. No.9863 was fitted only with Westinghouse, but ex works 25th February 1925, a vacuum ejector had been added. Note the straight run of the exhaust pipe compared with the others. Until after June 1928 they had single red lining on the black paint.

When new, all had two lamp irons over each buffer and No.9863 (later 9125) – see previous illustration – still had them in 1925, but had the inner pair removed later, No.9858 having lost them by May 1928 – see page 102, top. Note the shunters step fitted.

Between June and October 1946 they were renumbered 9120 to 9125, and Nos.9121, 9122 and 9123 were withdrawn as such in late 1947. Nos.9120, 9124 and 9125 had LNER restored at April 1946, July 1947 and October 1947 heavy repairs.

After Nationalisation the three survivors got full BR numbers but had different paint treatment. From a Cowlairs Light repair No.69124 still had LNER on plain black and kept it to its 3rd November 1950 withdrawal from being ex works 25th December 1948.

No.69120, ex Cowlairs 2nd April 1949, got the full treatment. A newly built boiler was put on and BR lining of red, cream, and grey was applied.

No.69125 became such ex Inverurie 27th April 1950, after a Heavy Intermediate overhaul. It remained unlined black but although the number was moved to the bunker, no emblem was put on. The correct Gill sans numbers, including the 6 and 9, were put on the smokebox plate but the bunker number contained the painted modified style. Although shedded as far apart as Aberdeen and Eastfield, Nos.69120 and 69125 were withdrawn on the same day, 25th March 1954, making Class N14 extinct.

Between June and August 1910 twelve more similar engines, numbered 386 to 393 and 396 to 399, were supplied by NBL Co., but these were fitted with steam brake only on the engine. They and all later builds had steam brake on the engine, so were allocated Part 1 of the class. Twenty more were built by NBL Co., during July and August 1912. Whereas the previous eighteen had been built by Hyde Park works, this batch came from the Queen's Park works. They were numbered 907 to 926. A further nine built in May 1913, Nos.219, 223, 224, 229, 230, 246, 252, 257, and 264, also came from the Queen's Park works.

From August 1916 to March 1917, twelve more engines numbered 47, 54, 61, 65, 69, 70, 276, 453, 142, 165, 166, and 259, were built by NBL Co., Glasgow, but at their Atlas works, shown by the different style of makers' plate on the sandbox.

* Safety valve on dome.

9007

N.B.Loco. 19159.

To traffic 6/1910.

REPAIRS:
StM. ?/?—7/3/24.**H.**
StM. ?/?—15/3/24.**N/C.**
StM. 3—23/3/25.**N/C.**
Vacuum ejector fitted.
Cow. ?/?—?/10/25.**G.**
Cow. ?/1—25/2/28.**G.**
Cow. ?/?—22/4/33.**G.**
Cow. ?/?—8/2/35.**G.**
Drop grate fitted.
Cow. ?/?—24/5/36.**L.**
Cow. ?/?—31/12/37.**L.**
Cow. 10—24/12/38.**G.**
Cow. ?/?—29/6/40.**L.**
Cow. ?/?—8/2/41.**L.**
Cow. ?/?—31/10/42.**H.**
Cow. 1—29/5/45.**G.**
Cow. 14—26/6/48.**G.**
Cow. 6—29/12/51.**C/H.**
Cow. 10/9/53.**N/C.**
Efd. 15/3—21/4/54.**C/H.**
Cow. 22/4/54.**N/C.**
Cow. 15/12/55—7/1/56.**G.**
Cow. 19—21/1/56.**N/C.**

BOILERS:
305.
242 *(ex??)* ?/10/25???.
242 *(ex9069)* 25/2/28???.
284 *(ex9528)* 22/4/33.
1270 *(ex9915)* 24/12/38.
1870 *(ex9174)* 29/5/45.
26442 *(ex9144)* 29/12/51.
26442 reno.26353 22/4/54.
26469 *(exC15 67455)* 7/1/56.

SHEDS:
St Margarets.
Eastfield 24/2/28.
St Rollox 12/8/57.
Dawsholm 3/1/58.

RENUMBERED:
7в 7/3/24.
9007 15/3/24.
9126 19/5/46.
69126 26/6/48.

CONDEMNED: 12/2/62.
Sold for scrap to G.H.Campbell,
Airdrie, 31/7/62.

9154

N.B.Loco. 19160.

To traffic 6/1910.

REPAIRS:
Cow. ?/?—?/11/25.**G.**
Vacuum ejector fitted.
Cow. ?/?—21/2/31.**G.**
Cow. ?/?—8/6/34.**G.**
Cow. ?/?—24/12/36.**G.**
Drop grate fitted.
Westinghouse removed.
Cow. ?/?—8/4/38.**L.**
Cow. 26/8—9/9/39.**G.**
Cow. ?/?—6/6/42.**L.**
Cow. ?/?—12/2/44.**H.**
Cow. ?/?—2/11/44.**L.**
Cow. 21/10—8/11/46.**G.**
Inv. 5—12/4/47.**L.**
Inv. 11/12/50—16/1/51.**G.**
Cow. 25/1—9/2/52.**C/L.**
Cow. 15—23/2/52.**C/L.**
Cow. 6—24/10/53.**H/I.**
Westinghouse replaced by steam
brake (vacuum ejector still
fitted).
Cow. 15/11/54.**N/C.**
Cow. 22/12/55—14/1/56.**G.**
Cow. 11—12/4/56.**N/C.**

BOILERS:
306.
241 *(ex9065)* ?/11/25.
275 *(ex9519)* 21/2/31.
1558 *(new)* 8/6/34.
246 *(ex9264)* 9/9/39.
1989 *(new)* 8/11/46.
1989 reno.26563 16/1/51.
26563 reno.26454 24/10/53.
26381 *(ex69141)* 14/1/56.

SHEDS:
Eastfield.
St Rollox 12/8/57.
Aberdeen 30/4/58.

RENUMBERED:
9154 ?/11/25.
9127 8/11/46.
69127 16/1/51.

CONDEMNED: 16/6/59.
Cut up at Inverurie, 11/9/59.

9209

N.B.Loco. 19161.

To traffic 6/1910.

REPAIRS:
NBL. ?/?—11/10/20.**G.**
Cow. ?/8—11/10/24.**G.**
Vacuum ejector fitted.
Cow. ?/?—?/?/30.**?.**
Air sanding fitted.
Cow. ?/?—23/4/32.**G.**
Inv. ?/?—22/9/33.**L.**
Cow. ?/?—11/5/35.**G.**
Cow. ?/?—16/12/37.**G.**
Cow. ?/?—22/6/40.**H.**
Inv. ?/?—4/7/41.**L.**
Inv. ?/?—18/12/43.**G.**
Cow. 2/7—9/8/47.**H/I.**
Cow. 27/9—28/10/50.**G.**
Inv. 8—13/11/51.**N/C.**
Inv. 13—29/1/54.**L/I.**
Inv. 8—12/2/54.**N/C.**
Inv. 18/4—18/5/55.**C/L.**
Inv. 9/7—9/8/57.**H/I.**

BOILERS:
289.
307 *(ex9210)* 11/12/24.
302 *(ex9924)* 23/4/32.
230 *(ex9907)* 16/12/37.
7 *(ex9911)* 18/12/43.
2058 *(new)* 28/10/50.
2058 reno.26592 13/11/51.
26592 reno.26483 29/1/54.
26390 *(ex??)* 9/8/57.

SHEDS:
Thornton Jct.
Aberdeen 20/5/32.
St Margarets 19/6/61.

RENUMBERED:
9209 11/10/24.
9128 20/10/46.
69128 28/10/50.

CONDEMNED: 1/10/62.
Sold for scrap to Motherwell
Machinery & Scrap,
Wishaw, 17/11/64.

9210

N.B.Loco. 19162.

To traffic 6/1910.

REPAIRS:
Cow. ?/?—?/7/24.**G.**
Vacuum ejector fitted.
Inv. ?/?—3/10/33.**L.**
Cow. 29/12/34—23/2/35.**G.**
Cow. ?/?—10/11/37.**H.**
Cow. ?/?—15/3/39.**L.**
Cow. ?/?—20/4/40.**G.**
Cow. ?/?—7/3/42.**H.**
Cow. ?/?—24/6/44.**G.**
Inv. ?/?—30/11/44.**L.**
Inv. ?/?—18/1/47.**H.**
Inv. 6/7—12/8/49.**G.**
Inv. 28/9—7/10/49.**C/L.**
Cow. 11—16/7/50.**C/L.**
Inv. 9—30/11/51.**L/I.**
Inv. 28/9—16/10/53.**G.**
Inv. 5—23/11/56.**L/I.**

BOILERS:
307.
308 *(ex9282)* ?/7/24.
1263 *(ex9023)* 23/2/35.
10 *(exG9 9356)* 20/4/40.
251 *(ex9926)* 24/6/44.
1401 *(ex9207)* 12/8/49.
1401 reno.26470 30/11/51.
26451 *(ex69150)* 16/10/53.

SHEDS:
Thornton Jct.
Aberdeen 7/1/29.

RENUMBERED:
9210 ?/7/24.
9129 20/1/46.
69129 12/8/49.

CONDEMNED: 2/12/58.
Cut up at Kilmarnock 1/59.

9251

N.B.Loco. 19163.

To traffic 6/1910.

REPAIRS:
Cow. ?/?—?/4/23.**G.**
Cow. ?/?—25/1/28.**L.**
Cow. ?/?—20/12/33.**G.**
Cow. ?/?—26/8/35.**G.**
Drop grate fitted.

In February and March 1920 the same NBL works supplied another ten – 20, 22, 29, 49, 96, 97, 106, 107, 108, and 240. Still steam braked on the engine, they had vacuum ejectors and piping for working train brakes. This extra brake facility was taken off in 1922/23 so that the equipment could be put to better use on J36 class. They were thus pure Part 1 when the LNER classification was compiled late in 1923.

During the latter part of 1922 the NBR authorised purchase of ten more N15 but it was the LNER which received them between 19th January and 26th March 1923. Numbered 519 to 528, they had NBR style number plates but were without indication of ownership on the tanks. They were built in Darlington by R.Stephenson & Co., thus having another style of makers' plate on the sandbox.

The class was completed by Cowlairs building twenty more from 30th October 1923 to 5th April 1924, all having LNER on their tank sides. The first sixteen to, 1st March 1924, had area suffix B to their numbers which were 19, 23, 31, 52, 55, 60, 67, 71, 74, 75, 76, 77, 78, 79, 99, and 125. The other four, from 8th March 1924 went into traffic as 9147, 9174, 9225, and 9227. All, including those built after Grouping had the NBR style of two lamp irons over each buffer. No.9227 was the last engine to be built by Cowlairs works (*see* opposite, bottom).

All ninety-nine had boilers with safety valves on the firebox when they were new, and not on the dome as with Class N14.

By interchange of boiler with N14 and G9 classes, fifteen got earlier built boilers which had lock-up safety valves on the dome. From April 1923 to December 1933 No.9251 had No.858's original boiler. These boilers are identified by an asterisk in the tables.

(above) The last such boiler on No.69222, from 19th May 1951 to 20th February 1957, was built in 1909 and started work on 0-4-4T No.354 in October 1909. It had also served N15 No.9387 from April 1939 to June 1945 and No.9914 from August 1945 to April 1950.

All those built to March 1923 had lock-up safety valves on their original boiler (*see* opposite, bottom). Only on the last twenty, those built by Cowlairs in 1923/24, were 'pop' safety valves used when new.

9251 cont./
Cow. ?/?—30/12/37.**G.**
Cow. ?/?—14/2/40.**G.**
Cow. ?/?—7/3/40.**L.**
Cow. ?/?—29/11/41.**H.**
Cow. ?/?—23/10/43.**H.**
Cow. 17/2—3/3/45.**L.**
Cow. 16/11—14/12/46.**G.**
Cow. 29/6—17/7/48.**H/I.**
Westinghouse replaced by steam brake (vac. ejector still fitted).
Cow. 20/10—12/11/49.**L/I.**
Cow. 9/8—1/9/51.**G.**
Cow. 18/8—10/9/54.**H/I.**
Cow. 4—12/2/55.**C/L.**

BOILERS:
  230.
  309 *(exN14 858)* ?/4/23*.
  1550 *(new)* 20/12/33.
  1869 *(new)* 14/2/40.
  1356 *(ex9153)* 14/12/46.
  26508 *(ex9191)* 1/9/51.
  26508 reno.26399 10/9/54.

SHEDS:
Eastfield.
Haymarket ?/3/40.
St Margarets 13/6/45.

RENUMBERED:
  9251 ?/6/25.
  9130 26/5/46.
  69130 17/7/48.

CONDEMNED: 27/12/57.
Cut up at Inverurie, 3/58.

9282

N.B.Loco. 19164.

To traffic 6/1910.

REPAIRS:
Cow. ?/?—22/8/23.**G.**
Cow. ?/?—?/2/26.**?.**
Cow. ?/?—24/3/28.**G.**
Cow. ?/?—17/7/31.**G.**
Cow. ?/?—17/1/34.**G.**
Cow. ?/?—13/4/37.**G.**
Drop grate fitted.
Cow. 22/10—3/11/38.**G.**
Cow. ?/?—7/4/39.**L.**
Cow. ?/?—6/6/39.**L.**
Cow. ?/?—2/11/40.**H.**
Cow. ?/?—7/9/43.**L.**
Cow. 13—27/11/43.**G.**
Cow. 16—23/6/45.**L.**
Cow. 24/3—4/4/47.**H/I.**
Cow. 7—16/5/47.**C/L.**
Cow. 22/9—21/10/50.**G.**
Cow. 14/10—7/11/53.**H/I.**

Cow. 24/11—3/12/53.**C/L.**
Westinghouse replaced by steam brake (vac. ejector still fitted).
Cow. 12—13/10/54.**N/C.**
Cow. 6—29/10/55.**C/L.**
Cow. 5/9—3/10/57.**G.**

BOILERS:
  308.
  310 *(exN14 860)* 22/8/23*.
  236 *(ex9029)* 24/3/28.
  1553 *(new)* 17/1/34.
  1613 *(new)* 3/11/38.
  234 *(exN14 9862)* 27/11/43.
  2057 *(new)* 21/10/50.
  2057 reno.26482 7/11/53.
  26424 *(ex??)* 3/10/57.

SHED:
Eastfield.

RENUMBERED:
  9282 ?/2/26.
  9131 25/8/46.
  69131 21/10/50.

CONDEMNED: 12/2/62.
Sold for scrap to G.H.Campbell, Airdrie, 10/7/62.

9386

N.B.Loco. 19165.

To traffic 6/1910.

REPAIRS:
Cow. ?/11/21—?/2/22.**G.**
Cow. ?/?—27/11/23.**G.**
Cow. ?/?—18/6/32.**G.**
Cow. ?/?—16/9/32.**L.**
Cow. ?/?—4/7/33.**H.**
Cow. 7—21/3/36.**G.**
Cow. ?/?—21/9/38.**H.**
Cow. 6—20/6/42.**G.**
Cow. ?/?—1/7/44.**H.**
Inv. 10—31/3/45.**H.**
Cow. 14/4—3/5/47.**G.**
Cow. 21/6—2/7/49.**H/I.**
Cow. 30/8—28/9/51.**G.**
Cow. 12/5—6/6/52.**C/H.**
Cow. 22/6—9/7/53.**H/I.**
THJ. 30/8—9/9/54.**C/L.**
Cow. 17/10—5/11/55.**G.**

BOILERS:
  265.
  7 *(new)* ?/2/22.
  306 *(ex9914)* 18/6/32.
  1276 *(ex9230)* 21/3/36.
  1891 *(new)* 20/6/42.
  1998 *(new)* 3/5/47.
  26513 *(ex69142)* 28/9/51.

26513 reno.26404 9/7/53.
26429 *(exC15 67461)* 5/11/55.

SHEDS:
Bathgate.
Parkhead *by* 31/8/32.
Thornton Jct. 23/1/35.
Motherwell 30/11/59.

RENUMBERED:
  386в 27/11/23.
  9386 ?/1/26.
  9132 20/1/46.
  69132 2/7/49.

CONDEMNED: 18/11/60.
Cut up at Inverurie, 29/12/60.

9387

N.B.Loco. 19166.

To traffic 6/1910.

REPAIRS:
Cow. ?/?—5/7/24.**G.**
Cow. ?/?—?/9/30.**G.**
Cow. ?/?—5/4/34.**G.**
Cow. ?/?—12/10/35.**G.**
Cow. ?/?—2/7/37.**H.**
Cow. ?/?—22/4/39.**G.**
Cow. ?/?—22/2/41.**H.**
Cow. ?/?—20/3/43.**H.**
Cow. 13/6—3/7/45.**G.**
Cow. 28/8—16/9/47.**H/I.**
Cow. 8—29/12/49.**G.**
Cow. 10—21/6/52.**L/I.**
Cow. 21/6—9/7/55.**G.**
Cow. 25/4—18/5/57.**H/I.**

BOILERS:
  287.
  263 *(ex9398)* 5/7/24.
  1555 *(new)* 5/4/34.
  219 *(exG9 9351)* 22/4/39*.
  1270 *(ex9007)* 3/7/45.
  1614 *(ex9216)* 29/12/49.
  1614 reno.26481 ??? 21/6/52.
  26450 *(ex69169)* 9/7/55.

SHEDS:
Haymarket.
St Margarets 27/2/25.

RENUMBERED:
  9387 5/7/24.
  9133 25/8/46.
  69133 29/12/49.

CONDEMNED: 3/8/60.
Cut up at Cowlairs 15/10/60.

9388

N.B.Loco. 19167.

To traffic 7/1910.

REPAIRS:
StM. ?/?—?/10/24.**H.**
Cow. ?/?—29/9/26.**G.**
Cow. ?/10—1/11/30.**G.**
Cow. ?/?—?/3/32.**?.**
Cow. ?/?—6/10/34.**G.**
Cow. 27/6—11/7/36.**G.**
Cow. ?/?—7/5/38.**G.**
Cow. ?/?—4/10/39.**L.**
Cow. ?/?—26/10/40.**H.**
Cow. ?/?—13/4/42.**L.**
Cow. 6/3—3/4/43.**G.**
Cow. 8—26/4/45.**H/I.**
Cow. 19/12/47—9/1/48.**G.**
Cow. 2—6/8/48.**C/L.**
Vacuum ejector fitted.
Cow. 30/5—16/6/50.**L/I.**
Cow. 6—22/11/52.**G.**
Cow. 22/5—9/6/53.**C/H.**
Cow. 11—27/11/54.**L/I.**
Cow. 19/11—14/12/57.**H/I.**

BOILERS:
  264.
  1399 *(new)* 29/9/26.
  1359 *(ex9925)* 1/11/30.
  306 *(ex9386)* 11/7/36.
  1610 *(ex9142)* 3/4/43.
  1894 *(ex9148)* 9/1/48.
  26360 *(ex69193)* 22/11/52.
  26438 *(ex??)* 14/12/57.

SHED:
St Margarets.

RENUMBERED:
  9388 ?/10/24.
  9134 25/8/46.
  69134 6/8/48.

CONDEMNED: 2/3/61.
Cut up at Inverurie, 31/3/61.

9389

N.B.Loco. 19168.

To traffic 7/1910.

REPAIRS:
Cow. ?/?—25/3/22.**G.**
Cow. ?/?—14/10/24.**G.**
Cow. ?/11—?/12/26.**G.**
Cow. ?/?—27/1/34.**G.**
Cow. ?/?—?/8/34.**L.**
Cow. ?/?—14/12/35.**G.**
Cow. ?/?—10/1/36.**L.**
Cow. ?/?—20/2/37.**G.**

9389 cont./
Cow. ?/?—25/3/39.**G.**
Cow. ?/?—16/3/40.**G.**
Cow. ?/?—10/5/41.**L.**
Cow. 6—27/6/42.**H.**
Cow. ?/?—16/12/44.**G.**
Inv. 15/6—6/7/46.**H.**
Cow. 12—15/7/47.**N/C.**
Cow. 13/7—14/8/48.**G.**
Cow. 30/1—23/2/51.**G.**
Cow. 17—29/11/52.**L/I.**
Cow. 22—27/3/54.**C/L.**
Cow. 7—25/9/54.**H/I.**
Cow. 28/1—16/2/57.**G.**

BOILERS:
300.
265 *(ex386)* 25/3/22.
303 *(ex9925)* ?/12/26.
294 *(ex9916)* 27/1/34.
299 *(ex9924)* 20/2/37.
1552 *(ex9076)* 25/3/39.
1917 *(new)* 16/12/44.
26542 *(ex69219)* 23/2/51.
26542 reno.26433 29/11/52.
26591 *(ex??)* 16/2/57.

SHEDS:
Dunfermline.
Dundee 15/8/57.
St Margarets 9/5/58.

RENUMBERED:
9389 14/10/24.
9135 20/1/46.
69135 14/8/48.

CONDEMNED: 1/10/62.
Cut up at Inverurie, 21/12/62.

_____

9390

N.B.Loco. 19169.

To traffic 7/1910.

REPAIRS:
Cow. ?/?—?/10/25.**G.**
Cow. ?/5—14/6/30.**G.**
Cow. ?/?—16/7/32.**G.**
Cow. ?/?—24/11/34.**G.**
Cow. ?/?—10/3/37.**G.**
Cow. ?/?—31/8/38.**L.**
Cow. 23/9—7/10/39.**G.**
Cow. ?/?—11/7/42.**H.**
Inv. ?/?—16/9/44.**G.**
Cow. 3—31/8/45.**H/I.**
Cow. 12—19/7/47.**N/C.**
Cow. 9—26/8/47.**H/I.**
Cow. 5—29/1/49.**G.**
Inv. 8—29/12/50.**H/I.**
Cow. 12/11—1/12/51.**H/I.**
Cow. 31/1—2/2/52.**C/L.**
DFU. 9—24/12/53.**C/L.**

Inv. 9/6—10/7/54.**G.**
Inv. 9/7—17/8/56.**H/I.**

BOILERS:
266.
1356 *(new)* ?/10/25.
296 *(ex9918)* 14/6/30.
304 *(ex9069)* 16/7/32.
265 *(ex9246)* 7/10/39.
1275 *(ex9060)* 16/9/44.
1613 *(ex9156)* 29/1/49.
1613 reno.26509 29/12/50.
26509 reno.26400 10/7/54.

SHEDS:
Dunfermline.
Dundee 15/7/57.
Thornton Jct. 14/12/59.

RENUMBERED:
9390 ?/10/25.
9136 1/12/46.
69136 29/1/49.

CONDEMNED: 11/5/61.
Cut up at Inverurie, 26/5/61.

_____

9391

N.B.Loco. 19170.

To traffic 7/1910.

REPAIRS:
Cow. ?/?—?/7/24.**G.**
Cow. ?/?—26/11/27.**G.**
Cow. ?/?—3/12/32.**G.**
Cow. ?/?—5/8/35.**G.**
Cow. ?/?—14/8/37.**H.**
Cow. ?/?—23/12/39.**G.**
Cow. ?/?—7/6/40.**L.**
Cow. ?/?—17/4/43.**H.**
Cow. ?/?—14/12/43.**L.**
Cow. 14/2—9/3/46.**G.**
Cow. 6—13/9/47.**L.**
Cow. 1—18/6/48.**H/I.**
Cow. 13/11—15/12/50.**G.**
Cow. 4—6/1/51.**N/C.**
Cow. 18/3—12/4/52.**H/I.**
Cow. 1—16/4/55.**G.**
Cow. 25—26/4/55.**N/C.**
Cow. 27/12/55—14/1/56.**C/H.**
Cow. 15/4—9/5/58.**L/I.**

BOILERS:
303.
267 *(ex9915)* ?/7/24.
264 *(ex9388)* 26/11/27.
297 *(ex9919)* 3/12/32.
1277 *(ex9019)* 23/12/39.
1939 *(new)* 9/3/46.
2064 *(new)* 15/12/50.
2064 reno.26489 12/4/52.
26431 *(ex69217)* 16/4/55.

SHED:
Polmont.

RENUMBERED:
9391 ?/7/24.
9137 12/5/46.
69137 18/6/48.

CONDEMNED: 21/5/62.
Cut up at Inverurie, 22/6/62.

_____

9392

N.B.Loco. 19171.

To traffic 7/1910.

REPAIRS:
Cow. ?/?—?/12/24.**G.**
Cow. ?/?—12/8/33.**G.**
Cow. ?/?—12/3/36.**G.**
Cow. ?/?—24/8/36.**L.**
Collision damage.
Cow. 4—18/3/39.**G.**
Cow. ?/?—10/4/43.**H.**
Cow. 2—16/12/44.**G.**
Cow. 14—21/9/46.**L.**
Cow. 5—23/1/48.**G.**
Vac. ejector & steam heat fitted.
Cow. 27/12/50—13/1/51.**H/I.**
EFD. 14—29/5/54.**C/L.**
Cow. 16/11—4/12/54.**G.**
Cow. 16—17/12/54.**N/C.**
Cow. 10—22/1/55.**C/L.**
Cow. 31/8—10/9/55.**C/L.**
Cow. 11—21/4/56.**C/H.**
Cow. 14/8—1/9/56.**C/L.**
Cow. 26/4—18/5/57.**C/H.**

BOILERS:
273.
268 *(ex9219)* ?/12/24.
280 *(ex9524)* 12/8/33.
1553 *(ex9282)* 18/3/39.
1906 *(new)* 16/12/44.
1278 *(exC15 7470)* 23/1/48.
26413 *(ex??)* 4/12/54.
26433 *(ex??)* 18/5/57.

SHEDS:
Eastfield.
St Rollox 24/6/57.
Aberdeen 31/8/57.
St Margarets 19/6/61.

RENUMBERED:
9392 ?/12/24.
9138 2/6/46.
69138 13/1/51.

CONDEMNED: 1/10/62.
*Sold for scrap to P.W.McLellan,
Langloan, 29/5/64.*

_____

9393

N.B.Loco. 19172.

To traffic 8/1910.

REPAIRS:
Cow. ?/10—?/12/25.**G.**
Cow. ?/6—18/6/32.**G.**
Cow. ?/?—8/2/35.**G.**
Cow. 28/8—8/9/37.**G.**
Cow. ?/?—16/12/39.**G.**
Cow. ?/?—20/12/41.**H.**
Cow. ?/?—16/2/43.**L.**
Inv. 15—29/1/44.**H.**
Cow. 24/11—13/12/46.**H/I.**
Cow. 14/9—8/10/48.**G.**
Cow. 13/2—3/3/50.**H/I.**
Cow. 21/1—14/2/53.**G.**
Cow. 29/10—20/11/54.**H/I.**

BOILERS:
269.
1357 *(new)* ?/12/25.
1400 *(ex9917)* 18/6/32.
1609 *(new)* 8/9/37.
1899 *(ex9179)* 8/10/48.
26414 *(ex69134)* 14/2/53.

SHEDS:
Parkhead.
St Margarets ?/12/40.
Carlisle Canal 5/3/45.

RENUMBERED:
9393 ?/12/25.
9139 10/2/46.
69139 8/10/48.

CONDEMNED: 26/4/58.
Cut up at Kilmarnock 7/58.

_____

9396

N.B.Loco. 19173.

To traffic 8/1910.

REPAIRS:
Cow. ?/?—?/1/23.**G.**
Cow. ?/?—9/8/30.**G.**
Cow. 8/8—13/9/36.**G.**
Cow. ?/?—25/3/39.**H.**
Cow. ?—?/4/39.**N/C.**
Cow. ?/?—25/7/39.**L.**
Cow. 13/6—4/7/42.**G.**
Cow. ?/?—6/5/44.**H.**
Inv. 8/2—15/3/47.**H.**
Cow. 22/2—12/3/49.**H/I.**
Cow. 8—24/11/51.**G.**
Cow. 8/9—2/10/54.**H/I.**
Cow. 5—6/10/54.**N/C.**
Cow. 4—21/9/57.**G.**

(above) **Replacement boilers built from 1933 onwards had 'pops' on wider spacing and not on mounting blocks, but some were still fitted with a circular casing around their base. Note change of whistle to standard bell shape from NBR deeper pattern as shown in the previous illustration.**

During the 1939-45 war, when new base casing was needed, a rectangular shape was introduced. No.9157 was formerly 9920 until 17th November 1946.

Lubrication of the cylinders was by tallow cups mounted on the front of the smokebox. There was also a single feed hydrostatic lubricator in the cab to feed the steam chest.

The coupled axleboxes were siphon lubricated from oilboxes but ex works 10th September 1932, No.9007 had its axlebox lubrication changed to Madison-Kipp mechanical type, driven from the left hand front coupling pin. It was the only N15 to get a mechanical lubricator.

(above) No.9007 had a change of mechanical lubricator in May 1945 when the Madison-Kipp type was replaced by a Wakefield which it then kept to 12th February 1962 withdrawal. No.9007 became 9126 from 19th May 1946 and 69126 on 26th June 1948.

(right) Other lubrication changes were very limited but Nos.69146, 69187 and 69202 did have their tallow cups moved from the front to the side of the smokebox where they were much higher. They were moved to the side on No.69202 when ex Inverurie on 13th November 1953. At least No.69146 had them moved back to the front.

Until 1935-37 the leading sandbox had a single filler which was located towards the rear of the box top.

(above) When shopped in 1935-37, an additional filler was fitted at the front end of the box to all the N15s.

Three of the class got shorter chimneys, as used on J36 class. Carried out at Inverurie over a ten year period, the three engines so fitted were Nos.9209 (18th December 1943), 69202 (13th November 1953), and 69136 (10th July 1954) – *see* page 113, bottom.

By 18th May 1954 No.69178 had a patched stovepipe top to its chimney having lost its cap. Note the protruding step has been added to the cab entrance.

When ex Inverurie on 23rd November 1951, No.69224 had been fitted with a chimney from an ex Caledonian 0-4-4T.

The last twenty engines came out new with a raised ventilator on the cab roof.

The raised ventilator on the cab roof was also fitted to three of the engines used as bankers on the Cowlairs incline – Nos.9154, 9251 and 9282. They also had blinds which could be unrolled to cover the cab entrance to help prevent smoke ingress when in the Queen Street tunnel.

9396 cont./
BOILERS:
   299.
   270 (ex918) ?/1/23.
   1280 (ex9225) 9/8/30.
   1581 (new) 13/9/36.
   282 (ex9257) 4/7/42.
26375 (ex69211) 24/11/51.
26375 reno.26336 ?/5/52.
26361 (ex??) 21/9/57.

SHEDS:
Kipps.
St Margarets 8/12/40.

RENUMBERED:
   9396 ?/3/25.
   9140 2/6/46.
   69140 12/3/49.

CONDEMNED: 13/6/58.
Sold for scrap to Motherwell
Machinery & Scrap,
Wishaw, 3/59.

_____

9397

N.B.Loco. 19174.

To traffic 8/1910.

REPAIRS:
Cow. ?/?—?/3/25.**G.**
Cow. ?/?—14/6/34.**G.**
Cow. ?/?—15/7/36.**G.**
Cow. ?/?—12/8/38.**H.**
Cow. 7—28/6/41.**G.**
Cow. ?/?—6/12/41.**L.**
Cow. 30/1—13/2/43.**G.**
Cow. ?/?—21/10/44.**H.**
Cow. 7—21/3/47.**G.**
Cow. 26/10—20/11/48.**H/I.**
Cow. 26/6—12/7/51.**G.**
Cow. 17/11—5/12/53.**L/I.**
Cow. 4—6/3/54.**N/C.**
Cow. 29/8—17/9/55.**G.**
Cow. 14—29/3/58.**L/I.**

BOILERS:
   257.
   271 (exN14 9863) ?/3/25*.
   1559 (new) 14/6/34.
   293 (ex9047) 28/6/41.
   1269 (exN14 9860) 13/2/43.
   1577 (ex9185) 21/3/47.
26484 (ex69222) 12/7/51.
26484 reno.26381 ?/11/52.
26401 (ex69133) 17/9/55.

SHEDS:
Kipps.
St Margarets 25/9/49.

RENUMBERED:
   9397 ?/3/25.
   9141 25/8/46.
   69141 20/11/48.

CONDEMNED: 2/9/60.
Cut up at Cowlairs 15/10/60.

_____

9398

N.B.Loco. 19175.

To traffic 8/1910.

REPAIRS:
Cow. ?/?—20/3/23.**H.**
Cow. ?/?—22/5/24.**G.**
Cow. ?/?—?/8/25.**H.**
Cow. ?/?—18/6/32.**G.**
Cow. ?/?—31/8/35.**G.**
Cow. ?/?—20/3/37.**G.**
Cow. ?/?—?/4/38.**L.**
Cow. ?/?—7/10/39.**G.**
Cow. 23/11—7/12/40.**G.**
Cow. 1—22/5/43.**G.**
Cow. ?/?—?/6/44.**L.**
Cow. 11—28/12/46.**G.**
Cow. 6—17/7/48.**L.**
Cow. 5—30/4/49.**H/I.**
Cow. 22/6—10/8/51.**G.**
Inv. 9—26/2/54.**L/I.**
Inv. 19/3/54.**N/C.**
Bgt. 30/6/54.**C/L.**
Hay. 29/10—14/11/55.**C/L.**

BOILERS:
   263.
   272 (ex9923) 22/5/24.
   283 (ex9527) 18/6/32.
   1356 (ex9519) 20/3/37.
   243 (ex9528) 7/12/40.
   306 (ex9388) 22/5/43.
   1869 (ex9130) 28/12/46.
26401 (ex9220) 10/8/51.
26401 reno.26341 ?/11/52.

SHED:
Bathgate.

RENUMBERED:
   9398 22/5/24.
   9142 1/9/46.
   69142 17/7/48.

CONDEMNED: 24/1/58.
Cut up at Cowlairs 3/58.

_____

9399

N.B.Loco. 19176.

To traffic 8/1910.

REPAIRS:
Cow. ?/?—17/4/24.**H.**
Cow. ?/?—7/3/25.**G.**
Cow. ?/?—22/3/30.**G.**
Cow. ?/?—23/2/35.**G.**
Cow. ?/?—?/3/36.**L.**
Cow. ?/?—30/8/37.**H.**
Cow. ?/?—14/7/38.**L.**
Cow. 23/3—6/4/40.**G.**
Inv. 21/11/42—6/2/43.**H.**
Cow. 25/11—9/12/44.**G.**
Cow. 27/6—12/7/47.**G.**
Cow. 31/10—25/11/49.**H/I.**
Cow. 9—12/4/51.**C/L.**
Cow. 14/2—8/3/52.**G.**
Cow. 14—15/3/52.**N/C.**
Inv. 3—25/2/55.**H/I.**
Inv. 16—23/3/55.**N/C.**
Cow. 16/5—8/6/57.**G.**

BOILERS:
   231.
   273 (ex9392) 7/3/25.
   243 (ex9070) 22/3/30.
   244 (ex9096) 23/2/35.
   1505 (exG9 9355) 6/4/40.
   280 (ex9125) 9/12/44.
   256 (ex9224) 12/7/47.
26375 (ex69208) 8/3/52.
26477 (ex??) 8/6/57.

SHEDS:
Bathgate.
Parkhead by 2/29.
Thornton Jct. 14/1/52.
Motherwell 30/11/59.

RENUMBERED:
   9399 17/4/24.
   9143 17/2/46.
   69143 25/11/49.

CONDEMNED: 16/9/60.
Cut up at Inverurie, 12/10/60.

_____

9907

N.B.Loco. 19828.

To traffic 7/1912.

REPAIRS:
Cow. ?/?—?/?/21.**G.**
Cow. ?/?—10/9/32.**G.**
Cow. ?/?—24/8/34.**G.**
Cow. ?/?—6/12/34.**L.**
Cow. ?/?—18/8/36.**G.**
Cow. ?/?—27/11/37.**G.**
Cow. ?/?—21/10/39.**G.**
Cow. ?/?—9/5/42.**H.**
Inv. ?/?—20/5/44.**H.**
Cow. 1—17/11/45.**G.**
Cow. 27/10—20/11/47.**H/I.**

Cow. 11—14/8/48.**L.**
Vacuum ejector fitted.
Cow. 7—24/6/49.**H/I.**
Cow. 8—24/11/51.**G.**
Cow. 3—15/8/53.**H/I.**
Cow. 12/3—6/4/57.**G.**

BOILERS:
   292.
   285 (ex924) ?/?/21.
   230 (exN14 9860) 10/9/32.
   1400 (ex9393) 27/11/37.
   1267 (ex9520) 17/11/45.
26572 (ex69132) 24/11/51.
26572 reno.26463 15/8/53.
26377 (ex??) 6/4/57.

SHED:
St Margarets.

RENUMBERED:
   9907 ?/1/26.
   9144 1/9/46.
   69144 14/8/48.

CONDEMNED: 25/2/60.
Cut up at Cowlairs 26/3/60.

_____

9908

N.B.Loco. 19829.

To traffic 7/1912.

REPAIRS:
Ghd. 11/6—23/9/25.**G.**
Cow. ?/?—3/10/31.**G.**
Cow. ?/?—27/6/35.**G.**
Cow. ?/?—9/8/37.**G.**
Cow. ?/?—9/5/39.**H.**
Cow. ?/?—25/10/41.**H.**
Cow. ?/?—12/6/43.**H.**
Cow. 21/3—13/4/46.**H/I.**
Cow. 7—26/6/48.**G.**
Cow. 19/1—8/2/51.**L/I.**
Cow. 2—14/3/53.**G.**
Cow. 18/5—5/6/54.**L/I.**
KPS. 21—25/4/55.**C/L.**
Cow. 31/8—22/9/56.**L/I.**
Cow. 1—4/10/56.**N/C.**

BOILERS:
   286.
   251 (ex9166) 3/10/31.
   283 (ex9398) 9/8/37.
   1895 (ex9221) 26/6/48.
   1895 reno.26524 8/2/51.
26419 (ex69139) 14/3/53.

SHEDS:
St Margarets.
Eastfield 6/4/46.
Parkhead 24/8/47.

The Cowlairs bankers had a slip coupling which could be operated by a wire from the cab. In this 31st July 1938 photograph No.9282 had a tall iron on the smokebox for carrying the guide wheel to give flexibility of position to tension the wire. No others were seen so fitted except No.9251 – *see* page 127, bottom – and as No.69131 on 15th May 1953 – *see* page 131, bottom – the long iron had been taken off and the guide wheel was no longer adjustable.

For use on the new wet ash pit at Eastfield shed, the twenty-three N15 allocated there were fitted with drop grates during 1935-37 overhauls. The retaining coil spring for it is between the middle and rear coupled wheels, the operating rod and lever being on the right hand side, and those fitted were Nos.9007, 9029, 9031, 9069, 9071, 9097, 9142, 9154, 9165, 9166, 9174, 9223, 9224, 9229, 9251, 9259, 9276, 9282, 9392, 9453, 9526, 9920, and 9926.

The twenty-nine engine built at Queen's Park works in 1912/13 had buffers with curved taper shanks, quite different from any NBR standard. By Grouping most had been replaced by the parallel shank type and No.9230, ex Cowlairs December 1925, was probably the last to carry them.

(above) The parallel shank type replacing them usually had an end collar to the shank.

No Group Standard buffers were used by N15 class but in later years some got a Great Northern type with a slightly taper shank and no end collar.

Buffer pairing was precise, so No.69186 with different types at the font was an exceedingly rare case.

From 1946 some had their smokebox replaced and had to make do with snap head instead of countersunk rivets. The wing plates were also less shapely. No.9135 (ex 9389) was so treated ex Inverurie 6th July 1946.

9908 cont./
Kipps 28/3/48.
Polmadie 30/11/59.

RENUMBERED:
9908 23/9/25.
9145 13/4/46.
69145 26/6/48.

CONDEMNED: 11/3/60.
Cut up at Cowlairs 16/4/60.

9909

N.B.Loco. 19830.

To traffic 7/1912.

REPAIRS:
StM. ?/?—29/10/24.**G.**
Cow. ?/?—?/9/26.**G.**
Cow. ?/?—11/5/35.**G.**
Cow. ?/?—10/8/37.**G.**
Cow. ?/?—15/6/40.**G.**
Cow. ?/?—6/6/42.**H.**
Inv. ?/?—10/6/44.**H.**
Cow. 22/9—6/10/45.**L.**
Cow. 27/1—5/2/47.**G.**
Cow. 28/3—16/4/49.**G.**
Cow. 5—19/12/50.**H/I.**
Cow. 11—28/6/52.**G.**
Cow. 2—21/5/55.**L/I.**
Cow. 21/12/55—21/1/56.**C/L.**
Cow. 4/7—8/8/57.**G.**

BOILERS:
298.
287 *(ex9387)* 29/10/24.
298 *(ex9920)* 11/5/35.
244 *(ex9399)* 15/6/40.
1992 *(new)* 5/2/47.
26452 *(ex69153)* 28/6/52.
26385 *(ex??)* 8/8/57.

SHED:
St Margarets.

RENUMBERED:
9909 29/10/24.
9146 1/9/46.
69146 16/4/49.

CONDEMNED: 7/7/59.
Cut up at Cowlairs 23/10/59.

9910

N.B.Loco. 19831.

To traffic 8/1912.

REPAIRS:
Cow. ?/?—?/1/26.**G.**

Cow. ?/?—3/10/31.**G.**
Cow. ?/?—29/8/33.**H.**
Cow. ?/?—21/6/35.**G.**
Cow. ?/1—24/2/37.**G.**
Cow. ?/?—4/10/38.**H.**
Cow. ?/?—23/5/40.**G.**
Cow. 13/12/41—10/1/42.**G.**
Cow. ?/?—11/3/44.**H.**
Cow. 30/6—11/8/45.**H.**
Cow. 1—24/10/47.**G.**
Cow. 29/12/48—22/1/49.**L/I.**
Cow. 15/11—8/12/51.**G.**
Cow. 30/11—19/12/53.**H/I.**
Cow. 14/2—9/3/57.**G.**

BOILERS:
288.
1360 *(new)* ?/1/26.
238 *(ex9049)* 3/10/31.
1584 *(new)* 24/2/37.
314 *(ex9096)* 10/1/42.
1868 *(exN14 9125)* 24/10/47.
26420 *(ex69213)* 8/12/51.
26420 reno.26344 19/12/53.
26366 *(ex??)* 9/3/57.

SHEDS:
St Margarets.
Annesley 10/7/24.
St Margarets 16/11/24.

RENUMBERED:
910B *by* ?/7/24.
9910 *by* 11/7/25.
9147 24/11/46.
69147 22/1/49.

CONDEMNED: 6/6/58.
Cut up at Kilmarnock 2/59.

9911

N.B.Loco. 19832.

To traffic 8/1912.

REPAIRS:
Cow. ?/?—11/7/23.**G.**
Cow. ?/?—?/12/24.**G.**
Cow. ?/7—10/9/27.**G.**
Cow. ?/?—12/8/33.**G.**
Cow. ?/?—13/8/35.**G.**
Cow. 4/9—12/10/37.**G.**
Cow. ?/?—9/3/40.**H.**
Inv. 14/11/42—2/1/43.**G.**
Inv. 3—24/3/45.**H.**
Cow. ?/?—8/12/45.**L.**
Cow. 27/11—19/12/47.**G.**
Cow. 11—27/12/50.**H/I.**
Cow. 29/12/52—15/1/53.**G.**
Cow. 17—21/11/53.**N/C.**
Cow. 3—11/12/53.**N/C.**
Cow. 29/6—15/7/55.**H/I.**
Cow. 3/8/55.**N/C.**

BOILERS:
244.
289 *(ex9209)* ?/12/24.
269 *(ex9393)* 10/9/27.
279 *(ex9523)* 12/8/33.
7 *(ex9252)* 12/10/37.
1894 *(new)* 2/1/43.
1920 *(exJ36 5221)* 19/12/47.
26354 *(ex69160)* 15/1/53.

SHEDS:
Berwick.
Tweedmouth 1/8/24.
St Margarets 1/4/29.

RENUMBERED:
9911 ?/12/24.
9148 16/6/46.
69148 27/12/50.

CONDEMNED: 6/6/58.
Cut up at Kilmarnock 3/59.

9912

N.B.Loco. 19833.

To traffic 8/1912.

REPAIRS:
Cow. ?/4—?/6/25.**G.**
Cow. ?/?—11/7/31.**G.**
Cow. ?/?—1/8/33.**G.**
Cow. ?/?—23/3/35.**G.**
Cow. ?/?—27/4/35.**L.**
Cow. ?/?—20/11/36.**G.**
Cow. ?/?—25/7/38.**H.**
Cow. ?/?—28/9/40.**H.**
Cow. 16/1—6/2/43.**G.**
Cow. 17/3—7/4/45.**H.**
Cow. 16/11/46—4/1/47.**L.**
Cow. 1—17/4/48.**G.**
Cow. 11/7—12/8/50.**H/I.**
Cow. 4—21/11/53.**G.**
Cow. 2—25/8/56.**H/I.**

BOILERS:
314.
290 *(ex9246)* ?/6/25.
245 *(ex9097)* 11/7/31.
1266 *(exN14 9859)* 20/11/36.
1896 *(new)* 6/2/43.
2015 *(new)* 17/4/48.
26471 *(ex69167)* 21/11/53.

SHED:
St Margarets.

RENUMBERED:
9912 ?/6/25.
9149 27/10/46.
69149 17/4/48.

CONDEMNED: 22/3/60.
Cut up at Cowlairs 7/5/60.

9913

N.B.Loco. 19834.

To traffic 8/1912.

REPAIRS:
Cow. ?/?—?/7/25.**G.**
Cow. ?/?—22/3/30.**G.**
Cow. ?/?—2/7/30.**L.**
Cow. ?/?—2/10/34.**G.**
Cow. ?/?—23/1/37.**G.**
Cow. ?/?—13/1/40.**G.**
Cow. ?/?—28/6/41.**G.**
Inv. ?/?—11/9/43.**H.**
Cow. 30/7—29/8/46.**G.**
Cow. 3—21/8/48.**H/I.**
Cow. 8—24/12/49.**H/I.**
Inv. 14—25/4/52.**G.**
Inv. 28/4—5/5/52.**N/C.**
Cow. 9—28/8/54.**H/I.**
Cow. 30/8—1/9/54.**N/C.**
Cow. 12/4—11/5/57.**G.**

BOILERS:
312.
291 *(exN14 9861)* ?/7/25*.
233 *(exN14 9863)* 22/3/30.
245 *(ex9912)* 23/1/37.
236 *(ex9067)* 28/6/41.
1966 *(new)* 29/8/46.
26385 *(ex69159)* 25/4/52.
26427 *(ex??)* 11/5/57.

SHEDS:
Thornton Jct.
Dundee 15/8/57.
St Margarets 12/5/58.

RENUMBERED:
9913 ?/7/25.
9150 2/6/46.
69150 21/8/48.

CONDEMNED: 1/10/62.
Cut up at Inverurie, 21/12/62.

9914

N.B.Loco. 19835.

To traffic 8/1912.

REPAIRS:
??. ?/?—?/2/22.**G.**
??. ?/?—?/2/27.**G.**
Cow. ?/?—21/5/32.**G.**
Cow. ?/?—26/6/34.**G.**
Cow. ?/?—1/6/35.**L.**
Cow. 27/2—20/3/37.**G.**

Although only the first six – those with Westinghouse brake – were equipped for working a passenger train, all the class were curiously fitted with clips on the smokebox front to carry a destination board.

By the late 1920s a start had been made on moving the upper lamp iron on to the smokebox door where a Group Standard type was fitted and the inner pair of irons above the buffers also began to disappear.

Not all had the redundant lamp irons removed. In addition to No.69191, still carrying them in this 18th May 1959 photograph, Nos.69166, 69193 and 69217 are known to have kept them.

The engines built from January 1923 had long footsteps at the rear and a horizontal rail on the bunker to allow the shunter to ride on the engine. Note no vertical step and handrail were then provided.

The NBR-built engines were gradually fitted from 1916 with shunters step except on those used as bankers on the Cowlairs incline which were only so equipped during or after the 1939-45 war. The Cowlairs bankers were duly equipped with shunters step and handrails so it is probable that all had them by the end of the LNER. No.9138 was previously 9392.

9914 cont./
Cow. 6/7—8/6/40.**G**.
Cow. ?/?—13/7/40.**L**.
Cow. ?/?—11/9/43.**H**.
Cow. 16/7—10/8/45.**G**.
Cow. 24—31/8/46.**L**.
Cow. 1—26/12/47.**H/I**.
Cow. 24/4—13/5/50.**G**.
Inv. 29/7—29/8/52.**H/I**.
Cow. 30/6—3/7/53.**C/L**.
Cow. 18/1—6/2/54.**C/L**.
Cow. 22/2—11/3/55.**H/I**.
Cow. 9—28/12/57.**L/I**.
Cow. 10—12/4/58.**C/L**.
Cow. 7—15/1/59.**C/L**.

BOILERS:
240.
292 *(ex907)* ?/2/22.
306 *(ex9154)* ?/2/27.
1279 *(ex9125)* 21/5/32.
238 *(ex9910)* 20/3/37.
1551 *(ex9071)* 8/6/40.
219 *(ex9387)* 10/8/45*.
2051 *(new)* 13/5/50.
2051 reno.26476 29/8/52.
26426 *(ex69181)* 11/3/55.

SHEDS:
Burntisland.
Thornton Jct. *by* 1/4/27.
Eastfield *after* 30/6/40.
Parkhead ?/12/41.
Eastfield 1/6/42.
Parkhead 18/1/43.

RENUMBERED:
9914 ?/8/24.
9151 3/11/46.
69151 13/5/50.

CONDEMNED: 23/2/59.
Sold for scrap to Motherwell
Machinery & Scrap,
Wishaw, 6/59.

9915

N.B.Loco. 19836.

To traffic 8/1912.

REPAIRS:
Cow. ?/?—22/11/24.**G**.
Cow. ?/?—?/6/27.**G**.
Cow. ?/?—27/1/34.**G**.
Cow. ?/?—28/6/36.**G**.
Cow. ?/?—20/12/36.**L**.
Cow. 13—27/8/38.**G**.
Cow. ?/?—20/4/39.**L**.
Cow. ?/?—17/1/42.**H**.
Cow. ?/?—16/10/43.**G**.
Inv. 24/3—7/4/45.**H**.
Cow. 27/12/46—18/1/47.**H/I**.

Cow. 10/11—4/12/48.**G**.
Cow. 22/5—8/6/50.**H/I**.
Cow. 22/6—12/7/53.**G**.
Cow. 22/6—12/7/56.**L/I**.

BOILERS:
267.
293 *(ex9921)* 22/11/24.
288 *(ex9910)* ?/6/27.
1270 *(ex9071)* 27/1/34.
1262 *(ex9225)* 27/8/38.
1583 *(ex9924)* 16/10/43.
1900 *(ex9184)* 4/12/48.
26418 *(ex69172)* 12/7/53.

SHEDS:
Thornton Jct.
St Margarets 28/10/40.

RENUMBERED:
9915 22/11/24.
9152 16/6/46.
69152 4/12/48.

CONDEMNED: 30/12/58.
Cut up at Kilmarnock 1/59.

9916

N.B.Loco. 19837.

To traffic 8/1912.

REPAIRS:
Cow. ?/?—?/4/25.**G**.
Cow. ?/?—2/12/33.**G**.
Cow. ?/?—30/11/35.**G**.
Cow. ?/?—8/7/37.**G**.
Cow. ?/?—29/4/39.**H**.
Cow. ?/?—8/2/41.**G**.
Cow. ?/?—7/11/42.**H**.
Inv. 14—28/10/44.**H**.
Cow. 17—31/10/46.**G**.
Cow. 18/8—9/9/48.**H/I**.
Cow. 18/3—12/4/52.**G**.
Cow. 25/1—18/2/56.**H/I**.

BOILERS:
294.
261 *(ex9264)* 2/12/33.
255 *(ex9049)* 8/7/37.
1356 *(ex9398)* 8/2/41.
1987 *(new)* 31/10/46.
26397 *(ex69195)* 12/4/52.

SHED:
Thornton Jct.

RENUMBERED:
9916 ?/4/25.
9153 25/8/46.
69153 9/9/48.

CONDEMNED: 22/9/58.

Cut up at Inverurie, 8/59.

9917

N.B.Loco. 19838.

To traffic 8/1912.

REPAIRS:
Cow. ?/?—18/7/24.**G**.
Cow. ?/?—?/10/26.**G**.
Cow. ?/?—21/5/32.**G**.
Cow. ?/?—21/6/34.**G**.
Cow. ?/?—8/4/36.**G**.
Cow. ?/?—19/2/38.**G**.
Cow. ?/?—4/10/39.**L**.
Cow. ?/?—7/6/40.**G**.
Cow. ?/?—18/4/42.**H**.
Inv. ?/?—26/2/44.**G**.
Cow. ?/?—4/7/44.**L**.
Cow. ?/?—29/12/44.**L**.
Cow. 3—20/7/46.**G**.
Cow. ?/?—15/10/46.**L**.
Cow. 14/5—3/6/48.**H/I**.
Cow. 17/8—2/9/50.**G**.
Cow. 1—25/4/52.**H/I**.
Cow. 3—27/2/53.**C/H**.
Cow. 23/11—11/12/54.**G**.
Cow. 10/1—2/2/57.**L/I**.

BOILERS:
295.
1400 *(new)* ?/10/26.
262 *(ex9106)* 21/5/32.
312 *(ex9060)* 19/2/38.
230 *(ex9209)* 26/2/44.
1965 *(new)* 20/7/46.
2053 *(new)* 2/9/50.
2053 reno.26478 25/4/52.
26472 *(ex69161)* 11/12/54.

SHEDS:
Dunfermline.
Dundee 15/8/57.
St Margarets 9/5/58.

RENUMBERED:
9917 18/7/24.
9154 10/11/46.
69154 3/6/48.

CONDEMNED: 18/11/59.
Cut up at Cowlairs 30/1/60.

9918

N.B.Loco. 19839.

To traffic 8/1912.

REPAIRS:
Cow. ?/?—?/?/22.**G**.
Cow. ?/?—?/5/25.**G**.

Cow. ?/?—22/3/30.**G**.
Cow. ?/?—1/12/34.**G**.
Cow. ?/?—13/5/37.**H**.
Cow. 27/5—17/6/39.**G**.
Cow. ?/?—28/6/41.**H**.
Cow. ?/?—25/9/43.**H**.
Cow. 15/2—22/3/46.**G**.
Cow. 18/2—6/3/48.**H/I**.
Cow. 6—25/3/50.**G**.
Cow. 22/12/52—10/1/53.**L/I**.
CAR. 5/2—19/3/54.**C/L**.
Cow. 1—30/3/57.**G**.

BOILERS:
270.
296 *(ex65)* ?/?/22.
310 *(ex9282)* 22/3/30*.
1264 *(ex9031)* 1/12/34.
1555 *(ex9387)* 17/6/39.
269 *(ex9065)* 22/3/46.
2049 *(new)* 25/3/50.
2049 reno.26474 10/1/53.
26480 *(ex??)* 30/3/57.

SHEDS:
Dunfermline.
Carlisle Canal ?/11/40.

RENUMBERED:
9918 ?/5/25.
9155 25/8/46.
69155 19/9/48 *(at shed)*.

CONDEMNED: 3/9/62.
Cut up at Cowlairs 14/6/63.

9919

N.B.Loco. 19840.

To traffic 8/1912.

REPAIRS:
Ghd. 12/6—29/9/25.**G**.
Cow. ?/?—8/10/32.**G**.
Cow. ?/?—4/11/32.**L**.
Cow. ?/?—16/5/35.**G**.
Cow. 15—29/1/38.**G**.
Cow. ?/?—29/4/38.**L**.
Cow. ?/?—24/5/41.**H**.
Cow. 4—18/12/43.**G**.
Cow. 24/12/45—23/1/46.**H/I**.
Cow. 29/6—17/7/48.**G**.
Cow. 28/5—16/6/51.**G**.
Cow. 1—16/7/52.**C/L**.
Cow. 24/12/53—16/1/54.**H/I**.
Cow. 5—24/8/57.**G**.

BOILERS:
297.
1357 *(ex9393)* 8/10/32.
302 *(ex9209)* 29/1/38.
1613 *(ex9282)* 18/12/43.
1552 *(exN14 9123)* 17/7/48.

After 1923 an additional plate type footstep was fitted at the rear end of the shunters step and a corresponding vertical handrail was fitted on the bunker.

There were normally two steps fitted on the back of the bunker at about one-third the way up with a cross rail just below the coal rails.

(below) Nos.9065, 9097 (9191 later) and 9106 were noted with a third step added between the other two. The length of cross rail could also vary appreciably. Note the rolled up blind above the cab entrance.

Until well into LNER years the coal rails on the bunker top were open type.

The increasing use of small coal which had to be made from the late 1920s, led to steel plating being put behind the coal rails and all were so fitted.

9919 cont./
26565 *(ex69210)* 16/6/51.
26565 reno.26456 1/53.
26442 *(ex??)* 24/8/57.

SHEDS:
Kipps.
Bathgate 6/2/33.

RENUMBERED:
9919 29/9/25.
9156 16/6/46.
69156 17/7/48.

CONDEMNED: 12/2/62.
Sold for scrap to Arnott Young,
Carmyle 4/6/63.

9920

N.B.Loco. 19841.

To traffic 8/1912.

REPAIRS:
Cow. ?/?—?/11/24.**G.**
Cow. ?/?—14/11/31.**G.**
Cow. ?/?—23/2/35.**G.**
Drop grate fitted.
Cow. ?/?—30/9/37.**H.**
Cow. ?/?—1/2/41.**H.**
Cow. ?/?—27/11/43.**H.**
Cow. ?/?—15/4/44.**L.**
Cow. 14—26/4/47.**G.**
Cow. 30/6—15/7/49.**H/I.**
Cow. 17/12/51—12/1/52.**G.**
Inv. 23/11—4/12/53.**L/I.**
Inv. 11—25/12/53.**N/C.**
Cow. 6—17/7/54.**N/C.**
Cow. 2—14/8/54.**N/C.**
Cow. 19—21/8/54.**N/C.**
Cow. 10—19/1/55.**C/L.**
Cow. 14—26/2/55.**C/H.**
Cow. 13/7—13/8/55.**L/I.**
Cow. 10—14/4/56.**N/C.**
Cow. 1—10/11/56.**C/H.**

BOILERS:
  252.
  298 *(ex9909)* ?/11/24.
  239 *(ex9054)* 23/2/35.
 1554 *(ex9204)* 26/4/47.
26424 *(ex69140)* 12/1/52.
26424 reno.26347 14/8/54.

SHEDS:
Eastfield.
Bathgate ?/5/44.
Parkhead 25/9/49.

RENUMBERED:
9920 ?/11/24.
9157 17/11/46.
69157 15/7/49.

CONDEMNED: 9/4/58.
Cut up at Kilmarnock 7/58.

9921

N.B.Loco. 19842.

To traffic 8/1912.

REPAIRS:
Cow. ?/?—14/4/23.**G.**
KPS. ?/?—3/5/24.**H.**
Cow. ?/?—6/9/30.**G.**
Cow. ?/?—9/11/33.**G.**
Cow. ?/?—10/8/35.**G.**
Cow. ?/?—15/10/37.**G.**
Cow. ?/?—25/11/37.**L.**
Cow. ?/?—3/3/38.**H.**
Cow. ?/?—6/4/40.**G.**
Cow. ?/?—6/3/43.**H.**
Cow. ?/?—8/7/44.**H.**
Cow. 10/2—6/3/47.**G.**
Cow. 9—14/8/48.**L.**
Cow. 4—21/5/49.**H/I.**
Cow. 8/2—5/3/52.**G.**
Hay. 18—25/8/54.**C/L.**
Cow. 5—22/1/55.**H/I.**
Bgt. 9—15/3/56.**C/L.**

BOILERS:
  293.
  299 *(ex396)* 14/4/23.
  291 *(ex9913)* 6/9/30*.
  287 *(ex9909)* 10/8/35.
 1550 *(ex9251)* 6/4/40.
 1993 *(new)* 6/3/47.
26382 *(ex69157)* 5/3/52.

SHED:
Bathgate.

RENUMBERED:
9921 3/5/24.
9158 6/10/46.
69158 14/8/48.

CONDEMNED: 21/5/58.
Cut up at Kilmarnock 7/58.

9922

N.B.Loco. 19843.

To traffic 8/1912.

REPAIRS:
Cow. ?/?—?/11/22.**G.**
Cow. ?/?—27/11/24.**G.**
Cow. ?/?—21/3/31.**G.**
Cow. ?/?—22/4/31.**L.**
Cow. ?/?—15/3/35.**G.**
Cow. 12—22/6/37.**G.**
Cow. 30/12/39—20/1/40.**G.**
Cow. ?/?—19/6/43.**H.**
Cow. 6—30/3/46.**G.**
Cow. 21/6—10/7/48.**H/I.**
Inv. 24/9—12/10/51.**G.**
Cow. 20/5—6/6/53.**H/I.**
Cow. 13—15/4/55.**C/L.**
BGT. 1—11/11/55.**C/L.**
Cow. 15/11—3/12/55.**G.**

BOILERS:
  229.
  300 *(ex389)* ?/11/22.
  273 *(ex9399)* 21/3/31.
 1279 *(ex9914)* 22/6/37.
 1274 *(ex9165)* 20/1/40.
 1558 *(ex9019)* 30/3/46.
26556 *(ex69164)* 12/10/51.
26422 *(ex69176)* 3/12/55.

SHED:
Bathgate.

RENUMBERED:
9922 27/11/24.
9159 30/3/46.
69159 10/7/48.

CONDEMNED: 30/10/61.
Sold for scrap to Arnott Young,
Carmyle, 4/6/63.

9923

N.B.Loco. 19844.

To traffic 8/1912.

REPAIRS:
Cow. ?/?—12/4/24.**G.**
Cow. ?/?—11/7/31.**G.**
Cow. ?/?—16/12/33.**G.**
Cow. ?/?—1/8/36.**G.**
Cow. ?/?—8/7/38.**G.**
Cow. ?/?—24/8/40.**H.**
Cow. 10—24/1/42.**G.**
Cow. ?/?—26/6/43.**H.**
Cow. 31/3—21/4/45.**H.**
Cow. 15—27/9/47.**G.**
Cow. 14—30/3/50.**L/I.**
Cow. 11—29/11/52.**G.**
Vacuum ejector fitted.
Cow. 11/1—6/2/54.**C/H.**
Cow. 20/4—7/5/55.**H/I.**

BOILERS:
  272.
  301 *(ex9252)* 12/4/24.
  260 *(ex9259)* 11/7/31.
 1359 *(ex9388)* 1/8/36.
 1399 *(ex9925)* 24/1/42.
 1268 *(ex9214)* 27/9/47.
26439 *(ex69137)* 29/11/52.

SHEDS:
Bathgate.
Dunfermline 19/1/39.
St Margarets 24/3/58.

RENUMBERED:
9923 12/4/24.
9160 9/6/46.
69160 30/3/50.

CONDEMNED: 14/8/58.
Cut up at Cowlairs 2/60.

9924

N.B.Loco. 19845.

To traffic 8/1912.

REPAIRS:
Cow. ?/?—?/?/21.**G.**
Ghd. 31/12/23—27/2/24.**L.**
Cow. ?/?—27/1/25.**G.**
Cow. ?/?—?/7/26.**G.**
Cow. ?/?—16/5/31.**G.**
Cow. ?/?—23/11/34.**G.**
Cow. ?/?—19/2/37.**G.**
Cow. ?/?—28/6/38.**H.**
Cow. ?/?—3/6/39.**N/C.**
Cow. ?/?—19/4/41.**H.**
Cow. ?/?—29/5/43.**G.**
Cow. 3—19/10/45.**H/I.**
Cow. 26/1—14/2/48.**G.**
Cow. 5—24/2/51.**C/L.**
Cow. 30/9—11/10/52.**H/I.**
Cow. 24/5—19/6/54.**G.**
Cow. 3—26/12/56.**H/I.**

BOILERS:
  285.
  233 *(ex229)* ?/?/21.
  302 *(ex9096)* 27/1/25.
  299 *(ex9921)* 16/5/31.
 1583 *(new)* 19/2/37.
  243 *(ex9398)* 29/5/43.
 1893 *(ex9189)* 14/2/48.
1893 reno.26522 24/2/51.
26522 reno.26413 11/10/52.
26379 *(ex69186)* 19/6/54.

SHEDS:
Bathgate.
Burnbank
Bathgate *by* 1/32.
Parkhead *by* 31/3/32.

RENUMBERED:
9924 27/2/24.
9161 10/11/46.
69161 24/2/51.

CONDEMNED: 16/8/60.
Cut up at Inverurie, 9/9/60.

The six Part 2 engines which could be used for passenger trains, were also equipped for coach heating and had pipe connections at both ends. When some of the part 1 engines had train brake added – transferring them to Part 2 – they too had carriage heating apparatus fitted.

Nos.251 and 282 were dual brake fitted before Grouping and the other four with Westinghouse brake had vacuum ejector added as follows: Nos.9007 (March 1925), 9154 (November 1925), 9209 (October 1924), and 9210 (July 1924). The slip coupling fitted to the Cowlairs bankers was carried in addition to the screw adjustable type normally fitted for use on coaching stock.

Part 1 engines had only steam brake acting on the engine and no facility for train braking.

(below) In March 1929 two more Cowlairs incline bankers were needed and Nos.9029 and 9165 were fitted with Westinghouse and vacuum brakes, and made Part 2. Note vertical handrail on the bunker but the shunters step was removed.

When more were needed with continuous brakes, No.9166 (March 1936) and No.9097 (April 1936) were chosen. By then the Westinghouse brake was obsolete in the southern Scottish area so they were fitted with a steam and vacuum combination. Note that the shunters step was not taken off this banking engine.

Between January 1948 and May 1954, twelve N15 had vacuum ejectors fitted to work in combination with their steam brake. Nos.69134, 69138, 69144, 69160, 69163, 69164, 69167, 69179, 69180, 69181, 69189, and 69203.

The final brake change was removal of Westinghouse and alteration to steam and vacuum combination. Five were done, Nos.69130, ex works 17th July 1948 and then 69127 (24th October 1953), 69188 (31st October 1953) and 69131 (7th November 1953), followed by 69182 (2nd July 1955).

9925

N.B.Loco. 19846.

To traffic 8/1912.

REPAIRS:
Cow. ?/?—28/9/23.**G.**
Cow. ?/?—?/10/25.**G.**
Cow. ?/?—9/8/30.**G.**
Cow. ?/?—19/10/34.**G.**
Cow. 9—23/1/37.**G.**
Cow. ?/?—3/6/39.**G.**
Cow. 29/11—27/12/41.**G.**
Cow. ?/?—18/9/43.**H.**
Cow. 27/6—14/7/45.**H/I.**
Cow. 15/12/45—2/2/46.**L.**
Cow. 10—31/10/47.**G.**
Cow. 5—22/4/50.**H/I.**
Cow. 16/9—4/10/52.**G.**
Cow. 18/1—11/2/56.**L/I.**

BOILERS:
258.
303 *(ex9391)* 28/9/23.
1359 *(new)* ?/10/25.
247 *(ex9107)* 9/8/30.
1399 *(ex9259)* 23/1/37.
267 *(ex9166)* 27/12/41.
1281 *(ex9205)* 31/10/47.
26416 *(ex69187)* 4/10/52.

SHED:
Polmont.

RENUMBERED:
9925 ?/10/25.
9162 24/11/46.
69162 22/4/50.

CONDEMNED: 2/3/59.
Sold for scrap to Arnott Young, Carmyle, 17/11/59.

9926

N.B.Loco. 19847.

To traffic 8/1912.

REPAIRS:
Cow. ?/11/25—?/1/26.**G.**
Cow. ?/?—26/12/31.**G.**
Cow. ?/?—27/7/34.**G.**
Cow. ?/?—18/8/37.**G.**
Drop grate fitted.
Cow. ?/?—15/11/40.**G.**
Cow. ?/?—22/1/44.**G.**
Cow. 3—24/11/45.**L.**
Cow. 30/8—12/9/46.**H/I.**
Cow. 7—14/6/47.**L.**
Cow. 16/8—7/9/48.**G.**
Cow. 3—20/5/50.**H/I.**
Cow. 18—23/6/51.**C/L.**

Cow. 29/4—24/5/52.**G.**
Cow. 26/4—15/5/54.**L/I.**
Vacuum ejector fitted.
Cow. 8—20/11/54.**C/L.**
Cow. 10—19/11/55.**C/L.**
Cow. 16—17/3/56.**N/C.**
Cow. 21/6—13/7/57.**G.**

BOILERS:
304.
234 *(ex9020)* ?/1/26.
290 *(ex9912)* 26/12/31.
251 *(ex9908)* 18/8/37.
1903 *(new)* 22/1/44.
1584 *(ex9167)* 7/9/48.
26442 *(ex69203)* 24/5/52.
26463 *(ex??)* 13/7/57.

SHEDS:
Eastfield.
Dawsholm 29/10/50.
Eastfield 24/5/54.
St Rollox 24/6/57.
Eastfield 12/8/57.

RENUMBERED:
9926 ?/1/26.
9163 2/6/46.
69163 7/9/48.

CONDEMNED: 12/2/62.
Sold for scrap to G.H.Campbell, Airdrie, 10/7/62.

9219

N.B.Loco. 20164.

To traffic 5/1913.

REPAIRS:
Cow. ?/?—?/12/24.**G.**
Cow. ?/?—19/4/31.**?.**
Cow. ?/?—5/6/32.**G.**
Cow. ?/?—12/5/34.**G.**
Cow. ?/?—15/10/35.**G.**
Cow. ?/?—10/11/37.**H.**
Cow. ?/?—5/8/39.**G.**
Cow. 16/8—15/9/41.**G.**
Cow. ?/?—7/8/43.**H.**
Cow. 29/1—18/2/46.**H/I.**
Cow. 14/12/46—1/2/47.**L.**
Cow. 6—23/4/48.**H/I.**
Cow. 17/1—15/2/51.**G.**
StM. 2—18/12/53.**C/L.**
Cow. 21/6—10/7/54.**H/I.**
Cow. 15—17/7/54.**N/C.**
Cow. 14/6—14/7/56.**G.**

BOILERS:
268.
252 *(ex9920)* ?/12/24.
291 *(ex9921)* 15/10/35*.
1577 *(ex9022)* 15/9/41.

1559 *(ex9188)* 1/2/47.
1867 *(ex69178)* 15/2/51.
1867 reno.26511 15/2/51.
26511 reno.26402 10/7/54.
26447 *(ex??)* 14/7/56.

SHEDS:
Thornton Jct.
Carlisle Canal *by* 1/33.
Eastfield 20/7/51.
St Margarets 23/12/51.

RENUMBERED:
9219 ?/12/24.
9185 18/2/46.
69185 23/4/48.

CONDEMNED: 27/7/59.
Cut up at Cowlairs 17/11/59.

9223

N.B.Loco. 20165.

To traffic 5/1913.

REPAIRS:
Cow. ?/?—8/9/34.**G.**
Cow. ?/?—9/6/37.**H.**
Drop grate fitted.
Cow. ?/?—30/12/38.**L.**
Cow. ?/?—11/9/40.**G.**
Cow. ?/?—11/3/44.**H.**
Cow. 7—29/6/46.**G.**
Cow. 9—16/11/46.**L.**
Cow. 22—29/3/47.**L.**
Cow. 28/5—12/6/48.**H/I.**
Cow. 13/2—10/3/51.**G.**
Cow. 12—18/12/52.**N/C.**
Cow. 19/10—7/11/53.**H/I.**
Vacuum ejector fitted.
Cow. 14/12/55—7/1/56.**G.**

BOILERS:
253.
1278 *(ex9099)* 8/9/34.
295 *(ex9031)* 11/9/40.
1962 *(new)* 29/6/46.
26518 *(ex69204)* 10/3/51.
26518 reno.26409 7/11/53.
26395 *(exC15 67465)* 7/1/56.

SHEDS:
Eastfield.
Dunfermline 3/2/43.
Dundee 16/7/58.

RENUMBERED:
9223 ?/9/24.
9164 3/11/46.
69164 12/6/48.

CONDEMNED: 15/4/59.
Sold for scrap to Motherwell Machinery & Scrap, Wishaw, 6/59.

9224

N.B.Loco. 20166.

To traffic 5/1913.

REPAIRS:
Cow. ?/?—12/7/30.**G.**
Cow. ?/?—13/10/33.**G.**
Cow. ?/?—16/5/36.**G.**
Cow. ?/?—7/7/37.**L.**
Cow. ?/?—20/4/38.**H.**
Cow. ?/?—10/2/40.**G.**
Cow. ?/?—25/1/41.**L.**
Cow. 18/12/43—8/1/44.**G.**
Cow. 9—23/6/45.**L.**
Cow. 8—18/1/47.**H/I.**
Cow. 12/10—12/11/49.**G.**
Cow. 25/9—13/10/51.**L/I.**
Cow. 5/7—7/8/54.**G.**
Cow. 22/2—2/3/55.**C/L.**
Cow. 2/7—11/8/56.**H/I.**

BOILERS:
254.
249 *(ex9142)* 12/7/30.
254 *(ex9097)* 16/5/36.
1902 *(new)* 8/1/44.
1901 *(ex9166)* 12/11/49.
1901 reno.26530 13/10/51.
26338 *(ex69186)* 7/8/54.

SHEDS:
Eastfield.
Parkhead 29/10/50.

RENUMBERED:
9224 ?/10/25.
9165 28/4/46.
69165 12/11/49.

CONDEMNED: 19/5/60.
Cut up at Cowlairs 11/6/60.

9229

N.B.Loco. 20167.

To traffic 5/1913.

REPAIRS:
Cow. ?/?—2/2/21.**G.**
Dar. 26/5—18/9/25.**G.**
Cow. ?/?—23/4/32.**G.**
Cow. ?/?—19/12/34.**G.**
Cow. ?/?—31/8/35.**L.**
Cow. ?/?—?/3/37.**L.**
Cow. 19/2—19/3/38.**G.**

Until after Grouping the exhaust steam from the Westinghouse pump entered the smokebox above the boiler handrail.

After Grouping, this pump exhaust was diverted to go below the running plate. This 15th May 1953 photograph shows the Westinghouse pump still fitted, less than six months before removal.

Three of the original Part 2 engines still had their Westinghouse pumps to withdrawal. These were Nos.69126 (to 12th February 1962), 69128 (to 1st October 1962), and 69129 (to 2nd December 1958). No.69128 was laid aside almost a year at St Margarets and was put into service as a Stationary Boiler in September 1963 as here on 18th September 1963. It was sold to Motherwell Machinery & Scrap for cutting up.

(above) Nos.519 to 524 entered traffic fitted with NBR number plates on the bunker – see page 108 – but Nos.525 to 528 had L.&N.E.R. on the tank sides over transfer applied figures in NBR style, and a LNER standard number plate on the bunker. Cowlairs quickly put the earlier engines into the same style.

This initial painting and lettering was unchanged when some got their 1924 number, and it appears to be unlined black. No.519 seen on 4th July 1923 was recorded as having red lining.

Cow. ?/?—15/3/41.**H.**
Cow. ?/?—23/10/42.**L.**
Cow. 18/12/43—1/1/44.**G.**
Cow. 5—20/3/47.**H/I.**
Cow. 7/6—1/7/49.**G.**
Cow. 2—5/5/50.**C/L.**
Inv. 21/9—5/10/51.**L/I.**
Cow. 7—9/1/52.**C/L.**
Cow. 15/4—3/5/52.**C/H.**
Cow. 22/2—13/3/54.**H/I.**
Cow. 3—22/10/55.**L/I.**
Cow. 6—10/3/56.**N/C.**
Cow. 11—22/9/56.**C/H.**

BOILERS:
233.
1 *(new)* ?/2/21.
1393 *(ex9020)* 23/4/32.
1611 *(new)* 19/3/38.
1901 *(new)* 1/1/44.
1892 *(exN14 9120)* 1/7/49.
1892 reno.26521 5/10/51.
26458 *(ex69158)* 3/5/52.

SHEDS:
Eastfield.
Parkhead 29/10/50.

RENUMBERED:
9229 18/9/25.
9166 10/11/46.
69166 1/7/49.

CONDEMNED: 7/12/59.
Cut up at Cowlairs 27/2/60.

_____

9230

N.B.Loco. 20168.

To traffic 5/1913.

REPAIRS:
Cow. ?/?—?/12/25.**G.**
Cow. ?/8—6/9/30.**G.**
Cow. ?/?—22/6/34.**G.**
Cow. 11—26/1/36.**G.**
Cow. ?/?—23/10/37.**G.**
Cow. ?/?—24/3/38.**L.**
Cow. ?/?—2/12/39.**G.**
Cow. 24/1—14/2/42.**G.**
Cow. ?/?—18/12/43.**H.**
Inv. 7—28/12/46.**H.**
Cow. 29/6—16/7/48.**G.**
Vacuum ejector fitted.
Cow. 24/4—5/5/51.**H/I.**
Cow. 2—20/9/52.**H/I.**
Cow. 26/10—14/11/53.**G.**
Cow. 3/12/53.**C/L.**
Cow. 15—20/3/54.**C/L.**
Cow. 26/3—3/4/54.**N/C.**
Cow. 16/11—4/12/54.**G.**
Cow. 13—17/12/54.**N/C.**

BOILERS:
255.
1276 *(ex9079)* 6/9/30.
1273 *(ex9528)* 26/1/36.
1584 *(ex9910)* 14/2/42.
2016 *(new)* 16/7/48.
2016 reno.26580 5/5/51.
26580 reno.26471 20/9/52.
26356 *(ex69194)* 14/11/53.

SHED:
St Margarets.

RENUMBERED:
9230 ?/12/25.
9167 14/9/46.
69167 16/7/48.

CONDEMNED: 20/12/57.
Cut up at Kilmarnock 7/58.

_____

9246

N.B.Loco. 20169.

To traffic 5/1913.

REPAIRS:
Cow. ?/?—?/5/25.**G.**
Cow. ?/?—?/7/26.**H.**
Cow. ?/?—19/5/34.**G.**
Cow. ?/?—3/7/36.**G.**
Cow. ?/?—24/3/37.**L.**
Cow. ?/?—9/9/39.**G.**
Cow. 29/6—13/7/40.**G.**
Cow. ?/?—31/1/42.**H.**
Cow. ?/?—4/3/44.**H.**
Cow. 8/3—18/4/47.**G.**
Cow. 4—23/4/49.**H/I.**
Cow. 17/7—22/8/52.**G.**
Cow. 24/9—4/10/52.**N/C.**
Cow. 20/2—14/3/53.**C/H.**
Cow. 28/4—12/5/53.**C/L.**
Cow. 2—19/11/55.**L/I.**
Cow. 1/12/55.**N/C.**
Cow. 15—26/5/56.**C/L.**
Cow. 23/1—16/2/57.**G.**

BOILERS:
290.
257 *(ex9397)* ?/5/25.
265 *(ex9070)* 19/5/34.
278 *(ex9077)* 9/9/39.
259 *(ex9174)* 13/7/40.
1269 *(ex9141)* 18/4/47.
26412 *(ex69166)* 22/8/52.
26412 formerly 26821.
26402 *(ex??)* 16/2/57.

SHED:
St Margarets.

RENUMBERED:
9246 ?/5/25.
9168 5/5/46.
69168 23/4/49.

CONDEMNED: 5/2/60.
Cut up at Cowlairs 19/3/60.

_____

9252

N.B.Loco. 20170.

To traffic 5/1913.

REPAIRS:
Cow. ?/?—?/12/23.**G.**
Cow. ?/?—?/4/25.**G.**
Cow. ?/?—8/10/32.**G.**
Cow. ?/?—1/2/35.**G.**
Cow. 14—25/8/37.**G.**
Cow. ?/?—19/10/38.**L.**
Collision damage.
Cow. ?/?—12/8/39.**G.**
Cow. 2—23/5/42.**G.**
Cow. ?/?—14/10/44.**H.**
Inv. 25/5—8/6/46.**G.**
Cow. 8—22/3/47.**C/L.**
Cow. 26/4—13/5/48.**H/I.**
Cow. 11—14/10/48.**L.**
Cow. 25/1—17/2/51.**G.**
Cow. 1—11/10/51.**C/L.**
Cow. 3—8/12/51.**N/C.**
Cow. 16—26/6/52.**C/L.**
Cow. 6—28/5/55.**G.**
Cow. 27/6/55.**N/C.**
Hay. 2—9/12/57.**C/L.**

BOILERS:
301.
258 *(ex9925)* ?/12/23.
7 *(ex9386)* 8/10/32.
1395 *(ex9240)* 25/8/37.
1890 *(new)* 23/5/42.
1274 *(ex9922)* 8/6/46.
26559 *(ex69154)* 17/2/51.
26559 formerly 1965.
26432 *(exC15 67476)* 28/5/55.

SHEDS:
St Margarets.
Annesley ?/7/24.
St Margarets ?/11/24.
Haymarket 13/6/45.

RENUMBERED:
9252 ?/4/25.
9169 5/5/46.
69169 13/5/48.

CONDEMNED: 9/2/59.
Sold for scrap to Chalmers,
Bonnington, Edinburgh 12/59.

_____

9257

N.B.Loco. 20171.

To traffic 5/1913.

REPAIRS:
KPS. ?/?—3/5/24.**H.**
Cow. ?/?—15/7/33.**G.**
Cow. ?/?—6/9/35.**G.**
Cow. ?/?—30/3/38.**H.**
Cow. ?/?—14/9/38.**L.**
Cow. ?/?—10/8/40.**G.**
Cow. 2—23/5/42.**G.**
Inv. ?/?—28/10/44.**G.**
Cow. 2—9/6/45.**C/L.**
Cow. 19—27/3/47.**G.**
Cow. 16/1—3/2/50.**H/I.**
Cow. 29/12/52—22/1/53.**G.**
Cow. 6—30/10/54.**H/I.**
Cow. 13/5—13/6/57.**C/L.**
Cow. 24—26/6/57.**C/L.**
Cow. 26—29/11/58.**N/C.**

BOILERS:
259.
281 *(ex9525)* 15/7/33.
282 *(ex9099)* 10/8/40.
1889 *(new)* 23/5/42.
1996 *(new)* 27/3/47.
26351 *(ex69215)* 22/1/53.

SHEDS:
Kipps.
Eastfield 26/6/44.

RENUMBERED:
9257 3/5/24.
9170 5/5/46.
69170 3/2/50.

CONDEMNED: 6/1/60.
Sold for scrap to J.N.Connell,
Coatbridge 3/60.

_____

9264

N.B.Loco. 20172.

To traffic 5/1913.

REPAIRS:
Ghd. 24/1—9/5/24.**G.**
Cow. ?/?—4/11/33.**G.**
Cow. ?/?—27/12/35.**G.**
Cow. ?/?—21/4/37.**H.**
Cow. 19—31/8/39.**G.**
Cow. ?/?—27/12/40.**L.**
Cow. ?/?—10/1/42.**H.**
Cow. ?/?—16/1/43.**H.**
Cow. 5/8—1/9/45.**G.**
Cow. 16—31/1/48.**H/I.**
Cow. 19/6—8/7/50.**G.**

Later in 1923, Cowlairs had discarded the ampersand and full points, but from September to the end of February 1924 they added the area suffix B to the number. No.386ʙ was ex works 27ᵗʰ November 1923.

Cowlairs always avoided re-painting until it was absolutely necessary and became notorious for hybrid appearances. L.&N.E.R. 921 was ex works 14ᵗʰ April 1923 and then Kipps works made it 9921 on 3ʳᵈ May 1924 without any attempt to centre the number. Some got their 1924 number on NBR unlined black, others on NBR black with double yellow lining, and No.9257 on 3ʳᵈ May 1924 was so numbered whilst still in pre-1914 green.

9264 cont./
Cow. 4—20/11/52.**N/C.**
Cow. 1—19/9/53.**H/I.**
Cow. 6—30/3/57.**G.**

BOILERS:
261.
246 (exN14 9863) 4/11/33.
263 (ex9065) 31/8/39.
1551 (ex9914) 1/9/45.
2052 (new) 8/7/50.
2052 reno.26477 19/9/53.
26453 (ex??) 30/3/57.

SHEDS:
Kipps.
Parkhead by 1/1/33.
Eastfield 24/2/52.

RENUMBERED:
9264 9/5/24.
9171 26/5/46.
69171 8/7/50.

CONDEMNED: 16/6/60.
Cut up at Cowlairs 2/7/60.

_____

9047

N.B.Loco. 21218.

To traffic 8/1916.

REPAIRS:
Dar. 3/6—12/10/25.**G.**
Cow. ?/?—25/2/28.**G.**
Cow. ?/?—14/7/34.**G.**
Cow. ?/?—17/9/36.**G.**
Cow. ?/?—14/11/38.**H.**
Cow. 8—22/3/41.**G.**
Cow. ?/?—27/12/41.**L.**
Cow. ?/?—22/5/43.**H.**
Inv. ?/?—14/4/44.**L.**
Inv. 1/9—6/10/45.**H.**
Cow. 20/4—4/5/46.**C/L.**
Cow. 23/2—12/3/48.**G.**
Inv. 5—30/3/51.**L/I.**
Cow. 21/4—16/5/53.**G.**
Cow. 17/1—4/2/56.**H/I.**

BOILERS:
237.
295 (ex9917) 25/2/28.
293 (ex9165) 14/7/34.
1575 (exC15 9039) 22/3/41.
1898 (ex9181) 12/3/48.
1898 reno.26527 30/3/51.
26415 (ex69145) 16/5/53.

SHED:
St Margarets.

RENUMBERED:
9047 12/10/25.
9172 21/7/46.
69172 30/3/51.

CONDEMNED: 13/11/58.
Cut up at Cowlairs 8/59.

_____

9054

N.B.Loco. 21219.

To traffic 8/1916.

REPAIRS:
STM. ?/?—7/11/24.**H.**
Cow. ?/8—?/9/28.**G.**
Cow. ?/8—?/9/32.**G.**
Cow. ?/?—3/11/34.**G.**
Cow. ?/?—22/8/36.**G.**
Cow. ?/?—3/5/38.**L.**
Cow. ?/?—14/12/38.**G.**
Cow. ?/?—1/2/41.**G.**
Cow. ?/?—24/4/43.**H.**
Cow. 10—28/4/45.**G.**
Cow. 20/10—7/11/47.**H/I.**
Cow. 24/3—15/4/50.**G.**
Cow. 3—13/4/51.**C/H.**
Cow. 2—25/10/51.**H/I.**
Cow. 22/12/52—9/1/53.**H/I.**
Cow. 7—23/4/53.**C/H.**
Cow. 14/2—10/3/56.**G.**
Cow. 10—22/6/57.**C/L.**
Cow. 14—31/5/58.**H/I.**

BOILERS:
239.
271 (ex9397) 3/11/34*.
309 (ex9075) 1/2/41*.
304 (ex9070) 28/4/45.
2050 (new) 15/4/50.
2050 reno.26584 25/10/51.
26584 reno.26475 9/1/53.
26484 (ex??) 10/3/56.

SHEDS:
St Margarets.
Haymarket 6/5/55.
St Margarets 30/6/55.

RENUMBERED:
9054 7/11/24.
9173 2/6/46.
69173 15/4/50.

CONDEMNED: 12/1/61.
Cut up at Inverurie 17/3/61.

_____

9061

N.B.Loco. 21220.

To traffic 9/1916.

REPAIRS:
Cow. ?/?—?/3/22.**G.**
Cow. ?/?—27/1/34.**G.**
Cow. ?/?—26/9/35.**G.**
Cow. ?/?—12/6/37.**H.**
Cow. ?/?—14/7/37.**L.**
Cow. ?/?—20/5/39.**G.**
Cow. ?/?—19/4/41.**H.**
Cow. ?/?—20/2/43.**H.**
Cow. 17/2—3/3/45.**G.**
Cow. ?—17/3/45.**N/C.**
Cow. 11—30/5/47.**H/I.**
Cow. 11—29/4/50.**G.**
Cow. 28/11—31/12/55.**G.**

BOILERS:
241.
240 (ex914) ?/3/22.
1272 (ex9076) 27/1/34.
292 (ex9108) 3/3/45.
1264 (ex9194) 29/4/50.
1264 reno.26350 3/52.
26490 (ex69197) 31/12/55.

SHEDS:
Burntisland.
Carlisle Canal by 11/4/27.

RENUMBERED:
9061 ?/8/24.
9174 3/11/46.
69174 19/9/48 (at shed).

CONDEMNED: 15/11/58.
Cut up at Cowlairs 12/58.

_____

9065

N.B.Loco. 21221.

To traffic 9/1916.

REPAIRS:
Cow. ?/?—?/5/22.**G.**
Cow. ?/?—26/9/25.**G.**
Cow. ?/9—?/10/28.**G.**
Cow. ?/?—9/8/32.**G.**
Cow. ?/?—29/5/34.**G.**
Cow. ?/?—8/5/37.**H.**
Cow. ?/?—22/8/39.**G.**
Cow. ?/?—6/9/41.**H.**
Cow. ?/?—18/12/43.**H.**
Cow. 14/1—4/2/46.**G.**
Cow. 1—17/4/48.**H/I.**
Cow. 23/11—3/12/48.**C/L.**
Cow. 20/3—13/4/51.**G.**
Cow. 10/7—16/8/51.**C/H.**
Cow. 13—30/5/52.**C/L.**
Cow. 18/5—5/6/54.**H/I.**
Cow. 15/10—2/11/57.**G.**

BOILERS:
296.
241 (ex61) ?/5/22.

9065 (right column continued)
314 (ex9912) 26/9/25.
263 (ex9387) 29/5/34.
269 (exG9 9350) 22/8/39.
1925 (new) 4/2/46.
26534 (ex69218) 13/4/51.
26534 reno.26425 5/6/54.
26363 (ex??) 2/11/57.

SHEDS:
Burntisland.
St Margarets 10/4/31.

RENUMBERED:
9065 26/9/25.
9175 21/7/46.
69175 17/4/48.

CONDEMNED: 7/10/58.
Cut up at Kilmarnock 3/59.

_____

9069

N.B.Loco. 21222.

To traffic 10/1916.

REPAIRS:
Cow. ?/?—11/6/27.**G.**
Cow. ?/?—26/5/32.**G.**
Cow. ?/?—10/4/35.**G.**
Drop grate fitted.
Cow. ?/?—9/8/37.**L.**
Cow. 18—30/6/38.**G.**
Cow. ?/?—19/12/41.**G.**
Inv. 17/6—8/7/44.**G.**
Inv. 22/3—27/4/46.**L.**
Cow. 31/10—21/11/47.**H/I.**
Cow. 7/11—3/12/49.**G.**
Cow. 2—31/5/52.**H/I.**
Cow. 22/4—14/5/55.**G.**
Cow. 16/4—3/5/58.**H/I.**

BOILERS:
242.
304 (ex9926) 11/6/27.
248 (ex9108) 26/5/32.
1393 (ex9229) 30/6/38.
1360 (ex9076) 8/7/44.
1902 (ex9165) 3/12/49.
1902 reno.26422 31/5/52.
26407 (exC15 67469) 14/5/55.

SHEDS:
Eastfield.
Dawsholm 29/10/50.

RENUMBERED:
9069 ?/3/25.
9176 25/8/46.
69176 3/12/49.

CONDEMNED: 12/8/59.
Cut up at St Rollox 2/10/59.

_____

The new engines which Cowlairs built in 1923/24 did have the LNER black with single red lining. To No.125, paint date 1st March 1924, they added suffix B to the number. Whilst the suffix was used on the tank, the bufferbeam number did not include it.

At the front end of the running plate angle iron, Scottish area engines had the paint date put on. Ex works 8th March 1924, No.9147 was the first of the new engines to have full LNER number, which was also applied to Nos.9174, 9225 and 9227 to complete the order.

From March 1924 until the June 1928 painting economies took effect, full LNER number and single red lining was put on, No.9524 being so treated when ex Darlington works 30th September 1925. That and five others, Nos.9047, 9229, 9240, 9453, and 9528 were sent there for repair and went back showing North Eastern Railway painting details: lining was carried round from the sides to the back of the bunker and instead of the number in the centre it was applied to the buffer beam which also carried the classification.

Cowlairs also applied red lining until June 1928 but sometime in 1924 ceased to put the paint date on the engine.

(below) There were some exceptions to the unlined black used from 1928 because the Cowlairs incline banking engines continued to be fully lined on account of their frequent presence in Glasgow (Queen Street) station. The two passenger pilot engines at Aberdeen station were also accorded lining, Nos.9209 and 9210 being so often under public observation.

9070

N.B.Loco. 21223.

To traffic 12/1916.

REPAIRS:
NBL. ?/?—12/8/20.**G**.
Cow. ?/1—25/2/28.**G**.
Cow. 10—24/3/34.**G**.
Cow. ?/?—9/10/36.**G**.
Cow. ?/?—8/4/38.**L**.
Slip coupling fitted.
Cow. ?/?—4/11/39.**G**.
Cow. ?/?—28/1/42.**L**.
Cow. ?/?—28/11/42.**H**.
Cow. 24/3—7/4/45.**G**.
Cow. 11—28/8/47.**H/I**.
Cow. 5/7—6/8/49.**H/I**.
Cow. 16/4—10/5/52.**G**.
Cow. 4—8/8/52.**N/C**.
Cow. 16—19/12/52.**N/C**.
Cow. 15—20/3/54.**C/L**.
Cow. 19/10—6/11/54.**L/I**.
Cow. 5/9—8/10/55.**C/L**.
Cow. 30/11—17/12/55.**C/H**.
Cow. 17/12/57—14/1/58.**H/I**.

BOILERS:
243.
265 (ex9389) 25/2/28.
303 (ex9389) 24/3/34.
304 (ex9390) 4/11/39.
305 (ex9079) 7/4/45.
26337 (ex69143) 10/5/52.
26487 (ex69204) 17/12/55.

SHEDS:
Aberdeen.
Eastfield *by* 1/11/32.
Dawsholm 29/10/50.

RENUMBERED:
9070 ?/8/25.
9177 10/11/46.
69177 6/8/49.

CONDEMNED: 9/8/60.
Cut up at Cowlairs 20/8/60.

9276

N.B.Loco. 21228.

To traffic 1/1917.

REPAIRS:
Cow. ?/?—?/11/25.**G**.
Cow. ?/?—10/9/32.**G**.
Cow. ?/?—25/5/35.**G**.
Cow. ?/?—11/6/35.**L**.
Cow. ?/11/37—24/1/38.**G**.
Cow. ?/?—12/10/40.**H**.
Cow. 4—18/12/43.**G**.

Cow. 13/7—2/8/45.**H/I**.
Cow. 31/8—7/9/46.**L**.
Cow. 25/5—8/6/48.**G**.
Cow. 3—19/8/50.**H/I**.
Cow. 22/10—3/11/51.**N/C**.
Vacuum ejector fitted.
Cow. 27/8—15/9/53.**G**.
Cow. 27/6—7/7/56.**C/L**.
Cow. 22/8—15/9/56.**L/I**.

BOILERS:
262.
312 (ex9913) ?/11/25.
296 (ex9390) 10/9/32.
226 (exG9 9352) 24/1/38*.
1899 (new) 18/12/43.
1266 (ex9199) 8/6/48.
26391 (ex69200) 15/9/53.

SHED:
Eastfield.

RENUMBERED:
9276 ?/11/25.
9179 2/6/46.
69179 8/6/48.

CONDEMNED: 29/9/60.
Cut up at Cowlairs 21/1/61.

9453

N.B.Loco. 21229.

To traffic 1/1917.

REPAIRS:
Dar. 12/6—20/10/25.**G**.
Cow. ?/?—26/11/27.**L**.
Cow. ?/?—22/2/30.**G**.
Cow. ?/?—29/6/32.**G**.
Cow. ?/?—5/10/35.**G**.
Drop grate fitted.
Cow. ?/?—13/9/38.**H**.
Cow. ?/?—31/10/40.**L**.
Cow. ?/?—27/9/41.**G**.
Inv. ?/?—24/6/44.**H**.
Cow. ?/?—17/1/45.**L**.
Cow. 19—28/3/47.**G**.
Cow. 8—26/8/50.**H/I**.
Cow. 1—10/11/50.**C/L**.
Cow. 21—23/5/51.**N/C**.
Cow. 3—13/12/51.**N/C**.
Cow. 26/2/52.**N/C**.
Cow. 17/2—7/3/53.**G**.
Vacuum ejector fitted.
Efd. 20/5—3/7/54.**C/L**.
Cow. 7/7/54.**N/C**.
Cow. 11/11—3/12/55.**H/I**.

BOILERS:
274.
305 (ex9007) 22/2/30.
1275 (ex9147) 5/10/35.

245 (ex9913) 27/9/41.
1550 (ex9158) 28/3/47.
26461 (ex69170) 7/3/53.

SHEDS:
Eastfield.
St Rollox 12/8/57.
Eastfield 30/6/58.
Kittybrewster 30/3/59.
Aberdeen 3/3/60.

RENUMBERED:
9453 20/10/25.
9180 22/9/46.
69180 26/8/50.

CONDEMNED: 20/3/61.
Cut up at Inverurie, 14/4/61.

9142

N.B.Loco. 21224.

To traffic 2/1917.

REPAIRS:
Cow. ?/?—?/6/26 .**?**.
Cow. ?/8—1/9/28.**G**.
Cow. ?/?—26/1/35.**G**.
Drop grate fitted.
Cow. ?/8—20/9/37.**G**.
Cow. ?/?—21/12/40.**H**.
Cow. 6—27/3/43.**G**.
Cow. ?/?—15/4/44.**L**.
Cow. 21/6—12/7/45.**H/I**.
Cow. 3/2—5/3/48.**G**.
Vac. ejector & steam heat fitted.
Cow. 9—21/4/51.**L/I**.
Cow. 8—11/5/51.**C/L**.
Cow. 11/1—5/2/55.**G**.
Cow. 16—22/2/55.**N/C**.
Cow. 21/10—9/11/57.**H/I**.

BOILERS:
249.
237 (ex9047) 1/9/28.
253 (ex9223) 26/1/35.
1610 (new) 20/9/37.
1898 (new) 27/3/43.
1906 (ex9138) 5/3/48.
1906 reno.26535 21/4/51.
26459 (exC15 67475) 5/2/55.

SHED:
Eastfield.

RENUMBERED:
9142 ?/6/26.
9181 21/7/46.
69181 21/4/51.

CONDEMNED: 12/2/62.
Sold for scrap to G.H.Campbell, Airdrie, 10/7/62.

9165

N.B.Loco. 21225.

To traffic 3/1917.

REPAIRS:
Cow. ?/?—23/3/29.**G**.
Changed from steam to Westinghouse brake with vacuum ejector.
Cow. ?/?—21/4/34.**G**.
Cow. ?/?—1/3/35.**L**.
Cow. ?/?—18/2/37.**G**.
Drop grate fitted.
Cow. ?/?—8/7/39.**G**.
Cow. ?/?—11/11/39.**L**.
Cow. ?/?—28/8/43.**H**.
Cow. 20/3—12/4/46.**G**.
Cow. 13—21/2/48.**L**.
Cow. 8/11—9/12/50.**G**.
Cow. 20/4—2/5/53.**C/H**.
EFD. 23/7—6/8/54.**C/L**.
Cow. 16/6—2/7/55.**G**.
Westinghouse replaced by steam brake (still with vac. ejector).
Cow. 5—9/7/55.**N/C**.
Cow. 9—19/5/56.**C/L**.

BOILERS:
250.
293 (ex9915) 23/3/29.
1274 (ex9227) 21/4/34.
1867 (new) 8/7/39.
1945 (new) 12/4/46.
2063 (new) 9/12/50.
26435 (exC15 67456) 2/7/55.

SHED:
Eastfield.

RENUMBERED:
9165 ?/4/25.
9182 12/4/46.
69182 9/12/50.

CONDEMNED: 2/9/59.
Cut up at Cowlairs 16/10/59.

9166

N.B.Loco. 21226.

To traffic 3/1917.

REPAIRS:
Cow. 28/9/23—?/?/? .**?**.
Cow. ?/?—16/5/31.**G**.
Cow. ?—23/5/31.**N/C**.
Cow. ?/?—22/12/33.**G**.
Cow. ?/?—21/3/36.**G**.
Vacuum ejector fitted.
Cow. ?/?—17/6/37.**L**.
Cow. ?/?—11/2/39.**G**.

From July 1942 only NE was put on, and by then N15s had begun to go to Inverurie for overhauls. Ex works 20th May 1944, No.9907 had 12in. NE which was the size they used for it.

For only NE, Cowlairs continued to use 7½in. letters, No.9910 having them when ex works 11th August 1945. Beginning in March 1938 the LNER classification was displayed on the front buffer beam.

In the 1946 re-numbering N15 class became 9126 to 9224 in date order except that Nos.9071 and 9219 were misplaced as 9178 and 9185. Nine numbers were used for N15s in both the 1924 and 1946 numberings: 9142, 9154, 9165, 9166, 9209, 9210, 9219, 9223, and 9224, whilst 9125 was used by an N15 then an N14. No.9133 was renumbered from 9387 on 25th August 1946.

9166 cont./
Cow. ?/?—28/12/39.**L.**
Cow. 2—30/8/41.**G.**
Cow. ?/?—3/7/43.**H.**
Inv. ?/?—6/5/44.**L.**
Cow. 14/3—10/4/46.**G.**
Inv. ?/?—26/3/49.**H/I.**
Cow. 28/11—22/12/51.**G.**
Cow. 16/9—3/10/53.**H/I.**
Efd. 4—13/3/54.**C/L.**
Cow. 24/12/56—26/1/57.**G.**

BOILERS:
251.
270 *(ex9396)* 16/5/31.
267 *(ex9079)* 21/3/36.
1 *(ex9029)* 30/8/41.
1943 *(new)* 10/4/46.
26438 *(ex69190)* 22/12/51.
26438 reno.26349 3/10/53.
26485 *(ex??)* 26/1/57.

SHED:
Eastfield.

RENUMBERED:
9166 ?/4/24.
9183 3/11/46.
69183 26/3/49.

CONDEMNED: 13/11/61.
Sold for scrap to Arnott Young,
Old Kirkpatrick, 17/9/63.

_____

9259

N.B.Loco. 21227.

To traffic 3/1917.

REPAIRS:
Cow. ?/?—21/3/31.**G.**
Cow. ?/?—27/3/34.**G.**
Drop grate fitted.
Cow. 12—31/10/36.**G.**
Cow. ?/?—8/7/39.**L.**
Cow. ?/?—30/3/40.**H.**
Cow. ?/?—12/6/42.**L.**
Cow. 11—25/12/43.**G.**
Cow. 25/5—8/6/46.**H/I.**
Cow. 11—30/10/48.**G.**
Cow. 4—22/9/51.**L/I.**
Cow. 13—16/11/51.**C/L.**
Cow. 20/10—19/11/53.**G.**
Cow. 11—13/1/54.**N/C.**
Cow. 30/11—11/12/54.**C/L.**
Cow. 29/11—22/12/56.**L/I.**
Cow. 10—11/1/57.**N/C.**

BOILERS:
260.
1399 *(ex9388)* 21/3/31.
260 *(ex9923)* 31/10/36.

1900 *(new)* 25/12/43.
1609 *(ex9139)* 30/10/48.
1609 reno.26505 22/9/51.
26392 *(ex69163)* 19/11/53.

SHEDS:
Eastfield.
Dawsholm 29/10/50.

RENUMBERED:
9259 ?/7/24.
9184 2/6/46.
69184 30/10/48.

CONDEMNED: 23/11/60.
Cut up at Cowlairs 4/3/61.

_____

9020

N.B.Loco. 22278.

To traffic 2/1920.

REPAIRS:
Cow. ?/10—?/12/25.**G.**
Cow. ?/2—?/3/28.**G.**
Cow. ?/?—?/1/29.**?.**
Cow. ?—31/12/31.**G.**
Cow. ?/?—19/12/33.**G.**
Cow. 3—16/9/35.**G.**
Cow. ?/?—22/10/36.**L.**
Cow. 10—30/9/38.**G.**
Cow. ?/?—9/11/40.**H.**
Cow. ?/?—16/1/43.**H.**
Cow. 31/3—18/4/45.**G.**
Cow. 12—27/3/48.**G.**
Cow. 18/1—5/2/49.**C/H.**
Cow. 12—28/4/51.**H/I.**
Cow. 1—27/2/54.**G.**
Inv. 4—21/6/57.**L/I.**

BOILERS:
234.
1393 *(new)* ?/12/25.
1360 *(ex9910)* 31/12/31.
248 *(ex9069)* 30/9/38.
1272 *(ex9061)* 18/4/45.
302 *(ex9200)* 5/2/49.
302 reno.26379 28/4/51.
26470 *(ex69149)* 27/2/54.

SHED:
St Margarets.

RENUMBERED:
9020 ?/12/25.
9186 26/5/46.
69186 27/3/48.

CONDEMNED: 31/7/59.
Cut up at Inverurie, 13/10/59.

_____

9022

N.B.Loco. 22279.

To traffic 2/1920.

REPAIRS:
STM. ?/?—9/5/24.**H.**
Cow. ?/?—30/1/26.**G.**
Cow. ?/?—?/6/28.**G.**
Cow. ?/?—6/9/30.**G.**
Cow. ?/?—31/3/34.**G.**
Cow. ?/?—4/9/35.**G.**
Cow. ?/?—23/6/37.**G.**
Cow. ?/?—18/2/39.**G.**
Cow. 28/6—12/7/41.**G.**
Cow. ?/?—14/8/43.**H.**
Cow. 26/11—19/12/45.**H/I.**
Cow. 15—30/4/48.**G.**
Cow. 3/7—5/8/50.**H/I.**
Cow. 21/8—12/9/52.**G.**
Cow. 1—18/12/54.**H/I.**
Cow. 23/8—24/9/55.**C/L.**

BOILERS:
235.
1395 *(new)* 30/1/26.
274 *(ex9453)* 6/9/30.
1577 *(new)* 4/9/35.
249 *(ex9527)* 12/7/41.
1896 *(ex9149)* 30/4/48.
26457 *(ex69146)* 12/9/52.

SHEDS:
St Margarets.
Dalry Road 8/1/50.

RENUMBERED:
9022 9/5/24.
9187 2/6/46.
69187 30/4/48.

CONDEMNED: 8/12/59.
Cut up at Cowlairs 5/3/60.

_____

9029

N.B.Loco. 22280.

To traffic 2/1920.

REPAIRS:
Cow. ?/?—31/1/24.**?.**
Cow. ?/?—?/9/25.**?.**
Cow. ?/?—?/6/27.**G.**
Cow. ?/?—?/3/29.**G.**
Westinghouse brake and
vacuum ejector fitted.
Cow. ?/?—3/12/32.**G.**
Inv. ?/?—12/11/34.**L.**
Cow. ?/?—10/10/35.**G.**
Drop grate fitted.
Cow. 20/5—24/6/39.**H.**

Cow. 5—19/7/41.**G.**
Cow. ?/?—19/2/42.**L.**
Cow. ?/?—21/1/43.**L.**
Cow. ?/?—26/2/44.**H.**
Cow. 5—20/12/46.**G.**
Cow. 25/11—21/12/49.**H/I.**
Cow. 1—31/10/53.**G.**
Westinghouse replaced by steam
brake (still with vac. ejector).
Cow. 27/9—19/10/57.**L/I.**
Cow. 24—25/8/61.**N/C.**

BOILERS:
236.
235 *(ex9022)* ?/6/27.
1 *(ex9229)* 3/12/32.
1555 *(ex9387)* 24/6/39.
1559 *(ex9397)* 19/7/41.
1503 *(ex9055)* 20/12/46.
26406 *(ex69192)* 31/10/53.

SHEDS:
Bathgate.
Eastfield by 8/6/29.
Aberdeen 14/11/34.
Eastfield ?/12/35.
Kittybrewster ?/2/36.
Eastfield ?/10/36.
Aberdeen ?/3/38.
Parkhead ?/12/41.
Eastfield 1/6/42.

RENUMBERED:
9029 ?/9/25.
9188 22/6/46.
69188 21/12/49.

CONDEMNED: 1/10/62.
Cut up at Cowlairs 7/12/62.

_____

9049

N.B.Loco. 22281.

To traffic 2/1920.

REPAIRS:
Cow. 23/5—13/6/31.**G.**
Cow. ?/?—6/7/34.**G.**
Cow. ?/?—?/3/36.**L.**
Cow. ?/?—2/3/37.**G.**
Cow. ?/?—17/11/38.**H.**
Cow. ?/?—13/4/40.**G.**
Cow. 24/10—14/11/42.**G.**
Cow. ?/?—14/10/44.**H.**
Cow. 28/9—16/11/46.**L.**
Cow. 23/12/47—16/1/48.**G.**
Vac. ejector & steam heat fitted.
Cow. 1—25/11/50.**L/I.**
Cow. 4—21/2/53.**G.**
Cow. 16/4—8/5/54.**C/H.**
Cow. 12/7—13/9/55.**L/I.**

The illustration in the middle of page 118 shows the original No.9219 and this is No.9099 as re-numbered to 9219 on Sunday 3rd March 1946 at St Margarets shed. At the rear, in the centre of the bunker, the NBR custom of showing the engine number was continued.

The Cowlairs applied NE proved long lasting. It was put on No.9921 ex works 8th July 1944 and 9921 became 9158 from 6th October 1946. Despite a General overhaul and change to a newly built boiler – 10th February to 6th March 1947 – no repainting was done. At a Light repair – 9th to 14th August 1948 – this alteration to a BR number was made, and NE was still carried when 69158 next went to works 4th May 1949 but out from that on 21st May, it had BRITISH RAILWAYS on the tanks.

(top) Ex Cowlairs 26th September 1947, Cowlairs banker No.9191 (formerly 9097) had red lining restored but it was the only N15 so favoured. *(middle)* LNER and the red lined black livery had to serve until it went to works on 5th January 1954. Note the shabby re-numbering to 69191 on 18th May 1951. *(bottom)* Despite odd ones such as 9191 with painted and unshaded Gill sans, Cowlairs could still find normal shaded transfers to the end of the LNER. No.9189 was ex works 16th January 1948 from a 'General' and kept LNER to 4th February 1953 although the number was patched to 69189 on 25th November 1950.

9049 cont./
BOILERS:
238.
255 *(ex9230)* 13/6/31.
1605 *(new)* 2/3/37.
1893 *(new)* 14/11/42.
1398 *(exC15 7465)* 16/1/48.
26430 *(ex69148)* 21/2/53.

SHEDS:
Aberdeen
Eastfield 1/11/32.
St Rollox 17/6/57.
Aberdeen 16/8/57.

RENUMBERED:
9049 ?/8/25.
9189 3/11/46.
69189 25/11/50.

CONDEMNED: 18/4/58.
Cut up at Kilmarnock 6/58.

9096

N.B.Loco. 22282.

To traffic 2/1920.

REPAIRS:
Cow. ?/10/24—8/1/25.**G.**
Cow. ?/?—1/12/34.**G.**
Cow. ?/?—15/1/37.**G.**
Cow. ?/?—6/5/38.**L.**
Cow. ?/?—29/7/39.**G.**
Cow. ?/?—1/6/40.**L.**
Cow. 18/10—8/11/41.**G.**
Inv. ?/?—26/2/44.**H.**
Cow. 4—21/6/46.**G.**
Cow. 31/5—12/6/48.**H/I.**
Cow. 14/5—2/6/51.**G.**
Cow. 11—13/6/51.**N/C.**
Klm. 11—13/7/51.**G.**
Cow. 25/10/51—19/1/52.**C/L.**
Cow. 22/2—13/3/54.**L/I.**
Cow. 19/4—18/5/57.**G.**
Cow. 20—21/11/58.**N/C.**

BOILERS:
302.
244 *(ex9911)* 8/1/25.
314 *(ex9065)* 1/12/34.
291 *(ex9219)* 8/11/41*.
1263 *(ex9071)* 21/6/46.
26573 *(ex69196)* 2/6/51.
26573 *reno.26464 13/3/54.*
26412 *(ex??)* 18/5/57.

SHEDS:
Thornton Jct.
Parkhead 23/9/27.

RENUMBERED:
9096 8/1/25.

9190 25/8/46.
69190 12/6/48.

CONDEMNED: 16/8/60.
Cut up at Inverurie 7/10/60.

9097

N.B.Loco. 22283.

To traffic 2/1920.

REPAIRS:
Cow. ?/?—?/5/25.**?.**
Cow. ?/?—18/4/31.**G.**
Cow. ?/?—12/1/34.**G.**
Cow. 21/3—23/4/36.**G.**
Vacuum ejector, slip coupling, and drop grate fitted.
Cow. ?/?—6/5/36.**L.**
Cow. ?/?—22/3/39.**H.**
Cow. 4—18/7/42.**G.**
Cow. 23/12/44—6/1/45.**H.**
Cow. 21/8—26/9/47.**G.**
Cow. 5—11/3/48.**C/L.**
Cow. 7—18/5/51.**H/I.**
Cow. 23/5—7/6/51.**C/H.**
Cow. 5/1—4/2/54.**H/I.**
Cow. 20/8—11/9/57.**G.**
Cow. 26—28/9/57.**N/C.**

BOILERS:
245.
254 *(ex9224)* 18/4/31.
1580 *(new)* 23/4/36.
1276 *(ex9386)* 18/7/42.
1612 *(exC15 7453)* 26/9/47.
26547 *(ex69206* 18/5/51.
26547 *reno.26438 4/2/54.*
26452 *(ex??)* 11/9/57.

SHEDS:
Bathgate.
Eastfield 2/4/26.

RENUMBERED:
9097 ?/5/25.
9191 3/2/46.
69191 18/5/51.

CONDEMNED: 1/10/62.
Cut up at Cowlairs 23/11/62.

9106

N.B.Loco. 22284.

To traffic 2/1920.

REPAIRS:
Cow. ?/2—?/4/27.**G.**
Cow. ?/?—27/2/32.**G.**
Cow. ?/?—16/1/34.**G.**

Cow. ?/?—?/3/36.**G.**
Cow. ?/?—2/4/38.**G.**
Cow. ?/?—9/6/38.**L.**
Cow. 15/2—8/3/41.**G.**
Cow. ?/?—28/6/41.**L.**
Cow. ?/?—3/7/43.**H.**
Inv. ?/?—22/1/44.**H.**
Cow. ?/?—31/10/44.**L.**
Cow. 5—27/2/46.**G.**
Cow. 14—16/7/47.**N/C.**
Cow. 9—28/2/48.**G.**
Cow. 30/6—14/7/49.**H/I.**
Cow. 28/9—10/10/49.**N/C.**
Cow. 9—21/10/50.**C/H.**
Cow. 19—29/12/51.**L/I.**
Cow. 24/8—10/9/53.**H/I.**
Cow. 9—14/8/54.**C/L.**
Cow. 4—22/10/55.**G.**
THJ. 20—25/4/56.**C/L.**

BOILERS:
246.
262 *(ex9276)* ?/4/27.
286 *(ex9908)* 27/2/32.
1554 *(new)* 16/1/34.
271 *(ex9054)* 8/3/41*.
1871 *(ex9078)* 27/2/46.
2059 *(new)* 21/10/50.
2059 *reno.26593 29/12/51.*
26593 *reno.26484 10/9/53.*
26488 *(ex69182)* 22/10/55.

SHEDS:
Thornton Jct.
Dunfermline 23/1/35.

RENUMBERED:
9106 ?/9/24.
9192 10/11/46.
69192 14/7/49.

CONDEMNED: 2/3/59.
Cut up at Inverurie 1/9/59.

9107

N.B.Loco. 22285.

To traffic 3/1920.

REPAIRS:
Cow. ?/?—3/9/24.**G.**
Cow. ?—29/9/28.**G.**
Cow. ?/?—?/7/33.**G.**
Cow. ?/?—11/7/35.**G.**
Cow. ?/?—14/7/37.**H.**
Cow. ?/?—18/11/39.**G.**
Cow. ?/?—9/7/41.**L.**
Cow. ?/?—21/10/42.**H.**
Inv. 23/9—7/10/44.**G.**
Cow. 15/9—11/10/47.**G.**
Cow. 5—22/12/49.**H/I.**
Cow. 10—27/9/52.**G.**
Cow. 9/7—2/9/54.**H/I.**

BOILERS:
247.
292 *(ex9914)* 29/9/28.
1868 *(new)* 18/11/39.
265 *(ex9390)* 7/10/44.
1276 *(ex9191)* 11/10/47.
26355 *(ex69168)* 27/9/52.

SHEDS:
Bathgate.
Parkhead 25/8/26.

RENUMBERED:
9107 3/9/24.
9193 14/7/46.
69193 22/12/49.

CONDEMNED: 7/8/58.
Cut up at Kilmarnock 12/58.

9108

N.B.Loco. 22286.

To traffic 3/1920.

REPAIRS:
Cow. ?/?—30/1/32.**G.**
Cow. ?/?—23/1/34.**G.**
Cow. ?/?—6/5/36.**G.**
Cow. ?/?—20/10/37.**G.**
Cow. ?/?—25/10/39.**L.**
Cow. ?/?—22/3/40.**G.**
Cow. ?/?—5/9/42.**H.**
Cow. ?/?—2/12/44.**G.**
Cow. 4—18/5/46.**L.**
Cow. 17/11—3/12/47.**H/I.**
Cow. 6—25/3/50.**G.**
Cow. 20/11—8/12/51.**H/I.**
Cow. 15/9—12/10/53.**G.**
Cow. 14/8—1/9/56.**H/I.**

BOILERS:
248.
300 *(ex9922)* 30/1/32.
290 *(ex9926)* 20/10/37.
292 *(ex9107)* 22/3/40.
1264 *(ex9077)* 2/12/44.
1270 *(ex9133)* 25/3/50.
1270 *reno.26445 8/12/51.*
26420 *(ex69179)* 12/10/53.

SHED:
Parkhead.

RENUMBERED:
9108 ?/1/25.
9194 3/2/46.
69194 25/3/50.

CONDEMNED: 22/10/60.
Cut up at Cowlairs 24/12/60.

No.9151 had LNER restored and got normal shaded transfers when ex works on 26th December 1947. Seen here in April 1950, note that a BR shed allocation plate had been fitted on the smokebox door, 65C indicating that it was a Parkhead engine.

(above) When ex works 24th October 1947, No.9147 had shaded transfers but this change was made at a Light repair 22nd January 1949 when the smokebox number plate was added. It kept LNER until it went to works 15th November 1951.

Even when ex works 17th April 1948 No.69199 still had LNER and its figures in shaded transfers. They were even used as usual on the buffer beam.

9240

N.B.Loco. 22287.

To traffic 3/1920.

REPAIRS:
Dar. 3/6—25/9/25.**G.**
Cow. ?/?—24/1/31.**G.**
Cow. ?/?—25/7/35.**G.**
Cow. ?/?—10/8/37.**G.**
Cow. ?/?—16/12/39.**G.**
Cow. ?/?—17/2/40.**L.**
Cow. 23/5—13/6/42.**H.**
Cow. ?/?—6/5/44.**H.**
Cow. 26/11—7/12/46.**H/I.**
Cow. 15/1—6/2/48.**G.**
Cow. 23/11—16/12/49.**H/I.**
Cow. 28/12/51—19/1/52.**G.**
Inv. 16/7—18/8/54.**L/I.**

BOILERS:
256.
1395 (ex9022) 24/1/31.
247 (ex9925) 10/8/37.
1610 (ex9134) 6/2/48.
26512 (ex69147) 19/1/52.
26512 reno.26403 18/8/54.

SHED:
Parkhead.

RENUMBERED:
9240 25/9/25.
9195 1/12/46.
69195 16/12/49.

CONDEMNED: 14/3/58.
Cut up at Kilmarnock 5/58.

9519

R.Stephenson. 3851.

To traffic 19/1/23.

REPAIRS:
KPS. ?/?—4/7/23.**N/C.**
Cow. ?/?—30/10/30.**G.**
Cow. 18/8—8/9/34.**G.**
Cow. 6/2—3/3/37.**G.**
Cow. ?/?—25/11/39.**G.**
Cow. 6/6—4/7/42.**H.**
Cow. ?/?—7/10/44.**H.**
Cow. 22/5—7/6/47.**G.**
Cow. 16/3—2/4/49.**H/I.**
Cow. 19/3—7/4/51.**G.**
Cow. 7—23/1/54.**H/I.**
Cow. 31/12/56—26/1/57.**G.**
Cow. 22/2—9/3/57.**C/L.**

BOILERS:
275.
1356 (ex9390) 30/10/30.

1606 (new) 3/3/37.
1999 (new) 7/6/47.
26461 (ex69223) 7/4/51.
26461 reno.26366 23/1/54.
26475 (ex??) 26/1/57.

SHEDS:
Kipps.
Hamilton 30/11/59.

RENUMBERED:
9519 ?/10/25.
9196 12/4/46.
69196 2/4/49.

CONDEMNED: 1/10/62.
Cut up at Cowlairs 15/11/63.

9520

R.Stephenson 3852.

To traffic 21/1/23.

REPAIRS:
Cow. ?/?—5/12/31.**G.**
Cow. ?/?—14/7/34.**G.**
Cow. ?/?—18/5/37.**H.**
Cow. ?/?—4/5/40.**G.**
Cow. ?/?—15/5/43.**H.**
Cow. 18/7—21/8/45.**G.**
Cow. 10/2—5/3/48.**H/I.**
Cow. 20/12/50—13/1/51.**G.**
Cow. 23/3—4/4/53.**H/I.**
Cow. 27/8—18/9/53.**G.**
Cow. 18/4—7/5/55.**G.**
Cow. 27—30/6/56.**C/L.**
Cow. 28/2—15/3/58.**L/I.**

BOILERS:
276.
277 (ex9521) 14/7/34.
1267 (ex9524) 4/5/40.
1921 (new) 21/8/45.
2066 (new) 13/1/51.
2066 reno.26490 4/4/53.
26476 (ex??) 7/5/55.

SHEDS:
Kipps.
Carlisle Canal 19/3/45.
Eastfield 20/7/51.

RENUMBERED:
9520 ?/8/25.
9197 5/5/46.
69197 19/9/48 (at shed).

CONDEMNED: 18/12/59.
Cut up at Cowlairs 20/2/60.

9521

R.Stephenson 3853.

To traffic 2/2/23.

REPAIRS:
Cow. ?/?—23/1/32.**G.**
Cow. ?/?—21/4/34.**G.**
Cow. ?/?—10/6/36.**G.**
Cow. ?/?—9/12/38.**G.**
Cow. 14—28/12/40.**G.**
Cow. ?/?—22/1/44.**H.**
Cow. 11/3—6/4/46.**G.**
Cow. 7—20/5/48.**H/I.**
Cow. 8/8—1/9/51.**G.**
Cow. 13/9/51.**N/C.**
Inv. 29/3—16/4/54.**L/I.**
Cow. 25/10—12/11/55.**G.**
Cow. 18/6—2/8/57.**C/L.**

BOILERS:
277.
1268 (ex9067) 21/4/34.
289 (ex9055) 28/12/40.
1277 (ex9391) 6/4/46.
26483 (ex69156) 1/9/51.
26483 reno.26380 16/4/54.
26467 (exC15 67470) 12/11/55.

SHED:
Parkhead.

RENUMBERED:
9521 ?/3/25.
9198 12/5/46.
69198 20/5/48.

CONDEMNED: 6/6/60.
Cut up at Cowlairs 18/6/60.

9522

R.Stephenson 3854.

To traffic 12/2/23.

REPAIRS:
Cow. ?/?—?/2/25.**?.**
Cow. ?/12/26—?/3/27.**G.**
Cow. ?/7—13/8/32.**G.**
Cow. ?/?—28/3/35.**G.**
Cow. ?/?—28/3/36.**L.**
Cow. ?/?—27/11/37.**G.**
Cow. ?/?—2/3/40.**H.**
Cow. ?/?—13/2/43.**G.**
Cow. ?/?—28/6/43.**L.**
Cow. 11—28/1/46.**H/I.**
Cow. 5—17/4/48.**G.**
Cow. 10—15/10/49.**C/L.**
Cow. 3—9/11/49.**N/C.**
Cow. 9/7—10/8/51.**H/I.**
Cow. 2—21/3/53.**G.**
Cow. 15/5—2/6/56.**H/I.**

Cow. 4/7/56.**C/L.**
Cow. 30/7—4/8/56.**C/L.**

BOILERS:
278.
272 (ex9398) 13/8/32.
300 (ex9108) 27/11/37.
1266 (ex9912) 13/2/43.
2013 (new) 17/4/48.
2013 reno.26577 10/8/51.
26371 (ex69189) 21/3/53.

SHED:
Parkhead.

RENUMBERED:
9522 ?/2/25.
9199 12/4/46.
69199 17/4/48.

CONDEMNED: 18/5/61.
Cut up Heatheryknowe 3/6/61.

9523

R.Stephenson 3855.

To traffic 23/2/23.

REPAIRS:
Cow. ?/4—?/6/28.**G.**
Cow. 11—25/3/33.**G.**
Cow. ?/?—29/5/36.**G.**
Cow. ?/12/38—19/1/39.**G.**
Cow. ?/?—1/3/41.**H.**
Cow. ?/?—29/1/44.**G.**
Cow. 12—19/5/45.**L.**
Cow. 24/2—8/3/47.**H/I.**
Cow. 29/11—24/12/48.**G.**
Cow. 26/6—13/7/51.**H/I.**
Cow. 6—17/7/53.**G.**
Cow. 18/8—3/9/55.**H/I.**

BOILERS:
279.
235 (ex9029) 25/3/33.
1614 (new) 19/1/39.
302 (ex9919) 29/1/44.
1583 (ex9152) 24/12/48.
1583 reno.26499 13/7/51.
26462 (ex69209) 17/7/53.

SHEDS:
Parkhead.
Polmont 19/1/34.

RENUMBERED:
9523 ?/12/25.
9200 1/12/46.
69200 24/12/48.

CONDEMNED: 12/6/58.
Cut up at Kilmarnock 2/59.

(above) No.9160 was ex Cowlairs 27th September 1947 with shaded transfers. Ex works again 30th March 1950, as shown here next day, the BR number had been patched on and the smokebox plate fitted. Although the engine also had a shed plate fitted, the shed name DUNFERMLINE was displayed on the buffer beam. Its LNER transfers lasted to 11th November 1952.

(left) LNER 9195 in shaded transfers was ex works 6th February 1948 and might have been expected to have an E prefix, a process which Cowlairs almost entirely ignored. Patching made it 69195 from 16th December 1949 when it also got the smokebox plate. The LNER remained to 28th December 1951.

This was an outstanding example of the reluctance of Cowlairs to discard LNER. Still using transfers, No.9181 was ex works 5th March 1948 to become 69181 at a Light repair 21st April 1951 but it then kept LNER until it went to works as late as 11th January 1955, seven years into BR ownership! Note that it got the correct 6 and 9.

Cowlairs did not use transfers exclusively. Ex works 7th June 1947 No.9196 had letters and figures in yellow painted and unshaded Gill sans but with modified 6 and 9. Out 2nd April 1949, the number was patched to 69196 and smokebox plate had been fitted. That guise remained to 19th March 1951.

No.69142 was an oddity in getting the widely spaced figures on the tank. Its LNER was restored by transfers when ex works 28th December 1946 and at a light repair 17th July 1948 it became 69142 as shown. Already almost impossible to discern, the LNER was carried until 5th April 1949.

When No.9214 became 69214 on 21st January 1950, after a Heavy Intermediate repair, no effort was made to change LNER or to alter 9214 on the back of the bunker. They survived to 12th November 1953.

9524

R.Stephenson 3856.

To traffic 1/3/23.

REPAIRS:
Dar. 3/6—30/9/25.**G.**
Cow. ?/1—?/3/27.**G.**
Cow. ?/?—25/2/33.**G.**
Cow. ?/?—6/5/35.**G.**
Cow. ?/?—12/10/37.**H.**
Cow. ?/?—23/3/40.**G.**
Cow. ?/?—3/10/42.**H.**
Inv. ?/?—20/5/44.**H.**
Inv. ?/?—6/7/45.**L.**
Inv. 23/3—20/4/46.**L.**
Inv. 31/1—20/2/47.**G.**
Cow. 22/4—5/5/48.**L.**
Cow. 13/9—1/10/49.**H/I.**
Inv. 14—23/5/51.**C/L.**
Cow. 27/4—16/5/53.**G.**
Inv. 14/6—1/7/55.**L/I.**
Inv. 6—24/2/56.**C/L.**
Inv. 9—29/3/56.**C/L.**

BOILERS:
280.
1267 *(ex9060)* 25/2/33.
1279 *(ex9922)* 23/3/40.
1279 reno.26455 23/5/51.
26468 *(ex69199)* 16/5/53.

SHEDS:
Dunfermline.
Aberdeen 18/12/49.
Keith 16/12/57.

RENUMBERED:
9524 30/9/25.
9201 12/1/47.
69201 5/5/48.

CONDEMNED: 10/1/58.
Cut up at Kilmarnock 3/58.

9525

R.Stephenson 3857.

To traffic 8/3/23.

REPAIRS:
Cow. ?—20/3/23.**N/C.**
For painting.
Cow. ?/?—12/3/25.**G.**
Cow. ?/8—?/10/27.**G.**
Cow. ?/?—25/2/33.**G.**
Cow. ?/?—28/12/35.**G.**
Cow. ?/?—16/12/37.**G.**
Cow. ?/?—26/1/40.**G.**
Inv. ?/?—5/12/42.**H.**
Cow. 27/1—3/2/45.**G.**
Cow. 22—29/9/45.**L.**

Cow. 14—21/9/46.**L.**
Cow. 8—23/5/47.**G.**
Cow. 25/1—19/2/49.**H/I.**
Cow. 31/1—27/2/52.**G.**
Inv. 19/10—13/11/53.**G.**
Cow. 7/5—2/6/56.**H/I.**
THJ. 18—25/12/56.**C/L.**
DFU. 14—28/11/57.**C/L.**

BOILERS:
281.
264 *(ex9391)* 25/2/33.
252 *(ex9219)* 28/12/35.
281 *(ex9209)* 23/5/47.
26443 *(ex69183)* 27/2/52.
26408 *(exC15 67464)* 13/11/53.

SHEDS:
Bathgate.
Dunfermline 19/1/39.

RENUMBERED:
9525 12/3/25.
9202 27/7/46.
69202 19/2/49.

CONDEMNED: 17/5/60.
Cut up at Cowlairs 4/6/60.

9526

R.Stephenson 3858.

To traffic 15/3/23.

REPAIRS:
Cow. ?/8—?/10/29.**G.**
Cow. ?/?—3/2/32.**G.**
Cow. 7—21/4/34.**G.**
Cow. ?/?—18/12/35.**G.**
Drop grate fitted.
Cow. ?/?—27/7/38.**H.**
Cow. ?/?—20/7/40.**G.**
Cow. ?/?—9/10/43.**H.**
Inv. 6—27/4/46.**G.**
Cow. 15—29/3/47.**L.**
Inv. 15—29/11/47.**L.**
Cow. 21/10—17/11/48.**H/I.**
Cow. 10—22/2/50.**L/I.**
Cow. 4/3—1/4/52.**G.**
Cow. 18—30/5/53.**C/L.**
Cow. 24/11—12/12/53.**H/I.**
Vacuum ejector fitted.
Daw. 7—15/7/54.**C/L.**
Daw. 12—15/1/55.**C/L.**
Daw. 18—29/10/55.**L/I.**
Daw. 25/11—21/12/57.**C/L.**

BOILERS:
282.
1271 *(ex9075)* 21/4/34.
237 *(exN14 9861)* 20/7/40.
1942 *(new)* 27/4/46.
26405 *(ex69126)* 1/4/52.

SHEDS:
Eastfield.
Dawsholm 29/10/50.

RENUMBERED:
9526 ?/2/26.
9203 1/12/46.
69203 17/11/48.

CONDEMNED: 26/6/58.
Cut up at Cowlairs 6/60.

9527

R.Stephenson 3859.

To traffic 22/3/23.

REPAIRS:
Cow. ?/?—?/8/25.**G.**
Cow. ?/3—?/5/27.**G.**
Cow. ?/?—26/3/32.**G.**
Cow. ?/?—1/5/34.**G.**
Cow. ?/?—7/7/36.**G.**
Cow. ?/?—7/12/38.**G.**
Cow. ?/?—27/1/39.**L.**
Cow. 15—29/3/41.**G.**
Cow. ?/?—13/9/41.**L.**
Cow. ?/?—18/9/43.**H.**
Cow. 21/4—5/5/45.**H.**
Cow. 24/3—5/4/47.**G.**
Cow. 15—17/7/47.**N/C.**
Cow. 20/10—13/11/48.**H/I.**
Cow. 21/11—15/12/50.**G.**
Cow. 23/6—5/7/52.**H/I.**
Cow. 4—24/9/53.**H/I.**
DFU. 21—23/8/54.**C/L.**
Cow. 27/6—15/7/55.**G.**

BOILERS:
283.
234 *(ex9926)* 26/3/32.
249 *(ex9224)* 7/7/36.
1554 *(ex9106)* 29/3/41.
1889 *(ex9170)* 5/4/47.
2062 *(new)* 15/12/50.
2062 reno.26487 5/7/52.
26398 *(exC15 67473)* 15/7/55.

SHEDS:
Dunfermline.
Dundee 15/7/57.
Thornton Jct. 14/12/59.

RENUMBERED:
9527 ?/8/25.
9204 12/1/47.
69204 13/11/48.

CONDEMNED: 16/7/62.
Cut up at Inverurie 19/10/62.

9528

R.Stephenson 3860.

To traffic 26/3/23.

REPAIRS:
Cow. ?—?/3/23.**N/C.**
For painting.
Dar. 26/5—30/9/25.**G.**
Cow. ?/?—31/12/32.**G.**
Cow. ?/?—12/6/34.**G.**
Cow. ?—13/7/35.**G.**
Cow. ?/?—31/3/37.**G.**
Cow. ?/?—7/4/39.**G.**
Cow. 2—16/11/40.**G.**
Cow. ?/?—6/11/43.**H.**
Cow. 1—15/9/45.**L.**
Cow. 13—20/10/45.**L.**
Cow. 13/9—9/10/47.**G.**
Cow. 14/11—3/12/49.**H/I.**
Cow. 16—26/8/50.**L/I.**
Cow. 18/8—12/9/52.**G.**
Cow. 5—24/10/53.**H/I.**
Cow. 28/3—2/4/55.**C/L.**
Cow. 8/10—3/11/56.**G.**

BOILERS:
284.
1273 *(ex9077)* 31/12/32.
243 *(ex9399)* 13/7/35.
1281 *(exN14 9863)* 16/11/40.
1273 *(ex9121)* 9/10/47.
1988 *(exC15 67463)* 12/9/52.
1988 reno.26453 12/9/52.
26481 *(ex??)* 3/11/56.

SHEDS:
St Margarets.
Haymarket 23/3/28.
Bathgate *by* 23/10/30.
Haymarket *by* ?/1/33.
Eastfield ?/3/40.
Dawsholm 29/10/50.

RENUMBERED:
9528 30/9/25.
9205 3/11/46.
69205 3/12/49.

CONDEMNED: 18/2/60.
Cut up at Cowlairs 5/3/60.

9019

Cowlairs.

To traffic 30/10/23.

REPAIRS:
Cow. ?/5—?/7/26.**G.**
Cow. ?/?—4/11/33.**G.**
Cow. ?/?—15/12/36.**G.**
Cow. 23/9—7/10/39.**G.**

No.69198, ex works 20ᵗʰ May 1948, was a hybrid. Although it got BRITISH RAILWAYS, this was so placed that first intention was to have the number still on the tank. Before it went into traffic the number was transferred to the bunker, which was the standard position from then on. The first N15 with a number on the bunker was 69187 ex works 30ᵗʰ April 1948.

(below) By mid-June 1948 BRITISH RAILWAYS had been centred on the tank and on the same level as the number. Although not yet of the same size, the BR number was also now appearing in the centre of the rear panel of the bunker. No.69206 was ex works 19ᵗʰ June 1948.

No.69159 as shown was ex works on 10ᵗʰ July 1948, and still had the front number on the buffer beam. Cowlairs did not begin to fit smokebox plates until 10ᵗʰ September 1948 and No.69139 on 8ᵗʰ October 1948 was probably the first N15 to have one. Note the lamp iron still on top of the smokebox.

9019 cont./
Cow. ?/?—27/3/43.**H.**
Cow. 7/2—5/3/46.**G.**
Cow. 16/11—7/12/46.**L.**
Cow. 9—22/8/47.**L.**
Cow. 7—19/6/48.**H/I.**
Cow. ?/?—?/4/49.**L.**
Cow. 24/4—12/5/51.**G.**
Cow. 10—28/8/53.**H/I.**
KPS. 19—21/9/55.**N/C.**
Cow. 5—30/6/36.**L/I.**

BOILERS:
1262.
1277 *(ex9078)* 4/11/33.
1558 *(ex9154)* 7/10/39.
1938 *(new)* 5/3/46.
26490 *(ex9185)* 12/5/51.
26490 reno.26386 28/8/53.

SHED:
Kipps.

RENUMBERED:
9019 ?/7/26.
9206 22/6/46.
69206 19/6/48.

CONDEMNED: 17/5/60.
Cut up at Cowlairs 4/6/60.

9023

Cowlairs.

To traffic 3/11/23.

REPAIRS:
Cow. ?/1—?/2/29.**G.**
Cow. ?/?—3/8/31.**G.**
Cow. ?/?—1/12/34.**G.**
Cow. ?/?—7/9/37.**H.**
Cow. ?/?—27/10/39.**L.**
Cow. 25/5—15/6/40.**G.**
Cow. 20/2—6/3/43.**H.**
Cow. 12—28/6/45.**H/I.**
Cow. 24/10—8/11/47.**H/I.**
Cow. 18/2—19/3/49.**G.**
Inv. 23/5—8/6/51.**L/I.**
Inv. 13/6/51.**N/C.**
Cow. 27/4—22/5/54.**G.**
KPS. 21—23/9/55.**C/L.**
Cow. 19/6—14/7/56.**G.**

BOILERS:
1263.
275 *(ex9154)* 1/12/34.
1401 *(exG9 9351)* 15/6/40.
2047 *(new)* 19/3/49.
2047 reno.26581 8/6/51.
26368 *(ex69214)* 22/5/54.

SHEDS:
Kipps.

Hamilton 30/11/59.
Polmadie 10/12/59.

RENUMBERED:
9023 ?/9/25.
9207 26/5/46.
69207 19/3/49.

CONDEMNED: 17/2/60.
Cut up at Cowlairs 12/3/60.

9031

Cowlairs.

To traffic 17/11/23.

REPAIRS:
Cow. ?/?—9/9/34.**G.**
Cow. ?/?—11/11/37.**H.**
Drop grate fitted.
Cow. ?/?—27/10/39.**L.**
Cow. ?/?—15/7/40.**G.**
Cow. ?/?—5/2/44.**H.**
Cow. 8—19/2/47.**G.**
Cow. 1—16/10/48.**L.**
Cow. 1—18/2/50.**H/I.**
Cow. ?/?—?/3/51.**L/I.**
Cow. 12/11—1/12/51.**G.**
Cow. 2—15/7/52.**C/L.**
Inv. 8—26/2/54.**L/I.**
Daw. 27/7—12/8/54.**C/L.**
Cow. 31/1—5/2/55.**N/C.**
Cow. 14/12/56—12/1/57.**G.**

BOILERS:
1264.
295 *(ex9047)* 9/9/34.
298 *(ex9909)* 15/7/40.
1394 *(exC15 7479)* 19/2/47.
26536 *(ex9135)* 1/12/51.
26536 reno.26427 26/2/54.
26384 *(ex??)* 12/1/57.

SHEDS:
Eastfield.
Dawsholm 29/10/50.

RENUMBERED:
9031 ?/11/25.
9208 3/11/46.
69208 16/10/48.

CONDEMNED: 25/11/59.
Cut up at Cowlairs 16/1/60.

9052

Cowlairs.

To traffic 13/11/23.

REPAIRS:
Cow. ?/?—12/8/26.**G.**
Cow. 4—11/7/31.**G.**
Cow. ?/?—25/1/34.**G.**
Cow. 4/7—11/8/36.**G.**
Cow. ?/?—10/6/38.**G.**
Cow. ?/?—3/8/38.**L.**
Cow. ?/?—26/10/40.**G.**
Cow. ?/?—5/6/43.**H.**
Cow. ?/?—18/11/44.**H.**
Cow. 14—25/4/47.**G.**
Cow. 24/5—4/6/49.**H/I.**
Cow. 22/5—8/6/51.**H/I.**
Cow. 7—28/4/53.**G.**
Cow. 17—19/8/53.**N/C.**
Cow. 13—23/4/55.**N/C.**
Cow. 10—28/5/55.**C/H.**
Cow. 28/6—5/7/55.**N/C.**
Cow. 28/12/56—24/1/57.**L/I.**
Cow. 26—30/8/58.**C/L.**

BOILERS:
1265.
241 *(ex9154)* 11/7/31.
1394 *(exN14 9860)* 11/8/36.
281 *(ex9257)* 26/10/40.
1997 *(new)* 25/4/47.
1997 reno.26571 8/6/51.
26378 *(ex69180)* 28/4/53.
26466 *(exC15 67477)* 28/5/55.

SHEDS:
Bathgate.
Parkhead *by* 2/29.

RENUMBERED:
9052 12/8/26.
9209 20/10/46.
69209 4/6/49.

CONDEMNED: 22/10/60.
Cut up at Inverurie 17/11/60.

9055

Cowlairs.

To traffic 17/11/23.

REPAIRS:
Cow. ?/6—?/7/28.**G.**
Cow. ?/?—13/10/31.**?.**
Cow. ?/?—24/2/34.**G.**
Cow. ?/?—21/2/36.**G.**
Cow. ?/?—8/6/37.**L.**
Cow. ?/?—22/2/38.**H.**
Cow. ?/?—17/8/39.**L.**
Cow. ?/?—4/11/39.**L.**
Cow. ?/?—3/8/40.**G.**
Cow. ?/?—27/2/42.**L.**
Cow. ?/?—8/5/43.**L.**
Cow. ?/?—17/7/43.**H.**
Inv. ?/?—19/10/44.**L.**
Cow. 12—30/11/46.**G.**

Cow. 9—27/11/48.**H/I.**
Cow. 16/4—4/5/51.**G.**
Cow. 18/2—22/3/52.**H/I.**
Cow. 7—12/9/53.**C/L.**
Cow. 8—27/2/54.**C/H.**
Cow. 15—28/6/54.**C/L.**
Cow. 29/4—14/5/55.**L/I.**
Cow. 20—24/11/56.**C/L.**

BOILERS:
1266.
289 *(ex9225)* 24/2/34.
1503 *(ex9078)* 3/8/40.
1991 *(new)* 30/11/46.
26450 *(ex69169)* 4/5/51.
26450 reno.26358 22/3/52.
26465 *(ex69221)* 27/2/54.

SHED:
Parkhead.

RENUMBERED:
9055 ?/9/26.
9210 27/1/46.
69210 27/11/48.

CONDEMNED: 29/10/57.
Cut up at Kilmarnock 2/58.

9060

Cowlairs.

To traffic 20/11/23.

REPAIRS:
Cow. ?/?—?/3/26.**?.**
Cow. ?/?—3/12/32.**G.**
Cow. ?/?—6/12/35.**G.**
Cow. 6—27/11/37.**G.**
Cow. ?/?—2/12/39.**G.**
Cow. ?/?—21/12/40.**L.**
Cow. 29/11—27/12/41.**G.**
Cow. ?/?—23/3/43.**L.**
Inv. 29/7—12/8/44.**H.**
Cow. 13/11—5/12/46.**G.**
Cow. 9/8—3/9/48.**H/I.**
Cow. 21/8—8/9/51.**G.**
Inv. 17/9—8/10/54.**L/I.**
Cow. 17/6—10/7/57.**G.**
Cow. 19/7—17/8/57.**C/L.**

BOILERS:
1267.
312 *(ex9276)* 3/12/32.
279 *(ex9911)* 27/11/37.
1275 *(ex9453)* 27/12/41.
1393 *(ex9069)* 12/8/44.
246 *(ex9154)* 5/12/46.
26453 *(ex69198)* 8/9/51.
26453 reno.26361 8/10/54.
26474 *(ex??)* 10/7/57.

This painting was put on No.69137 ex works 18th June 1948, and in addition to its number, the buffer beam also carried N15 and the name of the shed to which allocated. This was one engine on which the upper lamp iron had already changed position and pattern.

Starting in October 1948 the BR lining of red, cream and grey began to be put on, and No.69184 which was ex works 30th October 1948, was the first N15 to have it applied. No.69204 was ex Cowlairs 13th November 1948 duly lined but with letters and figures lower than usual, which did not look correct. Note that the boiler straps and the leading sandbox did not have any lining.

(below) Out from Cowlairs 4th December 1948 No.69152 had a much more acceptable appearance and this became the standard pattern for those with lining. Note that the numbers were still taller than the letters.

Inverurie also applied lining to the N15 class which it repaired but in an appreciably different style. No.69183 ex works 26th March 1949 had figures smaller than the letters which were bolder than the Cowlairs version. Nor did Inverurie line the sandbox and applied only a shallow panel on the bunker.

(below, left) This 27th April 1952 photograph of No.69136 raises unsolved queries. The lining style, letters and figures are of Cowlairs pattern except that sandbox is not lined. The painting probably stems from the 29th January 1949 'General' at Cowlairs, but this was followed by a 'Heavy' at Inverurie, which could account for no lining on the sandbox. Another 'Heavy' at Cowlairs 1st December 1951 might be when the emblem was put on, but 69136 is the only one known with emblem and letters.

(below) So far as has been traced, only two, Nos.69154 and 69166 of the ninety-nine N15 never got lining. No.69166 would be one of the last to get BRITISH RAILWAYS when ex Cowlairs 1st July 1949. This was blacked over and the emblem applied when out on 3rd May 1952 as here on 24th May 1952. Note that the number was altered to the correct 6 and 9.

9060 cont./
SHEDS:
Parkhead.
Thornton Jct. 23/1/35.
Haymarket 17/2/59.

RENUMBERED:
 9060 ?/3/26.
 9211 24/3/46.
 69211 3/9/48.

CONDEMNED: 1/10/62.
Sold for scrap to P.W.McLellan,
Langloan,29/5/64.

_____

9067

Cowlairs.

To traffic 12/12/23.

REPAIRS:
Cow. ?/1—?/2/29.**G.**
Cow. ?/?—?/7/31.**G.**
Cow. 10/2—24/3/34.**G.**
Cow. ?/?—23/5/36.**G.**
Cow. ?/?—23/11/36.**L.**
Cow. ?/?—28/10/38.**H.**
Cow. ?/?—4/11/39.**L.**
Cow. ?/?—1/3/41.**G.**
Cow. ?/?—4/10/41.**L.**
Cow. ?/?—19/2/44.**H.**
Inv. 20/10—1/12/45.**G.**
Cow. 21/6—5/7/47.**L.**
Cow. 12—23/4/48.**H/I.**
Cow. 31/10—2/12/50.**G.**
Cow. 2—13/12/52.**H/I.**
Cow. 22/12/54—15/1/55.**G.**
Cow. 28/10—16/11/57.**H/I.**
Cow. 10—11/3/59.**N/C.**
Cow. 24—26/6/59.**N/C.**

BOILERS:
 1268.
  236 *(ex9282)* 24/3/34.
  274 *(ex9074)* 1/3/41.
  277 *(exN14 9863)* 1/12/45.
 2061 *(new)* 2/12/50.
26421 *(ex69165)* 15/1/55.

SHEDS:
Parkhead.
Eastfield 17/6/57.

RENUMBERED:
 9067 ?/4/26.
 9212 16/6/46.
 69212 23/4/48.

CONDEMNED: 1/10/62.
Cut up at Cowlairs 6/11/62.

_____

9071

Cowlairs.

To traffic 13/12/23.

REPAIRS:
Cow. ?/9—?/12/26.**G.**
Cow. ?/?—9/12/33.**G.**
Cow. ?/?—14/8/35.**G.**
Drop grate fitted.
Cow. ?/?—2/9/37.**H.**
Cow. ?/?—8/4/38.**L.**
Slip coupling fitted.
Cow. ?/?—22/4/39.**L.**
Cow. 25/5—8/6/40.**G.**
Cow. ?/?—19/1/44.**G.**
Cow. ?/?—22/11/44.**H.**
Cow. 28/4—17/5/46.**G.**
Cow. 15—26/6/48.**H/I.**
Cow. 2—12/1/49.**L.**
Cow. 13/9—7/10/50.**G.**
Cow. 26/12/52—16/1/53.**L/I.**
Cow. 26/10—12/11/55.**G.**
Cow. 4/7/56.**N/C.**
Cow. 5—14/11/56.**C/L.**

BOILERS:
 1270.
 1551 *(new)* 9/12/33.
 1263 *(ex9210)* 8/6/40.
 1867 *(ex9165)* 17/5/46.
 2056 *(new)* 7/10/50.
 2056 reno.26481 16/1/53.
26489 *(ex69137)* 12/11/55.

SHEDS:
Eastfield.
Polmadie 26/6/61.
Hamilton 18/8/61.
Motherwell 10/12/62.

RENUMBERED:
 9071 ?/12/26.
 9178 17/5/46.
 69178 26/6/48.

CONDEMNED: 29/12/62.
Cut up at Cowlairs 10/63.

_____

9074

Cowlairs.

To traffic 20/12/23.

REPAIRS:
Cow. ?/1—?/2/29.**G.**
Cow. ?/?—26/4/33.**G.**
Cow. 8—22/2/36.**G.**
Cow. ?/?—10/8/38.**H.**
Cow. ?/?—11/11/39.**L.**
Cow. ?/?—25/1/41.**G.**

Cow. ?/?—14/8/43.**H.**
Inv. ?/?—10/5/44.**L.**
Cow. ?/?—18/10/44.**L.**
Cow. 16/11—1/12/45.**G.**
Cow. 24/5—5/6/48.**H/I.**
Cow. ?/?—?/8/49.**C/H.**
Cow. 13/8—1/9/51.**G.**
Cow. 7/1—1/2/52.**C/L.**
Cow. 21/9—9/10/54.**H/I.**
Cow. 20/9—17/10/57.**G.**

BOILERS:
 1269.
  274 *(ex9022)* 22/2/36.
  169 *(exG9 9475)* 25/1/41.
  278 *(ex9099)* 1/12/45.
26493 *(ex69141)* 1/9/51.
 26493 reno.26388 1/2/52.
26456 *(ex??)* 17/10/57.

SHED:
Parkhead.

RENUMBERED:
 9074 ?/4/26.
 9213 16/6/46.
 69213 5/6/48.

CONDEMNED: 19/10/59.
Cut up at Cowlairs 22/12/59.

_____

9075

Cowlairs.

To traffic 21/12/23.

REPAIRS:
Cow. ?/?—24/2/34.**G.**
Cow. ?/?—19/6/36.**H.**
Cow. ?/?—1/10/38.**H.**
Cow. ?/?—17/11/39.**L.**
Cow. ?/?—18/1/41.**G.**
Inv. ?/?—25/12/43.**H.**
Cow. 28/4—12/5/45.**L.**
Cow. 10/7—11/9/47.**G.**
Cow. 5—21/1/50.**H/I.**
Cow. 21—30/6/50.**C/L.**
Cow. 12—28/11/53.**G.**
EFD. 23—31/3/54.**C/L.**
Cow. 15/3—13/4/57.**H/I.**
Cow. 1—5/10/57.**C/L.**

BOILERS:
 1271.
  309 *(ex9251)* 24/2/34*.
 1268 *(ex9521)* 18/1/41.
 1361 *(exC15 7468)* 11/9/47.
26376 *(ex69188)* 28/11/53.

SHEDS:
Parkhead.
Eastfield 24/2/52.

RENUMBERED:
 9075 ?/8/26.
 9214 16/6/46.
 69214 21/1/50.

CONDEMNED: 7/5/59.
Cut up at Cowlairs 16/10/59.

_____

9076

Cowlairs.

To traffic 27/12/23.

REPAIRS:
Cow. ?/9—?/11/26.**G.**
Cow. ?/?—27/12/33.**G.**
Cow. ?/?—27/8/36.**G.**
Cow. ?/?—28/1/38.**L.**
Cow. ?/?—28/1/39.**G.**
Cow. ?/?—11/11/39.**L.**
Cow. ?/?—29/11/41.**H.**
Cow. ?/?—14/11/42.**L.**
Inv. ?/?—8/4/44.**H.**
Cow. 22/12/47—15/1/48.**G.**
Cow. 6—28/9/50.**H/I.**
Cow. 19/11—13/12/52.**G.**
Cow. 18/2—24/3/56.**H/I.**

BOILERS:
 1272.
 1552 *(new)* 27/12/33.
 1360 *(ex9020)* 28/1/39.
 1357 *(ex9225)* 8/4/44.
 1265 *(exN14 9122)* 15/1/48.
26417 *(exC15 67472)* 13/12/52.

SHEDS:
Kipps.
Carlisle Canal 19/3/45.

RENUMBERED:
 9076 ?/11/26.
 9215 3/11/46.
 69215 19/9/48 *(at shed)*.

CONDEMNED: 28/11/59.
Cut up at Cowlairs 18/12/59.

_____

9077

Cowlairs.

To traffic 27/12/23.

REPAIRS:
Cow. ?/?—?/7/26.**G.**
Cow. ?/8—?/9/27.**G.**
Cow. ?/10—8/11/32.**G.**
Cow. ?/?—17/12/36.**G.**
Cow. 29/7—12/8/39.**G.**
Cow. ?/?—2/10/39.**L.**

(above) **From the end of August 1949 the BRITISH RAILWAYS lettering was discarded and replaced by the 15½in. size emblem. No.69224 ex Cowlairs on 24th September 1949 and No.69201 on 1st October 1949 would be the first N15 to have the emblem. Cowlairs paint shop still continued to use the modified 6 and 9. No.69174 ex works 25th April 1950 having that style.**

(left) **When Cowlairs changed to correct Gill sans 6 and 9 they first used smaller figures than the standard 10in. Those on No.69185 ex works 15th February 1951 were no more than 7½in. Note two top lamp irons fitted, and number plate moved from bunker to sandbox.**

No.69224 got lining at Cowlairs ex works 24th September 1949 as shown by the sandbox having it. This 16th March 1952 photograph shows it after a 'general' ex Inverurie 23rd November 1951 when it got the Caledonian chimney and at least had the bunker repainted because the lining is the shallow panel style used by that works. The 6 and 9 have been changed to the correct Gill sans. Inverurie also put shopping dates at the front end of the running plate angle.

9077 cont./
Cow. ?/?—14/2/42.**H**.
Cow. 15/7—12/8/44.**G**.
Cow. 27/8—12/9/47.**H/I**.
Cow. 26/10—26/11/49.**G**.
Cow. 21/4—17/5/52.**L/I**.
THJ. 29—30/6/54.**C/L**.
Cow. 8—26/2/55.**G**.
Cow. 28/2—3/3/55.**N/C**.
Cow. 7—25/10/57.**H/I**.

BOILERS:
1273.
278 (ex9522) 8/11/32.
1264 (ex9918) 12/8/39.
1614 (ex9523) 12/8/44.
251 (ex9129) 26/11/49.
251 reno.26334 17/5/52.
26486 (ex69212) 26/2/55.

SHEDS:
Parkhead.
Bathgate ?/8/35.

RENUMBERED:
9077 ?/7/26.
9216 28/4/46.
69216 26/11/49.

CONDEMNED: 12/2/62.
Sold for scrap to Arnott Young,
Carmyle 4/6/63.

_____

9078

Cowlairs.

To traffic 9/2/24.

REPAIRS:
Cow. ?/?—?/10/25.**G**.
Cow. ?/?—?/8/26.**H**.
Cow. ?/11—?/12/27.**G**.
Cow. ?/?—7/10/33.**G**.
Cow. ?/?—26/9/35.**G**.
Cow. ?/?—8/3/38.**H**.
Cow. ?/?—27/11/39.**L**.
Cow. ?/?—1/6/40.**G**.
Cow. ?/?—15/8/42.**H**.
Inv. ?/?—5/8/44.**H**.
Cow. 11/12/45—8/1/46.**G**.
Cow. 9—28/2/48.**H/I**.
Cow. 5—24/3/51.**G**.
Cow. 16—28/6/52.**C/L**.
Cow. 18/5—6/6/53.**L/I**.
Cow. 8/2—5/3/55.**G**.
Cow. 5—11/4/56.**C/L**.
Cow. 29/4—17/5/58.**H/I**.

BOILERS:
1277.
1503 (exG9 9350) 7/10/33.
1871 (new) 1/6/40.
1400 (ex9907) 8/1/46.

26540 (ex69197) 24/3/51.
26540 reno.26431 6/6/53.
26479 (ex69219) 5/3/55.

SHEDS:
Bathgate.
Parkhead 9/11/29.
Dawsholm 3/8/57.

RENUMBERED:
9078 ?/10/25.
9217 16/6/46.
69217 24/3/51.

CONDEMNED: 16/10/59.
Cut up at Cowlairs 24/12/59.

_____

9079

Cowlairs.

To traffic 15/2/24.

REPAIRS:
Cow. ?/10—2/11/29.**G**.
Cow. ?/?—12/11/33.**G**.
Cow. ?/?—12/10/34.**L**.
Cow. 14—28/12/35.**G**.
Cow. ?/?—18/12/37.**G**.
Cow. ?/?—23/2/40.**G**.
Inv. 24/10—21/11/42.**H**.
Cow. ?/?—14/9/43.**L**.
Cow. ?/?—9/12/44.**G**.
Cow. 12—28/11/47.**H/I**.
Cow. 27/12/50—25/1/51.**G**.
Cow. 27/5—7/6/52.**L/I**.
Cow. 22/5—6/6/53.**C/H**.
Cow. 19/8—3/9/55.**L/I**.
Cow. 9/7—17/8/57.**G**.
Cow. 12/10/60.**N/C**.

BOILERS:
1276.
267 (ex9391) 2/11/29.
305 (ex9453) 28/12/35.
1905 (new) 9/12/44.
1551 (ex9171) 25/1/51.
1551 reno.26482 25/1/51.
26482 reno.26379 7/6/52.
26363 (ex69201) 6/6/53.
26413 (ex??) 17/8/57.

SHEDS:
Burntisland.
Carlisle Canal by 14/4/30.
Eastfield 20/7/51.
Dawsholm 7/8/61.
Eastfield 30/10/61.

RENUMBERED:
9079 ?/6/26.
9218 2/6/46.
69218 19/9/48 (at shed).

CONDEMNED: 1/10/62.
Cut up at Cowlairs 6/11/62.

_____

9099

Cowlairs.

To traffic 26/2/24.

REPAIRS:
Cow. ?/?—?/3/26.**G**.
Cow. ?/4—?/5/28.**G**.
Cow. ?/?—19/5/34.**G**.
Cow. ?/?—23/2/36.**G**.
Cow. ?/?—6/11/37.**G**.
Cow. ?/?—9/12/39.**L**.
Cow. 10—27/7/40.**G**.
Cow. ?/?—1/5/43.**H**.
Cow. 3—21/9/45.**G**.
Cow. 14—21/12/46.**L**.
Cow. 22/4—11/5/48.**H/I**.
Cow. 11/7—18/8/50.**G**.
Cow. 4—16/8/52.**L/I**.
Cow. 5—28/1/55.**G**.
Cow. 2—5/2/55.**N/C**.
Cow. 4—28/9/57.**H/I**.

BOILERS:
1278.
282 (ex9526) 19/5/34.
278 (ex9246) 27/7/40.
1923 (new) 21/9/45.
2054 (new) 18/8/50.
26478 (ex69154) 28/1/55.

SHED:
St Margarets.

RENUMBERED:
9099 ?/3/26.
9219 3/3/46.
69219 11/5/48.

CONDEMNED: 5/12/61.
Sold for scrap to Arnott Young,
Old Kirkpatrick, 16/8/63.

_____

9125

Cowlairs.

To traffic 1/3/24.

REPAIRS:
Cow. ?/?—?/6/25.**G**.
Cow. ?—?/11/29.**G**.
Cow. ?/?—31/12/31.**G**.
Cow. ?/?—3/4/32.**G**.
Cow. ?/?—7/9/34.**G**.
Cow. ?/?—11/9/36.**G**.
Cow. ?/?—20/5/39.**G**.
Cow. ?/?—16/12/39.**L**.
Cow. ?/?—18/4/42.**H**.

Inv. ?/?—9/7/43.**L**.
Cow. 2—16/9/44.**G**.
Cow. 21—28/9/46.**L**.
Cow. 18/11—5/12/47.**H/I**.
Cow. 23/5—15/6/51.**G**.
Inv. 20/10—6/11/53.**L/I**.
Cow. 18/8—11/9/54.**C/L**.
Cow. 31/1—5/2/55.**N/C**.
Cow. 17/4—19/5/56.**G**.
Cow. 22/6—12/7/56.**N/C**.
Cow. 1—17/8/57.**C/L**.

BOILERS:
1279.
301 (ex9923) 31/12/31.
280 (ex9392) 20/5/39.
10 (ex9210) 16/9/44.
26469 (ex9217) 15/6/51.
26469 reno.26373 6/11/53.
26454 (ex??) 19/5/56.

SHED:
Haymarket.

RENUMBERED:
9125 ?/6/25.
9220 20/10/46.
69220 15/6/51.

CONDEMNED: 18/11/58.

_____

9147

Cowlairs.

To traffic 8/3/24.

REPAIRS:
Cow. ?/?—?/4/26.**G**.
Cow. ?/9—?/10/28.**G**.
Cow. ?/?—30/6/33.**G**.
Cow. ?/?—30/8/35.**G**.
Cow. ?/?—10/9/37.**H**.
Cow. 7—28/9/40.**G**.
Cow. ?/?—30/11/40.**L**.
Cow. 16—30/1/43.**G**.
Inv. ?/?—29/6/44.**H**.
Cow. 21/4—3/5/47.**H/I**.
Cow. 5—21/4/48.**G**.
Cow. 21—30/12/49.**L/I**.
Cow. 27/11—1/12/50.**N/C**.
Cow. 9—24/11/51.**H/I**.
Cow. 19—23/5/52.**N/C**.
Cow. 16/11—5/12/53.**G**.
Cow. 18—27/8/55.**C/L**.
Cow. 9/7—18/8/56.**L/I**.

BOILERS:
1275.
250 (exN14 9861) 30/8/35.
238 (ex9914) 28/9/40.
1895 (new) 30/1/43.
2000 (new) 21/4/48.
2000 reno.26574 24/11/51.

No.69146 ex Cowlairs on 28th June 1952 shows all facets of their standard livery used from 1951 to April 1957. There is one small deviation in that the number plate is fitted on the leading wheel splasher instead of being centred on the sandbox.

Ex Inverurie 21st June 1957 No.69186 shows that works duly adjusted to the deep lining panel on the bunker, but not to putting any lining on the sandbox. Only one more N15 was painted by Inverurie, No.69128 ex works 9th August 1957 and it had the emblem – see page 132, top.

(below) Not all LNER number plates were moved from the bunker to avoid confliction with the painted BR number. On No.69159 it was just moved higher, only to cause a break in the lining.

No.69143 ex Cowlairs 8th June 1957 was the first N15 to have the BR crest instead of the emblem. Between then and the last N15 painting – No.69173 ex works 31st May 1958 – a total of twenty changed to the crest.

9147 cont./
26396 *(ex69184)* 5/12/53.

SHED:
Dunfermline.

RENUMBERED:
9147 as built.
9221 17/11/46.
69221 21/4/48.

CONDEMNED: 19/7/61.
Cut up at Inverurie 18/8/61.

9174

Cowlairs.

To traffic 15/3/24.

REPAIRS:
Cow. ?/3—?/5/27.**G.**
Cow. ?/?—12/8/33.**G.**
Drop grate fitted.
Cow. ?/?—7/10/35.**G.**
Cow. ?/?—4/5/37.**L.**
Cow. ?/?—22/1/38.**H.**
Cow. ?/?—7/12/39.**L.**
Cow. ?/?—6/6/40.**G.**
Cow. ?/?—11/7/41.**L.**
Cow. ?/?—24/10/42.**H.**
Cow. ?/?—28/1/43.**L.**
Cow. 31/3—14/4/45.**G.**
Cow. 2/11—14/12/46.**L.**
Cow. 23/7—21/8/47.**H/I.**
Cow. 10/1—5/2/49.**H/I.**
Cow. 28/8—3/9/49.**C/L.**
Cow. 2—19/5/51.**G.**
Cow. 4—20/9/52.**H/I.**
Cow. 24/5—12/6/54.**L/I.**
Cow. 6—18/9/54.**N/C.**
Cow. 20/2—16/3/57.**G.**
Cow. 22—24/8/57.**N/C.**

BOILERS:
1281.
  259 *(ex9257)* 12/8/33.
  1870 *(new)* 6/6/40.
  1553 *(ex9392)* 14/4/45.
26330 *(ex??)* 19/5/51*.
26330 reno.26491 20/9/52.
26349 *(ex??)* 16/3/57.

SHEDS:
Burntisland.
Eastfield *by* 7/7/28.
St Margarets 7/7/52.

RENUMBERED:
9174 as built.
9222 27/10/46.
69222 5/2/49.

CONDEMNED: 22/5/59.
Sold for scrap to Chalmers, Bonnington, Edinburgh 11/59

9225

Cowlairs.

To traffic 31/3/24.

REPAIRS:
Cow. ?/?—?/11/25.**G.**
Cow. ?/?—27/8/26.**?.**
Cow. ?/4—18/5/29.**G.**
Cow. ?/?—2/12/33.**G.**
Cow. ?/?—31/10/35.**G.**
Cow. ?/?—6/10/37.**L.**
Cow. 7—18/5/38.**G.**
Cow. ?/?—27/9/41.**H.**
Cow. ?/?—21/12/42.**L.**
Inv. ?/?—18/3/44.**G.**
Cow. 9—31/1/46.**G.**

Cow. 21/12/46—25/1/47.**G.**
Cow. 12/7—14/8/48.**H/I.**
Cow. 20—30/12/50.**G.**
Cow. 25/1—13/2/54.**H/I.**
Cow. 27/6—4/8/56.**G.**

BOILERS:
1280.
  289 *(ex9911)* 18/5/29.
  1262 *(ex9019)* 2/12/33.
  1357 *(ex9919)* 18/5/38.
  312 *(ex9917)* 18/3/44.
  169 *(ex9074)* 31/1/46.
  1393 *(ex9211)* 25/1/47.
  2065 *(new)* 30/12/50.
  2065 reno.26591 13/2/54.
26409 *(ex??)* 4/8/56.

SHEDS:
Thornton Jct.
Burntisland *at* 12/9/26.
Thornton Jct. 15/1/32.
Motherwell 30/11/59.

RENUMBERED:
9225 as built.
9223 3/11/46.
69223 14/8/48.

CONDEMNED: 13/8/60.
Cut up at Inverurie 23/9/60.

9227

Cowlairs.

To traffic 5/4/24.

REPAIRS:
Cow. ?/?—24/3/34.**G.**
Cow. ?/?—16/1/36.**G.**

Cow. ?/?—25/12/37.**G.**
Cow. ?/?—1/2/39.**H.**
Cow. ?/?—28/10/39.**L.**
Inv. ?/?—19/9/42.**H.**
Inv. ?/?—6/3/44.**L.**
Inv. 7/4—5/5/45.**H.**
Cow. 9—28/6/47.**G.**
Cow. 6—24/9/49.**H/I.**
Inv. 15/10—23/11/51.**G.**
Inv. 11—28/10/54.**L/I.**
Inv. 28/3—20/4/55.**C/L.**
Cow. 13/3—6/4/57.**G.**
Cow. ?/?—?/2/60.**G.**

BOILERS:
1274.
  240 *(ex9061)* 24/3/34.
  256 *(exN14 9858)* 25/12/37.
  1606 *(ex9196)* 28/6/47.
26458 *(ex9130)* 23/11/51.
26458 reno.26365 ?/4/54.
26445 *(ex??)* 6/4/57.
26377 *(ex??)* ?/2/60.

SHEDS:
Parkhead.
Thornton Jct. 11/5/32.
Dundee 15/8/57.
Keith 14/3/58.
Aberdeen 16/3/59.
Keith 21/12/59.
St Margarets 19/6/61.

RENUMBERED:
9227 as built.
9224 5/5/46.
69224 24/9/49.

CONDEMNED: 1/10/62.
Cut up at Inverurie 28/12/62.

As with the emblem, the crest was handed for the lion to face forward on both sides of the engine. On the left side this was acceptable to the College of Heralds, who had made the Grant of Arms of which the crest was part. No.69218 was ex Cowlairs on 17th August 1957. On the right hand side, for the lion to be looking to the front of the engine, it was facing to the right (*see* previous illustration) and this was a serious heraldic gaffe. During 1959 correction was begun but after 31st May 1958 when No.69173 was the last N15 to be painted, none of the class had a repair which involved repainting, so no correction was made to any N15.

Withdrawal of eleven N15 – of which No.69191 was one – took place 1st October 1962 and left only No.69178 in stock. Curiously that one had not had a significant overhaul after a 'General' at Cowlairs 12th November 1955. Consequently it still had the emblem and never got the1957 crest. It was not included in the mass 1st October 1962 withdrawals because from 26th June 1961 it had been allocated to ex Caledonian sheds. Its 29th December 1962 withdrawal made Class N15 extinct.